Preparing the Next Generation in Tanzania

DIRECTIONS IN DEVELOPMENT
Human Development

Preparing the Next Generation in Tanzania

Challenges and Opportunities in Education

Arun R. Joshi and Isis Gaddis, editors

© 2015 International Bank for Reconstruction and Development / The World Bank
1818 H Street NW, Washington, DC 20433
Telephone: 202-473-1000; Internet: www.worldbank.org

Some rights reserved

1 2 3 4   18 17 16 15

This work is a product of the staff of The World Bank with external contributions. The findings, interpretations, and conclusions expressed in this work do not necessarily reflect the views of The World Bank, its Board of Executive Directors, or the governments they represent. The World Bank does not guarantee the accuracy of the data included in this work. The boundaries, colors, denominations, and other information shown on any map in this work do not imply any judgment on the part of The World Bank concerning the legal status of any territory or the endorsement or acceptance of such boundaries.

Nothing herein shall constitute or be considered to be a limitation upon or waiver of the privileges and immunities of The World Bank, all of which are specifically reserved.

Rights and Permissions

This work is available under the Creative Commons Attribution 3.0 IGO license (CC BY 3.0 IGO) http://creativecommons.org/licenses/by/3.0/igo. Under the Creative Commons Attribution license, you are free to copy, distribute, transmit, and adapt this work, including for commercial purposes, under the following conditions:

Attribution—Please cite the work as follows: Joshi, Arun. R., and Isis Gaddis, editors. 2015. *Preparing the Next Generation in Tanzania: Challenges and Opportunities in Education*. Washington, DC: World Bank. doi:10.1596/978-1-4648-0590-5. License: Creative Commons Attribution CC BY 3.0 IGO

Translations—If you create a translation of this work, please add the following disclaimer along with the attribution: *This translation was not created by The World Bank and should not be considered an official World Bank translation. The World Bank shall not be liable for any content or error in this translation.*

Adaptations—If you create an adaptation of this work, please add the following disclaimer along with the attribution: *This is an adaptation of an original work by The World Bank. Views and opinions expressed in the adaptation are the sole responsibility of the author or authors of the adaptation and are not endorsed by The World Bank.*

Third-party content—The World Bank does not necessarily own each component of the content contained within the work. The World Bank therefore does not warrant that the use of any third-party-owned individual component or part contained in the work will not infringe on the rights of those third parties. The risk of claims resulting from such infringement rests solely with you. If you wish to re-use a component of the work, it is your responsibility to determine whether permission is needed for that re-use and to obtain permission from the copyright owner. Examples of components can include, but are not limited to, tables, figures, or images.

All queries on rights and licenses should be addressed to the Publishing and Knowledge Division, The World Bank, 1818 H Street NW, Washington, DC 20433, USA; fax: 202-522-2625; e-mail: pubrights@worldbank.org.

ISBN (paper): 978-1-4648-0590-5
ISBN (electronic): 978-1-4648-0591-2
DOI: 10.1596/978-1-4648-0590-5

Cover photo: © 2015 Arne Hoel/The World Bank
Cover design: Debra Naylor, Washington DC

Library of Congress Cataloging-in-Publication Data has been requested.

Contents

Foreword		*xiii*
Preface		*xv*
Acknowledgments		*xvii*
About the Editors and Authors		*xix*
Abbreviations		*xxiii*
Chapter 1	**Introduction and Overview**	1
	Arun R. Joshi and Isis Gaddis	
	Administrative Data Overestimate Primary Enrollment Rates	2
	Late Entry and Unequal Access to Education Remain Important Concerns	3
	Learning Outcomes Are Weak and Unequal	3
	Service Delivery Failures Undermine the Performance of the Education Sector	4
	Resource Allocations Are Often Misaligned, Unequal, and Inefficient	5
	References	6
Chapter 2	**Primary Education in Mainland Tanzania: What Do the Data Tell Us?**	7
	Isis Gaddis and Johannes Hoogeveen	
	Summary	7
	Introduction	8
	Children in Primary Schools	8
	Discrepancies between Survey-Based and Administrative Enrollments	10
	Late Entry to Primary School	15
	Fewer Opportunities and Lower Quality for Poor Pupils	18
	Challenges to Improving Primary School Enrollment	20
	The Way Forward	23
	Notes	24
	References	25

Chapter 3	**Addressing Tanzania's Gender Inequality Challenge in Secondary Schools** *Oyin Shyllon*	27
	Summary	27
	Introduction	28
	Gender Dimension of the Demand for Education Services	28
	Causes of Nonattendance in and Dropping from School	34
	Barriers, Remedies, and Drivers for Female Enrollment	37
	Notes	43
	References	44
Chapter 4	**Assessing Literacy and Numeracy in Tanzania's Primary Schools: The Uwezo Approach** *Suleman Sumra, Sara Ruto, and Rakesh Rajani*	47
	Summary	47
	Introduction	48
	Citizen-Led Assessment: The Key Tenets	48
	Findings	50
	Communicating with Key Actors	61
	What Comes Next?	62
	Notes	63
	References	64
Chapter 5	**An Educational Service Delivery Scorecard for Tanzania** *Waly Wane and Isis Gaddis*	65
	Summary	65
	Introduction	66
	The Service Delivery Indicators Project	66
	The Analytical Underpinnings of the Service Delivery Indicators	68
	Implementation of the Service Delivery Survey	71
	Indicators and Pilot Results	72
	Learning Outcomes: Test Scores in Education	79
	Lessons Learned, Trade-Offs, and Policy Recommendations for Scale-Up	82
	Notes	83
	References	85
Chapter 6	**Education Finance and Spending in Tanzania: Challenges and Opportunities** *Oyin Shyllon and Arun R. Joshi*	87
	Summary	87
	Introduction	88

	Education Finance in Tanzania	88
	Private and Public Education Spending	89
	Trends in Public Education Spending	92
	Structural Imbalances in Public Education Spending Patterns	96
	Public Education Unit Cost Estimates and Equitable Resource Allocations	105
	Policy Recommendations	107
	Annex 6A: Spending Patterns and National Education Strategies	108
	Notes	109
	References	110
Chapter 7	**Value for Money in Education** *Stevan Lee*	**113**
	Summary	113
	Introduction	114
	Education Spending and Results: National Trends	114
	Beyond the Averages: Unequal Funding, Unequal Outputs, and Local Inefficiencies	120
	The Scale of Inefficiency	130
	The Way Forward	133
	Notes	134
	References	135

Boxes

2.1	Administrative and Survey-Based Measures of Net Enrollment	11
3.1	Sumbawanga Parents Given Ultimatum to Send Girls to School	29
5.1	Microlevel Survey Instruments for Measuring Resource Flows and Service Delivery	67
5.2	Service Delivery Production Function	69

Figures

1.1	Trends in Enrollment and Exam Results, 2006–12	2
2.1	Net Primary Enrollment Rate since the Introduction of the PEDP	9
2.2	Net and Gross Primary Enrollment Rates by Region, 2010	9
2.3	Variations in Net Primary Enrollment Rates between Districts, 2006–07 (Selected Districts)	10
2.4	Discrepancies between Survey-Based and Administrative Net Primary Enrollment Rates by Region, 2010	11
2.5	Discrepancies between Survey-Based and Administrative Gross Primary Enrollment Rates by Region, 2010	12

2.6	Share of Children Enrolled in Primary School by Age, 2004–05 and 2010	16
2.7	Share of Children Enrolled in Primary School by Age in Selected East African Countries	17
2.8	Share of Children Enrolled in Secondary School by Age in Selected East African Countries	17
2.9	Correlation between the District-Level Poverty Incidence and the Pupil-Teacher Ratio, 2001–02	19
2.10	Reasons Cited by Parents for Not Sending Their Eight-Year-Old Children to Primary School, 2006–07	20
2.11	Primary Enrollment in Kagera by Age and Nutritional Status, 2004	21
2.12	Distance to School and Primary Enrollment among Seven-Year-Old Children in Kagera, 2004	21
3.1	Few Countries Are Less Effective at Ensuring Girls Get to School	31
3.2	Among Youth, Primary Schooling Is the Norm for Girls with Boys More Successful at Progressing to Secondary Schooling	33
3.3	Young Women Leave Schooling Earlier Partly Because They Get Jobs Much More Quickly than Young Men	36
3.4	Young Women Leave Schooling Earlier Also Because They Get a Smaller Wage Premium from Staying Longer in School than Young Men	37
3.5	Young Women Require Adult Female Role Models to Emulate	38
3.6	Young Women (and Men) from Poorer Households Need Financial Support	39
3.7	Young Women Need Secondary Schools Closer to Their Homes	40
3.8	First Generation Reforms Targeted at Affordability Have Been Successful	42
4.1	Performance by Class and Subject (2010–11)	51
4.2	Kiswahili Reading Levels by Class, 2011	52
4.3	English Reading Levels by Class, 2011	53
4.4	Numeracy Levels by Class, 2011	54
4.5	Performance by Schooling Status	56
4.6	Performance by Language Spoken at Home	57
4.7	Percentage of Pupils Meeting Standard 2 Proficiency by Location	58
4.8	Average Teacher Attendance	59
4.9	School Libraries	59
4.10	Student Profile	60
5.1	The Relationships of Accountability among Citizens, Service Providers, and Policy Makers	68
5.2	Education Expenditures (per Student) Reaching Primary Schools	78
5.3	Relationship between Student Performance and the Education Service Delivery Indicators	81

6.1	Private and Public Spending on Education in Tanzania, by Quintile	90
6.2	Recurring and Development Spending on Education, 2007–12	93
6.3	Distribution of Public Spending on Education	94
6.4	Mismatch between Enrollment Levels and Public Education Spending	97
6.5	Student Enrollment	98
6.6	Funding Sources for Higher Education	99
6.7	Numbers of Students Eligible and Ineligible for Higher Education	101
6.8	Repayment and Default Rates for Student Loans by Sector	101
6.9	Lessons on Sector Spending from Successful Reform Countries	104
6.10	Declining Value Derived from Public Investment in Secondary Schooling	104
7.1	Public Spending by Subsector	114
7.2	Primary School Leavers Pass Rates	115
7.3	Public Expenditure per PSLE Passer ("Cost per Passer")	116
7.4	Results of Uwezo's Standard 2 (8-to-9-Year-Old Level) Mathematics Test among Pupils from Standard 3 to Standard 7 (9-to-14-Year-Olds)	117
7.5	Children in Government Secondary School	118
7.6	Percentage of CSEE Candidates at Grade	118
7.7	Public Expenditure per University Student per Year	120
7.8	Primary Education Budget per Capita across Districts—Persistent Inequality	121
7.9	Children per Primary School Teacher—District Average Ranges from 30 to 80	121
7.10	PSLE Passers per 13-Year-Old—District Average Ranges from 0.2 to 1.1, 2008	122
7.11	Poverty Rates in Districts by Level of Spending	122
7.12	Poverty and Passers per 13-Year-Old, 2008 (−32% Correlation)	123
7.13	Child Health and Passers per 13-Year-Old, 2008 (−28% Correlation)	123
7.14	Adult Literacy and Passers per 13-Year-Old, 2008 (60% Correlation)	124
7.15	More Teachers Means More Exam Passers (Controlling for Social Conditions)	125
7.16	Distribution of Average Unit Cost: Recurrent Expenditure per PSLE Passer, 2008	126
7.17	"Frontier" Group Circled in Green, Highly Inefficient Districts Circled in Orange, 2008	129
7.18	Estimated PSLE Passers for an Extra T Sh 50 billion Spent in Each of Five Groups of Districts, Underserved to Best Served	132

Map

5.1	Map of the Sampling Areas	71

Tables

2.1	Estimated Primary Enrollment by Age, DHS and Administrative Data, 2010	13
2.2	Age Distribution in Standard 1, 2000–01, 2008–09, and 2010–11	15
2.3	Primary Enrollment and School-Age Population by Quintile, 2004–05 and 2010	18
2.4	Share of Children Aged 10–13 Who Never Attended School by Quintile/Area, 2010	19
2.5	Determinants of School Enrollment in Kagera, Children Aged Six to Eight, 2004	22
3.1	Girls Stop Attending School as Early as 13 Years of Age	30
3.2	More than Half of Tanzanian Females Aged 13–21 Are Not in School	35
4.1	Coverage of the Uwezo 1 (2010) and Uwezo 2 (2011) in Tanzania	50
4.2	Percentage of Standard 7 Pupils Meeting Standard 2 Proficiency by Parents' Schooling Levels	57
5.1	Indicators in an Education Service Delivery Report Card	70
5.2	Infrastructure in Tanzania (Percentage of Schools with Electricity, Water, and Sanitation)	73
5.3	Average Number of Children per Classroom in Tanzania	73
5.4	Student-Teacher Ratio	74
5.5	Textbooks per Student	74
5.6	Absence Rate (Percentage of Teachers Not in School)	75
5.7	Absence Rate from Classroom (Percentage of Time Teachers Not in the Classroom)	75
5.8	Time Children in School Are Being Taught per Day	76
5.9	Share of Teachers with Minimum Knowledge in Tanzania	77
5.10	Share of Teachers Answering Correctly on Specific Questions	77
5.11	Leakage of Capitation Grant (Percentage of Intended Resources Not Received by the Schools)	79
5.12	Delays in Salaries (Percentage of Teachers Whose Salary Is Overdue More than Two Months)	79
5.13	Average Score on Student Test in Tanzania	80
5.14	Language: Percentage of Students Who Can Read a Sentence (in English)	81
5.15	Mathematics: Percentage of Students Who Can Add Two Single Digits	81
6.1	Tuition and Instructional Costs of Higher Education in 2010–11	89
6.2	Participation in Levels of Education by Quintile	91

6.3	Sustained Increases in Nominal and Real Growth in Public Education Spending	92
6.4	Growth in Recurrent Spending, 2007–12	93
6.5	Development Projects for Secondary and Higher Education	95
6.6	Slower Relative Growth in Tertiary Education Is Required	96
6.7	Unit Costs of Expenditures Spent on Enrollees and Passers in Primary and Secondary Education Budgets	105
6.8	Actual and Budgeted Unit Cost of Public Investment in Education	106
6.9	Inequality in Recurrent Unit Cost Allocations for Primary Education	107
6A.1	Alignment of 2011–12 Approved Education Budget with MKUKUTA II Objectives	108
7.1	Trend in Tertiary Gross Enrollment Rates in East African Countries	119
7.2	Some of the Most Efficient Primary School Districts in Tanzania	127
7.3	Some of the Least Efficient Primary School Districts in Tanzania	128
7.4	District Expenditures on Education	131
7.5	Underserved Districts with Good Efficiency	133

Foreword

In 2013, Tanzania launched the Big Results Now in Education program as part of a major nationwide initiative to accelerate progress in priority sectors. The education program builds on Tanzania's rapid and historic gains in school enrollment by working toward improving the quality of basic education and equipping the next generation of Tanzanians with the foundational skills that they will need to succeed as working adults. Indeed, without quality basic education, investments at the secondary and tertiary levels of education will not deliver the desired outcomes. By investing in education and human capital, Tanzania is unblocking the constraints for overall growth and development.

The program introduces a highly innovative results-oriented approach to improving education service delivery and, as a consequence, learning outcomes. There is already early evidence of success. Innovative interventions built into the program are designed to transform the education ecosystem through changes in incentives and accountability structures. Global evidence from impact evaluation points to the importance of these measures.

The chapters in this volume provide a useful snapshot of the basic education sector in Tanzania at the start of the program. They highlight the current status and trends with respect to important thematic clusters—equity gaps, factors that influence learning outcomes, and variability in resource transfers to districts. Although improvements in access to basic education are evident, the book shows that major equity gaps persist, by income and gender. Learning outcomes need to improve significantly, and open data can play an important role in the reform process. The book also highlights the key service delivery pathways and "proximate" variables that have been shown to affect final learning outcomes. It is clear from the evidence that there needs to be more teaching time in the classroom and that an optimal learning environment must be created for students. Finally, the book highlights the major variability in resource transfers to districts, which generates and sustains a vicious cycle of inequality in inputs, outputs, and outcomes.

The lack of accountability stirs resentment in communities as children suffer the consequences of inadequate or inefficient investments and their impact on learning outcomes. The program offers a major opportunity for change. The key elements for success exist, and change can be brought about through strong commitment to efficient and effective implementation. The road toward better learning outcomes is never easy, but I believe that making early and effective investments in children's education will not only open new doors to them once they complete school, but also contribute to healthy economic growth and productivity at the level of the national economy.

Claudia Costin
Senior Director
Education Global Practice
The World Bank

Preface

Tanzania is facing a major challenge: preparing its youth, the next generation, to become competitive members of the East African and global economic community. Such human capital development is critical for setting Tanzania on a trajectory toward middle income status, a target it wants to reach by the year 2025 (Planning Commission 1999).

Human capital refers to a broad range of knowledge, skills, and capabilities that are needed for life and work and that are typically built through quality education. Countries that fail to invest consistently in education often do not experience robust economic growth because investments in physical infrastructure, such as dams, roads, and airports as well as developments in other economic sectors such as banking or information technology, are often constrained and yield low returns in the absence of an adequately educated workforce. It is projected that a significant share of Tanzania's economic growth over the coming decades will be concentrated in occupations that require citizens with postsecondary training and skills, as is already the case in middle-income countries.

The chapters in this volume lay out the central challenges facing the education sector in Tanzania and promising solutions. Tanzania has been successful in increasing access to primary and, more recently, secondary education. Although these are important past achievements, the education sector currently faces severe quality challenges. As discussed in chapter 2, the primary education sector still has significant remnants of an unequal system in which poorer students are more likely to either start school late or drop out early. Moreover, administrative data portray an overly optimistic picture of primary school enrollment in Tanzania. Gender inequalities remain entrenched at the secondary level (chapter 3). Furthermore, as highlighted in chapter 4, learning outcomes at the primary level are poor, evidenced by a large proportion of primary graduates who are unable to read simple Kiswahili and English and perform simple numerical operations. At the secondary level, the Form 4 pass rates have been very low and falling, which implies that an increasingly large cohort of secondary graduates lack basic labor market requirements (chapter 7).

The chapters here also provide evidence on service delivery failures that are behind these poor learning outcomes. These "proximate determinants" of education outcomes point to substantial weaknesses in the provision of incentives and accountability in the service provision chain (chapter 5), as well as to the overall misalignment of resource use and sector priorities (chapter 6). Out of this emerges a vicious circle of reduced value for money, weak service delivery, and poor educational quality. The chapters in this volume focus on highlighting these and other challenges, but they also lay out broad policy directions for breaking this vicious circle of underperformance. Recent discussions and the dialogue under the government of Tanzania's action plan Big Results Now in Education offer an excellent opportunity to craft a road map toward better resource use, enhanced service delivery, and improved learning outcomes.

Reference

Planning Commission. 1999. *The Tanzania Development Vision 2025*. Dodoma: United Republic of Tanzania.

Acknowledgments

The chapters in this volume were written by Johannes Hoogeveen, Isis Gaddis, Oyin Shyllon, Waly Wane, and Stevan Lee under the supervision of Arun R. Joshi and Paolo Zacchia. Chapter 4 was solicited separately for this volume, and we thank Suleman Sumra, Sara Ruto, and Rakesh Rajani for presenting the Uwezo approach, a highly innovative initiative for assessing literacy and numeracy in Kenya, Tanzania, and Uganda. The editors are grateful for the support and feedback received from Nobuyuki Tanaka, Andrew Trembley, Kaboko Nkahiga, Shwetlena Sabarwal, Gayle Martin, Emmanuel Mungunasi, David Evans, Juan Manuel Moreno, and Halsey Rogers. The volume received guidance from John McIntire, Philippe Dongier, Sajitha Bashir, Peter Materu, and Jacques Morriset.

The chapters were written between 2010 and 2013 as "just-in-time" reviews and policy notes to initiate discussions among the government and development partners on important education policy issues. The contents of these papers were used extensively by the government and the development partners in debating and formalizing a strategic framework for education reform entitled the Education Reform Compact (2012), as well as in preparing the detailed Big Results in Education Program (2013).

In Tanzania, the chapters benefited from many individuals. In particular, the contents benefited from the dialogue and exchanges held with Honorable Minister Sukuru Kwambwa, Sifuni Mchome, Issa Omari, Hamisi Dihenga, Ian Attfield, Tom LeBlanc, and Herme Mosha.

Any errors and omissions are those of the authors and the editors.

About the Editors and Authors

Arun R. Joshi is a Lead Education Specialist in the Education Global Practice at the World Bank. His experience spans policy reform and program development in a diverse range of countries in the Middle East, Africa, and South Asia. Before his current assignment, he was based in Dar es Salaam, Tanzania, between 2009 and 2013, when he was able to, among other tasks, contribute to the design of the government's Big Results Now in Education program. He has taught education sector policy analysis at George Washington University. He has a master's degree in international education policy and a doctorate in human development from Harvard University.

Isis Gaddis is an economist with the World Bank's Gender Group in Washington, DC. She previously worked in the Poverty Reduction and Economic Management unit as poverty economist for Tanzania and was based in Dar es Salaam. Her research interests are in the areas of labor economics, gender, poverty and inequality analysis, and public service delivery. Before joining the World Bank, she worked as a consultant for development agencies in the Arab Republic of Egypt, Kenya, Uganda, and Zambia, primarily in the fields of poverty measurement, labor market policy, fiscal policy, and statistical development. She holds a Ph.D. in economics from the University of Göttingen, where she was a research associate from 2006 to 2012.

Johannes Hoogeveen is a senior economist at the World Bank. He received a Ph.D. in economics from the Free University in Amsterdam and joined the World Bank in 2001. He has extensive experience with the implementation and analysis of household and firm surveys and has published on a variety of topics including the determinants of entrepreneurship in Zimbabwe, poverty mapping in Uganda, and the impact of land reform in South Africa and of nutrition programs in Tanzania. His latest publication is on the efficiency of the education system in Togo, which he coauthored with Prof. Cristina Rossi. Dr. Hoogeveen lived in Tanzania from 2004 until 2011, where he worked as poverty economist at the World Bank and as manager at Twaweza. In the latter capacity, he coauthored a report on education in East Africa using data from the Uwezo surveys. He also prepared various policy briefs on the status of the education sector in Tanzania.

Dr. Hoogeveen presently lives in Washington, DC, where his sons Abe and Reimer benefit from an excellent education in the public school system.

Stevan Lee, Bsc., M.A., Ph.D., has worked as a professional economist in development since 1993. He has lived and worked for nine years in East Africa as well as working in several other countries in Africa and the Middle East. At the time of writing the chapter in this volume, he was part of the World Bank's Africa Poverty Reduction and Economic Management team in Dar es Salaam, Tanzania.

Rakesh Rajani directs the Ford Foundation's work in democratic participation and governance, overseeing three grant-making initiatives focused on Increasing Civic and Political Participation; Promoting Electoral Reform and Democratic Participation; and Promoting Transparent, Effective, and Accountable Government. A global leader on issues of social justice, Rakesh has been at the forefront of citizen engagement and government accountability for two decades. He serves on the board of the Hewlett Foundation, the board of directors at the International Budget Partnership, the advisory board of the Open Contracting Partnership, and the steering committee of Making All Voices Count. Before joining the foundation in 2015, Rakesh was based in Tanzania, where he served as head of Twaweza ("We Can Make It Happen"), an organization he founded to promote basic learning, advance access to information, and increase government responsiveness.

Previously, Rakesh served as the lead civil society chair for the Open Government Partnership, an initiative to promote government transparency and accountability. He founded and served as executive director for HakiElimu ("Education Rights"), combining pioneering research with humor and satire to engage citizens in education reform. An earlier venture, Kuleana Centre for Children's Rights, which Rakesh cofounded in his hometown of Mwanza, Tanzania, became one of Africa's leading centers for children's rights and established Tanzania's first center for sexual health, linking work on HIV/AIDS, sexuality, youth, gender, and human rights. Rakesh holds a master's degree in theological studies from Harvard University, and he earned his bachelor's degree in philosophy and English and American literature from Brandeis University.

Sara Ruto serves as the director of Citizen-Led Assessments International (CLA International), based in Nairobi. CLA International complements the work of nine citizen-led learning assessments across Africa, Asia, and Latin America, helping to ensure the centrality of learning and measurement in policy and practice at the global level. Previously, Sara established and led the first citizen-led learning assessment on the African continent in Kenya in 2009. She later moved on to serve as the Regional Manager for Uwezo across East Africa, using evidence to draw public attention to children's learning. She sits on several boards and committees including Women Educational Researchers of Kenya and the Global Reading Network. Sara is a trained teacher and holds a master's degree from Kenyatta University and a Ph.D. from Heidelberg University.

Oyin Shyllon is a corporate economist with the City of Calgary focusing on municipal finance, economic forecasting, and policy analysis. His responsibilities include monitoring and forecasting trends in the Canadian and U.S. economies as well as the Calgary labor market. He has prior experience with the Washington, DC–based Results for Development Institute and the World Bank working on the economics of human development, public policy, and public finance. Before joining the City of Calgary, he also served as a budget officer with the government of Alberta. Oyin has graduate degrees with specialization in development economics (Dalhousie University) and public administration (Harvard University). He enjoys coaching and playing soccer and spending time with family and friends when not at work.

Suleman Sumra holds a Ph.D. from Stanford University. He retired from the University of Dar es Salaam in 2002 after a teaching career spanning 30 years. At the university, he held several posts including that of Associate Dean for Research and Publications, Director of the Bureau of Research and Evaluation (BERE), and the national coordinator for the Language of Instruction in Tanzania and South Africa (LOITASA), a joint research project between the University of Dar es Salaam, University of Western Cape in South Africa, and University of Oslo in Norway. He has carried out consultancies for various organizations and has written widely on primary education in Tanzania. He coordinated Uwezo Tanzania from August 2008 to April 2012.

Waly Wane is a senior economist in the Education Global Practice Department at the World Bank. Before joining the department he worked in the Poverty Reduction and Economic Management group as the poverty economist for Tanzania and Uganda based in Dar es Salaam and in the Research Group of the World Bank. Service delivery is among his main areas of interest and research. He has led several public expenditure tracking surveys in Africa and East Asia, and he was a member of the original team that designed and piloted the Service Delivery Indicators in Senegal and Tanzania. He has published in peer-reviewed journals such as the *Journal of Public Economics, Social Science and Medicine*, and *Journal of African Economies*. He has recently blogged about Tanzania and is based in Nairobi.

Abbreviations

ASER	Annual Status of Education Report
BRNEd	Big Results Now in Education
CCT	conditional cash transfer
CSEE	Certificate of Secondary Education Examination
CWIQ	Core Welfare Indicators Questionnaire
DC	District Commissioner
DHS	Demographic and Health Survey
DMI	Dar es Salaam Maritime Institute
DUCE	Dar es Salaam University College of Education
EA	enumeration area
ECD	early childhood development
EMIS	Education Management Information System
GDP	gross domestic product
GER	gross enrollment rate
GPA	grade point average
GPI	gender parity index
HBS	Household Budget Survey
HESLB	Higher Education Student Loans Board
HETI	higher education training institution
HH	households
IAE	Institute of Adult Education
ICT	information and communication technology
IJMC	Institute of Journalism and Mass Communication
ILFS	Integrated Labor Force Survey
KHDS	Kagera Health and Development Survey
LGA	Local Government Authority
LMIC	low- and middle-income country
MDG	Millennium Development Goal
MNMA	Mwalimu Nyerere Memorial Academy

MoEVT	Ministry of Education and Vocational Training
MUCE	Mkwawa University College of Education
NACTE	National Council for Technical Education
NAR	net attendance rate
NBS	National Bureau of Statistics
NER	net enrollment rate
NM-AIST	Nelson Mandela African Institute of Science and Technology
NPS	National Panel Survey
PE	personnel emoluments
PEDP	Primary Education Development Program
PETS	Public Expenditure Tracking Survey
PHDR	Poverty and Human Development Report
PPP	purchasing power parity
PSLE	Primary School Leaving Examination
PTR	pupil-teacher ratio
QSDS	Quantitative Service Delivery Survey
REPOA	Research on Poverty Alleviation
SACMEQ	Southern and Eastern Africa Consortium for Monitoring Educational Quality
SAS	Staff Absence Survey
SDI	Service Delivery Indicators
SEDP	Secondary Education Development Program
SSA	Sub-Saharan Africa
STHEP	Science and Technology in Higher Education Development Project
TTI	technical training institution
UDOM	University of Dodoma

CHAPTER 1

Introduction and Overview

Arun R. Joshi and Isis Gaddis

Tanzania has made strong progress in expanding access to education. In 1999, Tanzania adopted its Vision 2025, which put strong emphasis on expanding access to education (Planning Commission 1999). Through the Primary Education Development Program (PEDP), it eliminated tuition fees and expanded schools throughout the country. Primary school enrollment increased from 4.8 to 8.4 million between 2001 and 2010. From 2004, partly as a reaction to the large influx of students from primary schools, the country embarked on the Secondary Education Development Program (SEDP), with emphasis on building schools in every ward. Enrollment in secondary schools almost quadrupled between 2005 and 2010, highlighting the magnitude of enrollment growth in a country that is still in the middle of a demographic transition.

Although educational opportunities have expanded for large numbers of students, learning outcomes are often weak and have even declined further in recent years. In 2012, only 31 percent of those who sat for the Primary School Leaving Examination (PSLE) exams passed, down from 58 percent in 2011. At the secondary level, the pass rate of the Certificate of Secondary Education Examination (CSEE) has also declined in the past few years (figure 1.1). Results from the 2011 Uwezo Tanzania learning assessment show that the large majority of students in Standard 3 does not possess Standard 2 level literacy and numeracy skills.

Poor learning outcomes point to deeply rooted failures in service delivery, as well as misalignments, inefficiencies, and inequities in resource allocation that need to be addressed in the short and medium term. Rapid enrollment expansion appears to have placed primary and secondary school systems under increased pressure, further exposing their weaknesses.

Tanzanian policy makers are prepared to act on these challenges. In January 2013, the president launched a transformative action plan called "Big Results Now in Education" (BRNEd), which is part of the government of Tanzania's multisectoral flagship program "Big Results Now." The initiative is expected to

Figure 1.1 Trends in Enrollment and Exam Results, 2006–12

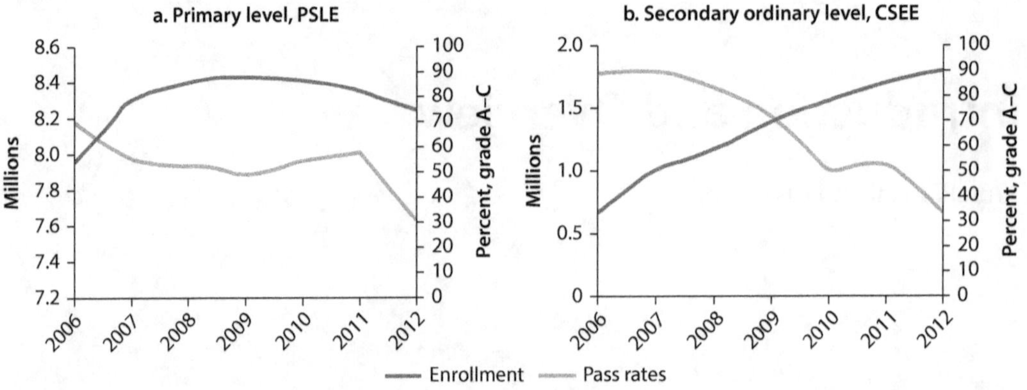

a. Primary level, PSLE

b. Secondary ordinary level, CSEE

— Enrollment   — Pass rates

Source: World Bank 2014.
Note: CSEE = Certificate of Secondary Education Examination; PSLE = Primary School Leaving Examination.

fast track improvements in the delivery of basic education services to produce tangible improvements in learning outcomes. In the longer term, the program is expected to lay the foundation of an outcome-based performance culture in the education sector in Tanzania.

The objective of this book is to present a broad-based diagnosis of the challenges faced by the Tanzanian education system. It provides a knowledge base to inform the government of Tanzania and other stakeholders in their endeavor to improve learning outcomes among Tanzanian students. The main findings of this book are summarized in the following section.

Administrative Data Overestimate Primary Enrollment Rates

A comparison of enrollment rates reported by the Education Management Information System (EMIS) with representative household surveys shows that the EMIS overestimates net enrollment rates by almost 16 percentage points and gross enrollment rates by almost 7 percentage points. In 2010, about half of the discrepancy in net enrollment rates can be attributed to inaccurate reporting of the age of students in the EMIS; the other half was related to inaccurate population projections that feed into the EMIS and underestimate the primary school age population (chapter 2).

The quality of administrative statistics in the education sectors deserves urgent attention from policy makers because they heavily affect the notion of whether key sector targets, including the Millennium Development Goal of universal primary education by 2015, are being achieved. The recently concluded 2012 Population and Housing Census will provide an opportunity to update population estimates and projections, and to revise enrollment rates in the EMIS accordingly.

Late Entry and Unequal Access to Education Remain Important Concerns

Late and nonenrollment at the primary level continue to be important challenges in the Tanzanian education sector: 59 percent of children age seven years were enrolled in school in 2010, which is a significant increase compared with 29 percent in 2004–05, although it falls short of the government's target of complete enrollment at the age of seven.

Children from poor families have increased their share of overall primary enrollments but continue to be disadvantaged. In 2010, 16 percent of children age 10–13 years from the poorest quintile had not entered primary school, compared with only 2 percent of children from the wealthiest group. Children from poor households are also more likely to attend lower quality schools (chapter 2).

Age, nutritional status, and the number of teachers per child are important determinants of primary school enrollment among young children. Although a child's age cannot be affected by policy, the government can influence the parents' perception about the appropriate age to start school, for instance, by reducing the compulsory age of entry from seven to six years, such as in neighboring Kenya and Uganda (chapter 2).

Higher levels of the education sector are further characterized by gender inequality: Gender parity is found in enrollments at the preprimary and primary school levels, but girls make up only 45 percent of lower secondary students and 35 percent of upper secondary students. Among the main proximate causes why girls drop out from secondary schools are teenage pregnancies. At a more fundamental level, the large number of females out of school points to a variety of market failures, such as imperfect information on the benefits of female education, poverty combined with liquidity, credit and capital market constraints, as well as supply-side limitations, for example, large distances to the nearest secondary school, lack of sufficient toilet facilities, and the absence of female teachers as role models and mentors (chapter 3).

Learning Outcomes Are Weak and Unequal

Learning outcomes in Tanzania are clearly unsatisfactory. In 2011, Uwezo, an initiative of Twaweza to improve learning outcomes in East Africa, conducted the second "Annual Learning Assessment," which measured student learning outcomes in literacy and numeracy. The results revealed that only three out of 10 students in Standard 3 are able to read a Standard 2 level Kiswahili story. Only three out of 10 Standard 3 students master Standard 2 level numeracy, such as adding, subtracting, and multiplying. Only one out of 10 students is able to read a second-grade English story. Uwezo also finds large disparities in students' learning achievements between districts and shows that students in urban areas perform significantly better than their rural counterparts (chapter 4).

Other indicators of learning outcomes are the PSLE and CSEE results. Chapter 7 documents that pass rates in both exams deteriorated between 2007 and 2010, a trend that has further continued over the last few years. Moreover, the chapter shows striking regional inequality in pass rates. Whereas in some districts only 15 percent of 13-year-old students pass the PSLE, more than 90 percent pass in other districts.

The Uwezo results in conjunction with the deteriorating PSLE and CSEE results highlight that the Tanzanian education system more and more produces graduates who lack the basic skills and competencies required to participate in the labor market. International evidence shows that basic numeracy, literacy, and social skills are a necessary precondition to enter productive employment and to acquire further skills on the job. Where the education system fails to provide such basic skills, graduates remain caught in a low-skill trap, with few opportunities to improve their employment situation and earnings. Similarly, at the macro level, countries require a skilled work force to climb the productivity ladder (World Bank 2012). For all of these reasons, the weak learning outcomes in Tanzania are a pressing policy concern. This volume sheds light on some of the factors that are responsible for the poor quality of education.

Service Delivery Failures Undermine the Performance of the Education Sector

Critical in the process to improve learning outcomes is the quality of the services delivered to students. Weak incentives for teachers (apparent by high levels of teacher absenteeism) are often described as a chief determinant of poor student performance in developing countries (Bruns, Filmer, and Patrinos 2011; Chaudhury et al. 2005; Glewwe, Holla, and Kremer 2008; Verspoor et al. 2008). Teacher salaries are the most expensive budget item in the education sector, and so poor teacher utilization becomes the single most important factor that bleeds public resources.

Chapter 5, based on pilot results from the Service Delivery Indicators (SDI) project conducted in Senegal and Tanzania, shows that teacher absenteeism is a serious problem. About one out of four teachers is absent from school in Tanzania, and the absentee rate in urban schools is significantly higher than in rural schools. Furthermore, teachers are absent from the classroom more than half the time even when they are in school. Students in primary schools are taught 2 hours a day on average, instead of the scheduled 5 hours and 12 minutes. It is difficult for children to learn consistently and to enhance their skills under these circumstances.

Unfortunately Tanzania has so far paid insufficient attention to creating incentives and accountability mechanisms for teachers, especially for attracting them to relocate to hard-to-reach areas (World Bank 2011). The SDI project provides a unique opportunity to benchmark the performance of schools (and other service providers) within and across districts. The indicators can be used to track progress over time and enhance active monitoring of service delivery.

Initiatives like the SDI and Uwezo can create public pressure for policy change, enhance the quality of services, and improve public accountability, governance, and development outcomes in the education sector.

Resource Allocations Are Often Misaligned, Unequal, and Inefficient

Besides teachers' incentives, a key challenge in improving service delivery is to ensure an adequate allocation of public resources across subsectors. World Bank (2005) analyzes per-student spending by education level and compares fast- and slow-growing economies. It reveals that the fast-growing economies had much more balanced per-student spending. For example, although per-student expenditure at the secondary level was only about 40 percent higher than per-student expenditure at the primary level in fast-growing economies, it was 120 percent higher in slow-growing economies. Similarly, although per-student expenditure at the tertiary level was only about three times that of per-student expenditure at the secondary level in fast-growing economies, it was 11 times higher in slow-growing economies. Even though these results do not necessarily imply causality, they suggest that a more balanced allocation of resources between education subsectors may contribute to faster human capital formation and higher economic growth.

Tanzania needs further reforms to rebalance intrasector resource allocations. In particular, more resources need to be transferred to the expanding secondary subsector to ensure adequate funding. Historically, secondary education has been underfinanced, but tertiary education has received a disproportionate share of the education budget, mostly to finance an untargeted students' loans scheme. A major challenge for the entire education sector is therefore to generate repayments under this loans program as a means of cost recovery and to free up resources and enhance spending in other subsectors (chapters 6 and 7).

Recent years have seen progress in the right direction: The share for secondary education has increased markedly from 14 percent in 2007–08 to 21 percent in the 2011–12 budget due in large part to the agreements reached in the context of the World Bank's support to the SEDP II (2010–15). The allocation to the higher education subsector has declined from an unusually higher share of 27 percent in 2010–11 to the norm of 24 percent in the 2011–12 budget. However, secondary education is still not sustainably financed to meet the needs of a rapidly expanding system. In particular, the planned secondary allocation is inconsistent with the resource needs for an expanded secondary subsector as well as inconsistent with practices in other countries that have implemented secondary education quality and enrollment expansion reforms. (Chapter 6 highlights these issues in greater detail.)

Regional inequalities in resource allocation and budget execution are additional challenges. For instance, student teacher ratios in primary schools vary between below 30 and 80 across districts, and there is a strong correlation to PSLE pass rates. In general, the worst served districts tend to have poor social conditions and weak learning outcomes. Such uneven spending patterns are not only inequitable but also inefficient, because the marginal benefit of an additional teacher is likely to be higher in underserved districts (chapter 7).

Going against this general tendency, some districts achieve remarkably strong education outcomes despite low resource allocations. This group of districts, which appear to operate on the Tanzanian productivity frontier, had far better PSLE pass rates than could be expected given their social conditions and spending levels, an indication of low unit cost (spending per passer) and, as a corollary, high spending efficiency. Further estimations suggest that if all districts achieved a similar unit cost as these cost-effective "frontier" districts, the primary education sector would have accumulated savings of more than T Sh 250 billion for 2008 and of T Sh 310 billion for 2010. This is equivalent to nearly 1 percent of gross domestic product being wasted on inefficiency in the primary education sector each year. Hence, a strong need is seen to examine the factors behind these inefficiencies, which are most likely related to poor school management and weak teacher incentives (chapter 7).

References

Bruns, Barbara, Deon Filmer, and Harry Anthony Patrinos. 2011. *Making Schools Work: New Evidence on Accountability Reforms*. Washington, DC: World Bank.

Chaudhury, Nazmul, Jeffrey Hammer, Michael Kremer, Karthik Muralidharan, and Halsey Rogers. 2005. "Missing in Action: Teacher and Health Worker Absence in Developing Countries." *Journal of Economic Perspectives* 20 (1): 91–116.

Glewwe, Paul, Alaka Holla, and Michael Kremer. 2008. "Teacher Incentives in the Developing World." In *Performance Incentives: Their Growing Impact on American K-12 Education*, edited by M. Springer, 295–326. Washington DC: Brookings Institution Press.

Planning Commission. 1999. *The Tanzania Development Vision 2025*. United Republic of Tanzania.

Verspoor, Adriaan, and SEIA Team. 2008. *At the Crossroads: Choices for Secondary Education in Sub-Saharan Africa*. Washington, DC: World Bank.

World Bank. 2005. *Expanding Opportunities and Building Competencies for Young People: A New Agenda for Secondary Education*. Washington, DC: World Bank.

———. 2011. *United Republic of Tanzania Public Expenditure Review 2010*. Washington, DC: World Bank.

———. 2012. *World Development Report 2013: Jobs*. Washington, DC: World Bank.

———. 2014. "Big Results Now in Education (BRNEd) Program." Program Appraisal Document, World Bank, Washington, DC.

CHAPTER 2

Primary Education in Mainland Tanzania: What Do the Data Tell Us?

Isis Gaddis and Johannes Hoogeveen

Summary

Tanzania has seen a remarkable increase in primary enrollments since the inception of the Primary Education Development Program (PEDP) in 2001, which led to the abolishment of school fees in early 2002. However, large regional variation is found in gross and net enrollment rates (NER), which indicates that not all regions have benefited equally from the PEDP. Moreover, in comparing enrollment rates estimated from representative household surveys with administrative data from the Education Management Information System (EMIS), we see that the EMIS significantly overestimates net enrollment rates (by almost 16 percentage points) and to a lesser extent gross enrollment rates (by almost 7 percentage points). In 2010 about half of the discrepancy in net enrollment rates can be attributed to inaccurate reporting of the age of students in the EMIS, and the other half is related to the EMIS using population projections that underestimate the primary school-age population. Both issues deserve urgent attention from policy makers because they heavily affect the notion of whether key government targets are being achieved or not.

Children from poor families have increased their share of overall primary enrollments in recent years but continue to be disadvantaged. Children from the poorest quintile have an eight times higher probability not to go to school between the ages of 10 and 13 compared with children from the wealthiest quintile. When they do go, they are more likely to visit schools of lower quality (i.e., schools with high student-teacher ratios).

Encouragingly, late entry into primary school has declined over the past few years. According to Demographic and Health Survey (DHS) data, 59 percent of children aged seven years were enrolled in school in 2010, which is a significant increase compared with 29 percent in 2004–05. Nonetheless this falls still short of the government's target of complete enrollment at the age of seven, showing that late and nonenrollment remain important challenges. In addition, remarkable progress has been made in reducing the number of older children in primary school, mainly due to increased (and earlier) transition to secondary school. But still too many students complete primary school at a time when they are ready to enter the labor force. Bringing children into primary school earlier—through improvements in early childhood nutrition, a reduction in the compulsory school age, and investments in school quality—remains an important objective to ensure optimal learning, facilitate the transition to secondary school, and increase lifetime earnings.

Introduction

Since 2001, Tanzania has implemented the PEDP, which aims to deliver sustainable, universal basic education of good quality. As part of the PEDP, primary school fees were abolished at the beginning of the 2002 academic year. This chapter explores for Tanzania mainland the increase in primary enrollment since the introduction of the PEDP, compulsory enrollment at the age of seven, and the quality of the EMIS. In addition, the chapter discusses whether poor households have benefited from the PEDP, and it explores some of the factors that keep poor children out of school.

Children in Primary Schools

From December 2009 to May 2010, a nationally (and regionally) representative DHS was implemented by the National Bureau of Statistics (NBS). This survey collected, among other things, information about the educational attainment of household members aged 5 years and above and current enrollment for those aged 5–24 years. The survey also collected information about asset ownership, which was used to construct an index of household wealth. Comparable DHSs were fielded in 1996 and 2004–05, which allow for comparisons over time (for details see NBS and ICF Macro 2011; NBS and Macro International Inc. 1997; NBS and ORC Macro 2005).[1] Although the DHSs are the main data source used here, we also draw on other surveys, particularly the National Panel Survey (NPS; see NBS 2012) and the 2000–01 Household Budget Survey (HBS). The latter survey was fielded just before the PEDP was introduced and is used to obtain baseline estimates of primary school enrollment.[2]

As shown in figure 2.1, the NER, defined as the proportion of children aged 7–13 years enrolled in primary school, increased from 59 percent in 2000–01 to 71 percent in 2004–05[3] and almost 80 percent in 2010. Even though enrollment was already rising before the introduction of the PEDP, strong evidence suggests that the significant increase in enrollment since 2001 can be attributed to the abolition of school fees in 2002 (Hoogeveen and Rossi 2013).

This impressive progress masks the existence of significant regional variation in enrollment. The NER varies from 65.7 percent in Tabora to 91.3 percent in Kilimanjaro (figure 2.2). Likewise the gross enrollment rates (GER), defined as

Primary Education in Mainland Tanzania: What Do the Data Tell Us?

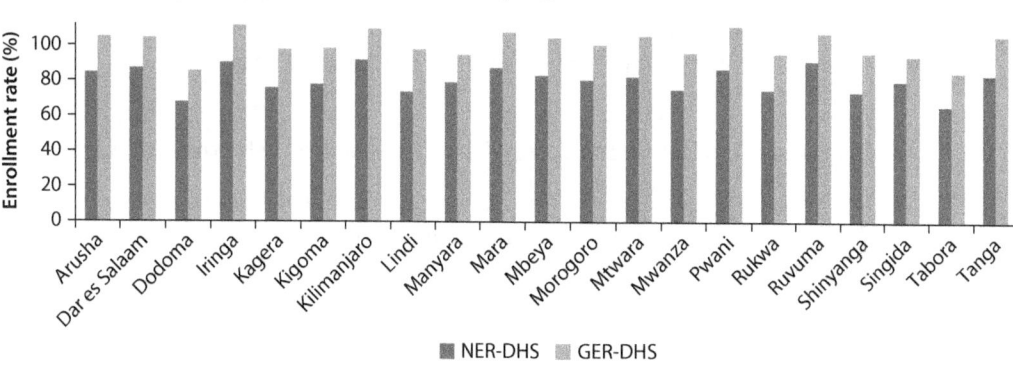

Figure 2.1 Net Primary Enrollment Rate since the Introduction of the PEDP

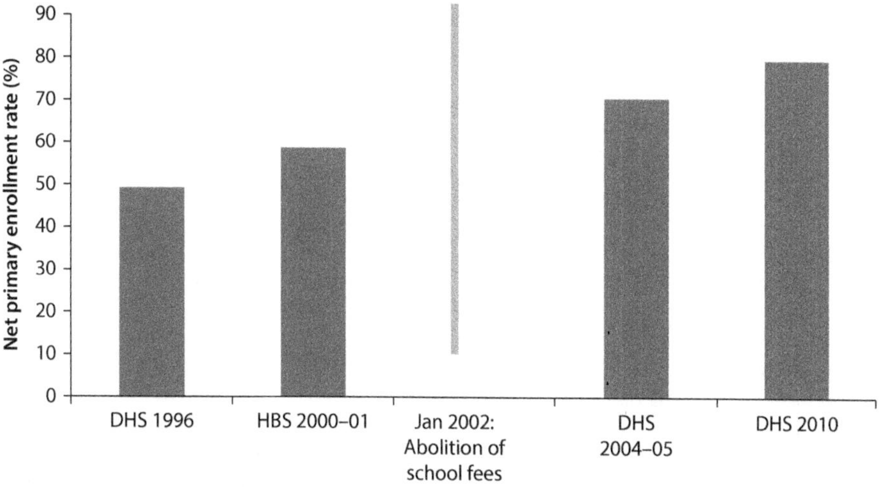

Sources: Authors' calculations based on DHS 1996, 2004–05, and 2010 results and HBS 2000–01.
Note: PEDP = Public Education Development Project; DHS = Demographic and Health Survey; HBS = Household Budget Survey.

Figure 2.2 Net and Gross Primary Enrollment Rates by Region, 2010

Source: Authors' calculations based on DHS 2010.
Note: DHS = Demographic and Health Survey; GER = gross enrollment rate; NER = net enrollment rate.

enrollment by children of any age as a proportion of the school-age population, differs from 84.7 percent in Tabora to 110.6 percent in Pwani and 111.3 percent in Iringa.

At the district level, variations are even larger. This can be illustrated with data from the 2006–07 Core Welfare Indicators Questionnaire Surveys (CWIQs), which covered 25 districts in Tanzania. These surveys are representative at the district level and also collect information about enrollment.[4] Districts covered by the CWIQs were purposively selected and are located in 11 out of Tanzania's 21 regions. Some regions are very well represented in the CWIQ (e.g., seven of the eight districts in Shinyanga); others, such as Arusha, had only

Figure 2.3 Variations in Net Primary Enrollment Rates between Districts, 2006–07 (Selected Districts)

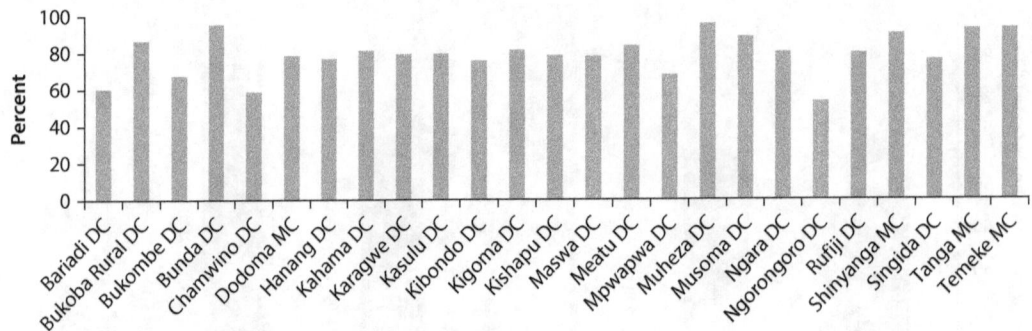

Source: Calculations based on Core Welfare Indicator Surveys, 2006–07.

one district included. The CWIQ survey is neither nationally nor regionally representative, and so it is not possible to draw general conclusions from this data set, but the estimates show considerable variation in net enrollment rates between districts, from as low as 53 percent in Ngorongoro to as high as 96 percent in Muheza (figure 2.3). And as seven of the eight districts in Shinyanga were covered, the CWIQ data illustrate considerable variation even within regions. For example, the net enrollment rate varies from 60 percent in Bariadi to 90 percent in Shinyanga MC (both in Shinyanga region).

Discrepancies between Survey-Based and Administrative Enrollments

The EMIS of the Ministry of Education and Vocational Training measures enrollment administratively through an annual census of schools and other education facilities. In combination with population projections, it permits the computation of net and GERs. This information is published in the Basic Education Statistics Tanzania report. This section argues that the EMIS data overestimate net enrollment by 15.9 percentage points and gross enrollment by 6.8 percentage points, and it sheds light on the proximate factors that explain these differences.

Whereas according to the DHS net enrollment in primary school in 2010 was 79.5 percent, the EMIS shows a net enrollment rate of 95.4 percent. Less of a difference is found for gross enrollment, where the DHS data show a GER of 99.6 percent for 2010, compared with 106.4 percent in the EMIS. These differences between data sources carry over to the regions as illustrated in figures 2.4 and 2.5. It is evident that in some regions, discrepancies are much larger than in others (compare, e.g., Dodoma and Ruvuma).

Enrollments measured administratively and through household surveys reflect a fairly similar concept, so one would expect gross or net enrollment rates from the two sources to correspond closely to each other, even though some discrepancies could occur, for instance, because children who report for school at the beginning of a school year may drop out during the year (see box 2.1 for a discussion).

Box 2.1 Administrative and Survey-Based Measures of Net Enrollment

Net enrollment is an administrative measure defined as the number of children of primary school age (7–13 years) who are *enrolled* in primary education as a percentage of the total children of the official school-age population. Enrollment information is collected from schools, which, at the start of the school year, report the number of students that have registered with the school, and the school-age population is obtained from population projections from the latest available census.

Net enrollment can also be measured through household surveys, in which case it is typically defined slightly differently as the number of children of official primary school age (7–13 years) who *attend* primary education as a percentage of the total children of the official school-age population. Information on attendance *and* school-age population are collected from households at the time of the survey (although absolute numbers also depend on population projections from the latest census through the respective survey weights/expansion factors).

Strictly going by definition, enrollment measured by administrative and survey data reflects different concepts because being enrolled differs from attending, for example, because children drop out from class during the school year or are temporarily absent from school. However, these differences in definitions cannot easily explain the large discrepancies observed between the DHS and the EMIS. Moreover we observe similar differences using data from the DHS 2004–05, which included a question phrased "During the academic year that started in 2004, did [NAME] attend school at any time?" Attendance at any time during the current school year arguably corresponds more closely to the concept of administrative enrollment than the 2010 question "Is [NAME] currently attending school?" Further differences could occur because the surveys collect information on children's age at the time of interview, whereas the administrative data system obtains age at the time of registration, and because about 10 percent of the 2010 DHS data were gathered in late 2009, just before the beginning of the 2010 school year; but again the difference should be small.

Figure 2.4 Discrepancies between Survey-Based and Administrative Net Primary Enrollment Rates by Region, 2010

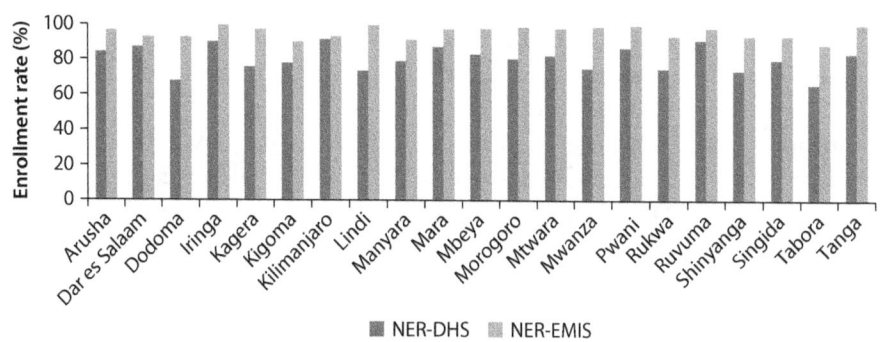

Sources: Authors' calculations based on DHS and EMIS.
Note: DHS = Demographic and Health Survey; EMIS = Education Management Information System; NER = net enrollment rate.

Figure 2.5 Discrepancies between Survey-Based and Administrative Gross Primary Enrollment Rates by Region, 2010

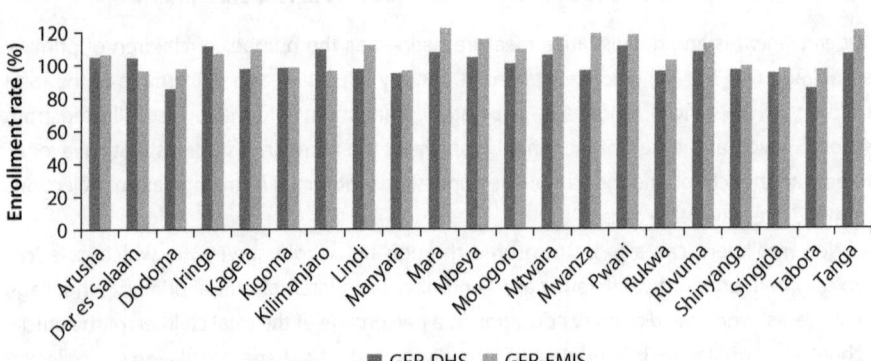

Sources: Authors' calculations based on DHS and EMIS.
Note: DHS = Demographic and Health Survey; EMIS = Education Management Information System; GER = gross enrollment rate.

In practice, however, enrollment rates in Tanzania depend strongly on the way they are measured. Survey-based measures are systematically lower than administratively determined measures (see figures 2.4 and 2.5 and table 2.1), with a gap of almost 16 percentage points between net enrollment measured by the DHS and by the EMIS, and a 7 percentage point gap in gross enrollment in 2010. This raises questions whether the survey underreports or whether the administrative data overreport enrollments. Two independently conducted surveys, the DHS 2010 and the NPS 2010–11, report virtually identical enrollment rates,[5] and so we have solid grounds to believe that the administrative data overreport primary enrollment rates.

To explain these discrepancies, we compare absolute numbers of enrollment by age (see table 2.1). As expected, given the large discrepancy in net enrollment rates, the DHS records a significantly lower number of students aged 7–13 than the EMIS (671,000 fewer students). However, overall enrollments (irrespective of age) are fairly comparable and in fact slightly higher in the DHS than in the EMIS (8.6 versus 8.4 million). Hence it seems that although the administrative data system often misreports the age of school-going children, it does a fairly good job in capturing total enrollments.

Incorrectly recorded age leads to a significant overestimation of the net enrollment rate by the EMIS as the number of enrolled children in the 7–13 age group exceeds the DHS estimate by around 671,000. However, this discrepancy only explains about half the difference in NERs between the EMIS and DHS (671,000 children represents about 8.0 percent of the primary school-age population, whereas the difference in NER is 15.9 percent). Nor does incorrectly recorded age explain the difference in GERs, because the latter is independent from the age of enrolled children. In fact, since total enrollments estimated from the DHS are slightly *higher* than enrollments captured in the

Table 2.1 Estimated Primary Enrollment by Age, DHS and Administrative Data, 2010

	DHS	EMIS	Discrepancy
Primary enrollments by age (years)			
<7	411,230	207,448	−203,782
7	805,052	889,623	84,571
8	848,677	1,197,327	348,650
9	1,148,130	1,212,941	64,811
10	1,128,655	1,194,477	65,822
11	1,010,955	1,081,532	70,577
12	1,017,403	1,036,410	19,007
13	917,843	935,496	17,653
>13	1,326,232	664,051	−662,181
Total 7–13	6,876,715	7,547,806	671,091
Total	8,614,177	8,419,305	−194,872
Primary school-age population			
Population 7–13	8,646,703	7,911,583	−735,120
Enrollment rates	Percent	Percent	Difference (percentage points)
NER	79.5	95.4	−15.9
GER	99.6	106.4	−6.8

Sources: Authors' calculations based on DHS and EMIS.
Note: DHS = Demographic and Health Survey; EMIS = Education Management Information System; NER = net enrollment rate; GER = gross enrollment rate.

EMIS (by 195,000 children), we would expect that the DHS shows a *higher* GER. The opposite is the case, because the DHS reports a GER of 99.6 percent and the EMIS reports 106.4 percent.

The explanation for this phenomenon lies in the denominator of the enrollment rates, that is, the underlying primary school-age population, which is significantly larger according to the DHS (8.6 million children) than according to the EMIS (7.9 million children). According to the 2010 DHS, 20.7 percent of the population of mainland Tanzania are in the age group 7–13 years. Given an overall population projection of 41.8 million (43 million including Zanzibar), this corresponds to approximately 8.6 million children of primary school age.[6] However, enrollment rates in the EMIS are based on the assumption of a primary school-age population of only 7.9 million. This discrepancy in the population numbers thus explains that the EMIS reports higher GERs than the DHS, despite capturing a slightly smaller absolute number of enrollments. It also explains the remainder of the difference in primary net enrollment rates between the EMIS and DHS.

Since the EMIS does not estimate the school-age population but draws on external population projections, we take a closer look at the official population projections, which were derived by the NBS in 2006 and are based on the 2002 Population and Housing Census (NBS 2006). These report a primary school-age population (7–13 years) of 7,375,709, which is even lower than the school-age population projection underlying the EMIS (7,911,583) and much lower than the DHS estimate (8,646,703). Even more strikingly, the official primary school-age population is lower than the number of enrolled children of primary school age captured by the EMIS (7,547,806), which would have led to a NER of above 100 percent had the EMIS used the NBS (2006) school-age population projection. This is obviously impossible because net enrollment rates are per definition bound by universal enrollment of the school-age population and thus cannot exceed 100 percent.

Although it would go beyond the purpose of this chapter to review the method used for the population projections, it appears that the official projections significantly underestimate the primary school-age population. The same conclusion was reached by the recently conducted Statistics Review Tanzania (Harris 2011a, 2011b), which also shows that the NBS population projections report an unexplained dramatic increase in the number of newborn children for 2003, the first year of the projection, which generates an uneven kink that moves through the population pyramid and distorts relative population shares. In sum, there is ample reason to believe that the NBS projections underestimate the primary school-age population.

We do not have further information on the population projections underlying the EMIS, but it appears that staff from the Ministry of Education and Vocational Training noticed some of the above inconsistencies and revised the official school-age population estimates. The comparison with population estimates derived from DHS data, however, suggests that these revisions were not able to fully resolve the underestimation of primary school-age children. Evidently there is an urgent need to derive updated and improved projections based on the 2012 Population and Housing Census and to reconcile the projections used by various branches of the government of Tanzania.

The overreporting of net enrollment has a number of important implications:

- Because net enrollment is overestimated by approximately 16 percentage points in the EMIS, Tanzania did not achieve the target of 99 percent net primary school enrollment by 2010 outlined under the National Strategy for Growth and Reduction of Poverty (known by its Kiswahili acronym MKUKUTA). In addition, it seems highly unlikely that the country will reach the MKUKUTA II and Millennium Development Goal (MDG) targets of universal primary enrollment by 2014–15 and 2015, respectively.
- The EMIS does relatively well in reporting the overall number of students. No evidence from the data considered in this study indicates that schools overreport total enrollments (e.g., to increase revenues from the capitation grant, which is allocated on a per-pupil basis).
- Improving the quality of age-specific enrollments in the EMIS requires clarity about why parents or teachers have incentives to incorrectly report age at entry and what can be done to address this misreporting.

- Enrollment rates are strongly affected by projections of the school-age population. It seems that the population projections that feed into the EMIS significantly underestimate the primary school-age population. Improved population projections based on the 2012 Population and Housing Census will be important to adequately track enrollment rates in the administrative data system.
- The success in enhancing the quality of the EMIS can be reviewed regularly by comparing EMIS enrollment rates with NPS-based enrollment rates, which are available every two years, as well as based on data from the less-frequent HBS and DHS surveys.

The analyses in this section have shown that despite substantial improvements in enrollment rates since the introduction of PEDP, Tanzania is still far from achieving universal primary education because many children still remain out of school. It is thus important to understand who they are and what policies are required to get them enrolled. The following sections will investigate some potential factors, such as late entry into primary school and low degrees of access for the poor, as well the constraints faced by poor households in sending their children to school.

Late Entry to Primary School

Late enrollment into primary school continues to be a problem, although considerable progress has been achieved. Table 2.2 shows the age distribution of Standard 1 students based on data from the 2000–01 HBS as well as the more recent 2008–09 and 2010–11 NPS.[7] The data show clearly significant progress in reducing late enrollment since the introduction of PEDP: The share of Standard 1 students aged nine years or above declined from almost 56 percent in 2000–01 to just over 21 percent in 2008–09 and 2010–11.

Table 2.2 Age Distribution in Standard 1, 2000–01, 2008–09, and 2010–11

Age (years)	2000–01	2008–09	2010–11
5	0.6%	3.2%	3.8%
6	4.7	17.4	20.2
7	16.9	32.0	28.4
8	22.2	26.0	25.8
9	18.7	10.6	11.1
10	17.5	5.2	6.5
11	8.7	2.5	2.3
12	5.7	1.0	1.0
13+	5.0	2.2	1.0
9+	55.6	21.5	21.8
Total	100.0	100.0	100.0

Sources: Authors' calculations based on HBS 2000–01, NPS 2008–09, and NPS 2010–11.

This suggests that the PEDP, with its emphasis on enforcing compulsory enrollment at the age of seven, has achieved considerable success, even though there are still a number of children who enroll at later ages. Much of the improvement appears to have occurred over the past few years, and not immediately after the introduction of the PEDP. In particular, figure 2.6 shows, based on DHS data, that late enrollment was still very common in 2004–05, when only 29 percent of children at the age of seven years were attending school. This share had doubled to 59 percent by 2010.

Figure 2.6 also shows that most children eventually go to school. Almost 90 percent of 11-year-old children are enrolled in primary school. However, a substantial fraction of children still enrolls late, and so they stay in school well longer than the official age to leave primary school of 13 years. More than 21 percent of 16-year-old children were still enrolled at the primary level in 2010, down from 37 percent in 2004–05.

Late enrollment bears high costs for individuals and society at large. Although delayed entry does not necessarily lead to fewer years of completed schooling, late enrollment leads to lower expected lifetime earnings. To maintain total years of schooling with delayed entry, an individual has to enter the workforce when older. It has been estimated that for each year of delay in entry to primary school, a child loses 3–5 percent of his or her lifetime wealth (Alderman, Hoogeveen, and Rossi 2009; Glewwe and Jacoby 1995).

Figure 2.7 shows that although Tanzania managed to significantly reduce the effective age at which children enter primary school between 2004–05 and 2010, it still falls behind other countries in the region. In particular, Kenya and Uganda, where the age of enrollment is six years (instead of seven years), have a larger

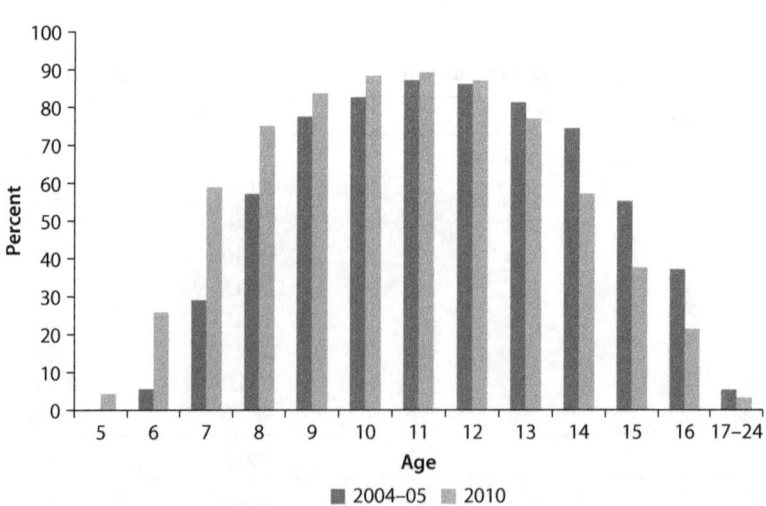

Figure 2.6 Share of Children Enrolled in Primary School by Age, 2004–05 and 2010

Sources: Authors' calculations based on DHS 2004–05 and 2010.

fraction of children in school by the age of seven: 69 percent of children in Uganda and 66 percent of children in Kenya, contrasted with 59 percent in Tanzania. Yet the data also show Tanzania's remarkable progress in reducing the age of school entry and the share of overage students. In this respect, Tanzania is well ahead of Kenya and Uganda, which continue to have much larger numbers of students older than 13 in primary school.[8]

Figure 2.8 shows that Tanzania's success in reducing the number of overage students in primary school appears to be related to the fact that many more children now go to secondary school. In 2004–05, only 2 percent of 14-year-olds were enrolled in secondary school; in 2010, this had increased to 14 percent. In addition, the mean age of children in secondary school slightly declined from 17.5 to 17.1 years. As a result, the average Tanzanian secondary student is about a year younger than his or her counterpart in Kenya, where the mean age of children in secondary school is 18.1 years.

Figure 2.7 Share of Children Enrolled in Primary School by Age in Selected East African Countries

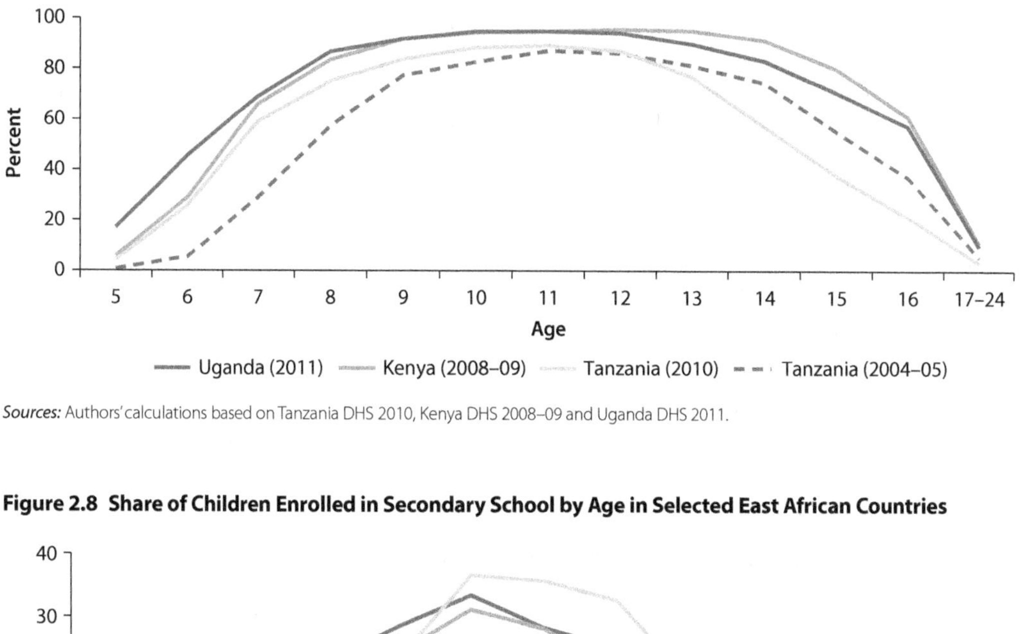

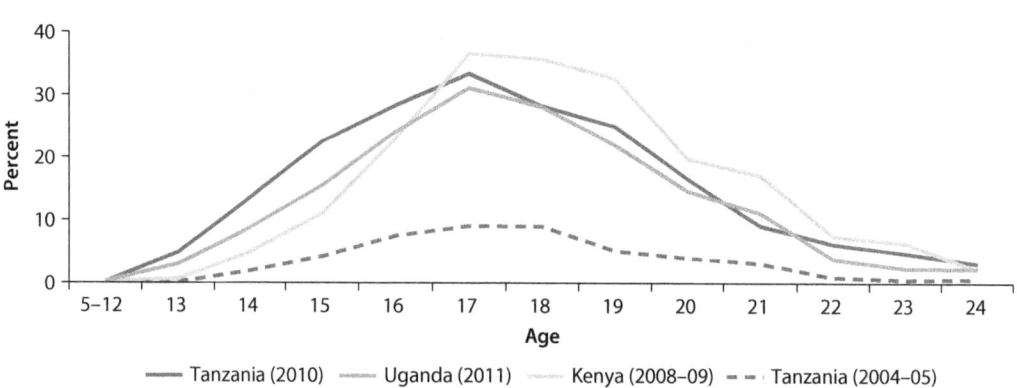

Sources: Authors' calculations based on Tanzania DHS 2010, Kenya DHS 2008–09 and Uganda DHS 2011.

Figure 2.8 Share of Children Enrolled in Secondary School by Age in Selected East African Countries

Sources: Authors' calculations based on Tanzania DHS 2010, Kenya DHS 2008–09, and Uganda DHS 2011.

Fewer Opportunities and Lower Quality for Poor Pupils

Among the children going to primary school in 2010, the fraction originating from the poorest wealth quintile is about the same as that from the wealthiest quintile (18.7 percent versus 18.3 percent). Encouragingly, the share of children from the poorest wealth quintile increased from 16.5 percent in 2004–05 to 18.7 percent in 2010, indicating that a more than proportionate share of the additional enrollments came from the bottom quintile: In other words, the effects of the PEDP favored the poor. Children from middle-class households are slightly overrepresented in primary school, but children from the wealthiest households are underrepresented.[9]

Because poorer households tend to have more children, children from the bottom wealth quintiles represent a larger share of the school-age population. This can be seen in table 2.3 as the share of the school-age population originating from the poorest wealth quintile is 21.6 percent, whereas that of children from the wealthiest quintile is 17.0 percent. Because of this and despite the progress made in enrolling children from poor households, children from poorer households still have a lower probability of going to school compared with children from wealthier backgrounds. For primary enrollments to be equitably distributed in relation to needs for education services (measured by the school-age population), the proportion of children from the poorest households in primary school ought to equal to their share of the school-age population. At present, however, it is lower for the poorest (18.7 versus 21.6) and higher for the wealthiest (18.3 versus 17.0) (see Demery and Gaddis 2012 for a more general discussion).

Another way to show that children from poor families are less likely to benefit from primary education is to consider children that have never attended school (table 2.4). Approximately 7.7 percent of all children aged 10–13 had not even entered Standard 1 in 2010. In rural areas, where 9.0 percent had not entered school, the situation is worse than in urban areas, where 2.6 percent had not entered school. Children from poor households are particularly disadvantaged: 15.5 percent of children from the poorest quintile had not entered primary school,

Table 2.3 Primary Enrollment and School-Age Population by Quintile, 2004–05 and 2010

Wealth quintile	2004–05		2010	
	Share of enrollment	Share of school-age population	Share of enrollment	Share of school-age population
Poorest	16.5%	20.7%	18.7%	21.6%
2	18.6	20.1	19.2	20.3
3	20.9	20.3	22.2	21.2
4	24.3	21.3	21.5	20.0
Wealthiest	19.7	17.6	18.3	17.0
Total	100.0	100.0	100.0	100.0

Sources: Authors' calculations based on DHS 2004–05 and 2010.

compared with only 1.8 percent of children from the wealthiest group. In other words, a child from the poorest quintile is eight times more likely not to have entered Standard 1 between the ages of 10 and 13 than a child from the wealthiest quintile.

Furthermore, evidence indicates that children from poor backgrounds tend to visit schools of lower quality, although unfortunately the latest available poverty maps for 2001–02 are somewhat dated.[10] Figure 2.9 shows a significant positive correlation between the 2001–02 poverty incidence at the district level and the average pupil teacher ratio, indicating that children in poorer areas access lower quality schools.[11] It will be interesting to explore if and how these patterns have changed with the continued expansion of primary enrollments in recent years.

Table 2.4 Share of Children Aged 10–13 Who Never Attended School by Quintile/Area, 2010

Wealth quintile/area	Never attended
Poorest quintile	15.5%
2	11.5
3	5.4
4	3.6
Wealthiest quintile	1.8
Urban	2.6
Rural	9.0
Total	7.7

Source: Authors' calculations based on DHS 2010.

Figure 2.9 Correlation between the District-Level Poverty Incidence and the Pupil-Teacher Ratio, 2001–02

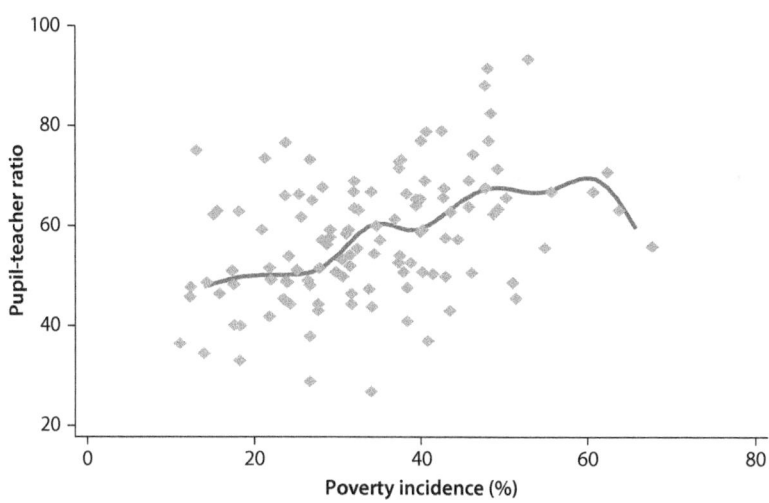

Source: Authors' calculations based on PHDR (United Republic of Tanzania 2005).

Challenges to Improving Primary School Enrollment

The preceding sections have demonstrated that the PEDP was generally successful in reducing the age at entry and in increasing enrollment in primary school, particularly of children from poor households. Nonetheless, many students, in particular those from poorer backgrounds, still do not go to primary school, and others fail to start at age seven, at which primary education is compulsory. Continued policy attention is required to further increase primary school enrollment and to reduce age at entry.

This section explores some of the underlying factors that prevent (poor) households from enrolling their children in primary school, and it suggests policies to address these constraints. Based on international evidence, we view improved early childhood nutrition, investments in school quality in rural areas, and a reduction in the compulsory age at entry from seven to six years as key candidate factors for interventions aimed at reducing late and nonentry. Our analyses are based on data from the 2006–07 CWIQ and the 2004 Kagera Health and Development Survey (KHDS; see Alderman, Hoogeveen, and Rossi 2009 for details).

Figure 2.10 reports reasons given by parents for not sending their eight-year-old children to school based on the 2006–07 CWIQ. Age and distance to school are among the most frequently mentioned reasons, along with the answer that the child is working or sick. The parents' responses require some interpretation. "Working," for instance, could refer to a child that for some reason does not attend school and is hence put to work, but could also refer to a child that because of poverty is forced to contribute to the family's income and withdrawn from school. Both interpretations are plausible, and the direction of causality cannot be disentangled from the parents' responses. Likewise, "too young" could refer to a child that is physically or mentally not yet ready for school, but it could also describe a child that appears physically young because he or she is malnourished and small for his or her age.

Figure 2.10 Reasons Cited by Parents for Not Sending Their Eight-Year-Old Children to Primary School, 2006–07

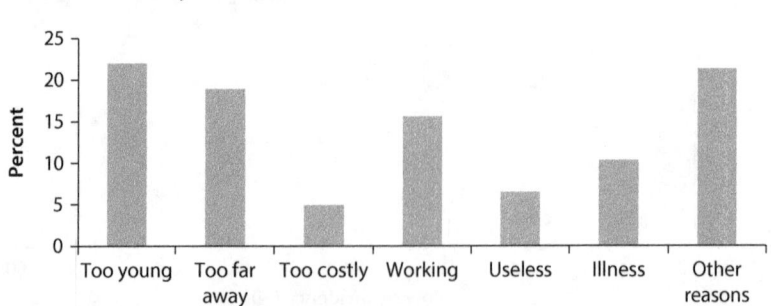

Source: Authors' calculations based on 2006–07 CWIQ.

Support for the latter interpretation comes from the Kagera survey, where the literature shows that malnourished children delay entry into primary school by 1.3 years and are four times more likely not to enroll at all (Alderman, Hoogeveen, and Rossi 2009). This pattern is described in figure 2.11, which shows that 77 percent of nonstunted children aged seven, but only 45 percent of the stunted children of the same age, went to primary school in 2004.

The importance of distance to school as an obstacle to entry can also be illustrated with the data from Kagera. Figure 2.12 plots the relationship between the percentage of children that is enrolled by the age of seven and distance to the

Figure 2.11 Primary Enrollment in Kagera by Age and Nutritional Status, 2004

Source: Authors' calculations based on KHDS 2004.

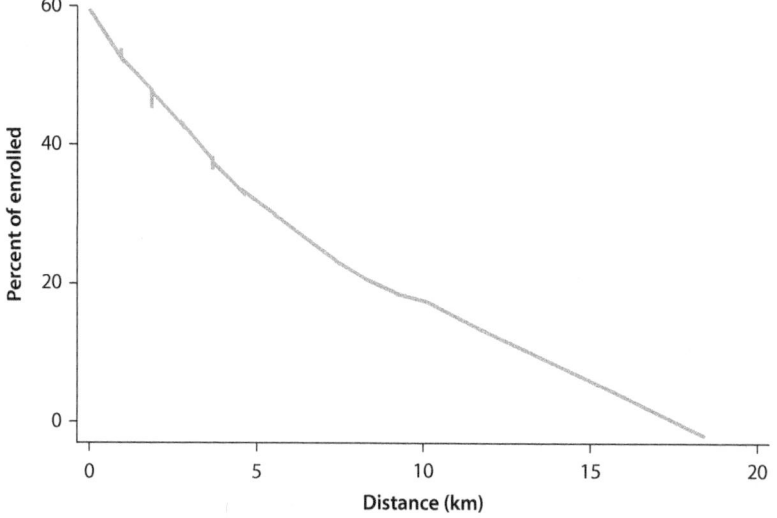

Figure 2.12 Distance to School and Primary Enrollment among Seven-Year-Old Children in Kagera, 2004

Source: Authors' calculations based on KHDS 2004.

nearest primary school. It demonstrates that enrollment strongly declines with distance. Children aged seven years living at a five-kilometer distance to a school exhibit an enrollment rate of 30 percent, half of the enrollment rate (60 percent) of children aged seven years living closest to a school.

To disentangle the relationship between these various correlated factors and the parents' decision to enroll their children in school, we use regression analysis to explain school enrollment of children aged six to eight years (results are shown in table 2.5). The coefficients in this table show "marginal effects," that is, the effects of a change in the independent variables on the predicted probability of being enrolled in school.[12] The regression confirms that age, household income, distance to school, and nutritional status are significant determinants of school enrollment. Enrollment increases with age and household income and decreases with distance and nutritional status. Among these factors, nutrition is the most influential in explaining enrollment. At age seven (eight), the probability of going to school is 33 (29) percentage points lower for stunted children compared with the nonstunted children. This is a much larger impact than, for instance, distance to school. A child with "average" characteristics living 15 kilometers from school has a 3 percentage point lower chance of visiting school than the same child living right next to a school.

The regression also includes various other variables that potentially could impact enrollment. Surprisingly, gender and being an orphan do not affect school enrollment, nor does the highest education attainment within the household. The number of teachers per child, on the other hand, has a strong impact on enrollment. One additional teacher per child increases enrollment by 11 percentage points.

Table 2.5 Determinants of School Enrollment in Kagera, Children Aged Six to Eight, 2004

	Marginal effect	Student's t
Age 7	0.380	8.61***
Age 8	0.449	9.66***
Stunted and aged 6	−0.317	−3.54***
Stunted and aged 7	−0.335	−5.18***
Stunted and aged 8	−0.294	−3.93***
Distance to primary school (km)	−0.002	−1.80*
Log per capita expenditure	0.167	4.82***
D-Female	−0.004	−0.12
D-Mother still alive	0.054	0.48
D-Father still alive	−0.026	−0.34
D-Father living in the household	−0.006	−0.11
D-Mother living in the household	−0.036	−0.66
Maximum years of education in the household	−0.006	−0.81
Number of classes per child	−0.534	−0.14
Number of teachers per child	11.904	3.23***
Observations	835	

Source: Authors' calculations based on KHDS 2004.
Significance level: * = 10 percent, ** = 5 percent, *** = 1 percent.

This is a quantitatively large effect, especially if one considers that additional teachers would most likely also improve education quality and learning outcomes.

Although this regression should not be seen as rigorously identifying causal impact, the results are suggestive of how to address the challenge of late (and non-) enrollment in primary school because age, nutritional status, and the number of teachers per child emerge as significant factors. Whereas a child's age cannot be affected by policy, the perception of what is the appropriate age to start school is a policy-relevant variable, for instance, by reducing the compulsory age of entry.

The Way Forward

Inadequate administrative data are likely to have persuaded policy makers into believing that Tanzania is on track to reach the MDG target of universal primary education by 2015. However, our analysis shows that this is not the case and hence raises the question how to close the remaining gap. This chapter identifies the following main policy areas to bring more children into school at an early age:

- Increases in the number of teachers in rural areas: The analysis here suggests that additional teachers significantly raise enrollments; additional positive effects on educational quality can also be expected.
- A reduction in the compulsory age at entry from seven to six years, combined with further efforts to promote early enrollment of children in school.
- Improvements in the nutritional status of children—through interventions in the areas of health, water, sanitation, and food security. Early childhood development programs, with an emphasis on nutrition and school readiness, may also play an important role in this context.

Public interventions in the above areas should be combined with a program of rigorous empirical evaluation and experimentation to identify cost-effective approaches that can be implemented nationwide.

To avoid the possibility that policy makers are (mis-)informed by incorrect data, an urgent need can be stated to further improve the quality of the administrative data system:

- As soon as possible, the EMIS enrollment rates should be revised based on updated and improved population projections from the 2012 Population and Housing Census.
- Further empirical investigations are needed to understand clearly the incentives (by parents and/or teachers) to misreport age at entry.
- The quality of enrollment rates reported by the EMIS can be regularly monitored using nationally representative household surveys (i.e., NPS, DHS, and HBS). Pending improvements of the administrative data system, reported education indicators from the EMIS (e.g., for MDG and MKUKUTA II progress reports) should be supplemented with survey-based enrollment estimates.

Notes

1. The DHS also includes Zanzibar, but the estimates here refer to mainland Tanzania only.
2. PEDP was launched in July 2001, just after the end of data collection for the 2000–01 HBS. Primary school fees were effectively abolished in January 2002.
3. The 2004–05 DHS report shows a slightly different net enrollment rate of 73.1 percent because it uses a somewhat different definition of enrollment. In particular, the NER published in the 2004–05 DHS report refers to enrollment "during the 2004 academic school year," but the enrollment rate shown here refers to "current enrollment," which is more comparable to the definitions used in the 1996 and 2010 DHS surveys and the 2000–01 HBS (see also box 2.1).
4. The recently completed 2012 Population and Housing Census will allow computing updated district-level enrollment rates, because the "long" questionnaire, administered to 30 percent of enumeration areas, captures information on school enrollments. However, since the census data are not yet available, the 2006–07 CWIQ remains, to our knowledge, the most recent survey that allows for the computation of district-specific enrollment rates.
5. The NPS 2010–11 reports a NER for primary education of 80 percent (NBS 2012), very similar to 79.6 percent in the DHS.
6. The 2010 DHS reports a total population of 43 million for the United Republic of Tanzania (NBS and ICF Macro 2011).
7. The NPS is a nationally representative longitudinal survey, which is fielded every two years.
8. Slight differences in definitions might play a role, as both Kenya and Uganda base enrollment on attendance at any time during the current school year rather than current attendance (as does Tanzania). The Tanzania DHS 2004–05, which allows computing enrollment rates for both definitions, shows that enrollment among overage children is higher if we consider enrollment at any time during the academic school year. This is not surprising, since overage children are more likely to drop out during the school year or to attend school irregularly. However, it is unlikely that these variations in definitions explain the substantial differences that we see between the East African countries.
9. A more progressive distribution emerges if we use consumption quintiles and NPS 2010–11 data. In this case, the share of enrollments from the poorest quintile is larger (20 percent) than the share from the wealthiest quintile (15.4 percent). The remaining patterns still hold.
10. District-level poverty maps are based on data from the 2002 census and the 2000–01 HBS; updated poverty maps can be generated once the 2012 census and 2011 HBS microdata are released. Pupil-teacher ratios also refer to 2002. Data are tabulated in the 2005 Tanzania Poverty and Human Development Report (PHDR; United Republic of Tanzania 2005).
11. The correlation coefficient is 0.26 and significant at the 1 percent level of confidence.
12. With binary variables, marginal effects measure the effect of a discrete change in the explanatory variable (e.g., from 0 to 1); with continuous variables they measure the effect of an incremental change.

References

Alderman, Harold, Hans Hoogeveen, and Mariacristina Rossi. 2009. "Preschool Nutrition and Subsequent Schooling Attainment: Longitudinal Evidence from Tanzania." *Economic Development and Cultural Change* 57 (2): 239–60.

Demery, Lionel, and Isis Gaddis. 2012. "Benefit Incidence Analysis, Needs and Demography: Measurement Issues and an Empirical Study for Kenya." Courant Research Centre Discussion Paper 122, University of Göttingen, Göttingen, Germany.

Glewwe, Paul, and Hanan G. Jacoby. 1995. "An Economic Analysis of Delayed Primary School Enrollment and Childhood Malnutrition in a Low Income Country." *Review of Economics and Statistics* 77 (1): 156–69.

Harris, Tim. 2011a. "Basic Education Statistics in Tanzania (BEST)." Statistics Review Tanzania, Dar es Salaam, Tanzania. http://www.statisticsreviewtanzania.org/reports.

———. 2011b. "Assessment of Tanzania's Population Projections." Statistics Review Tanzania, Dar es Salaam, Tanzania. http://www.statisticsreviewtanzania.org/reports.

Hoogeveen, Johannes, and Mariacristina Rossi. 2013. "Enrollment and Grade Attainment Following the Introduction of Free Primary Education in Tanzania." *Journal of African Economies*. doi:10.1093/jae/ejt003.

NBS (National Bureau of Statistics). 2006. *Tanzania Regional and District Projections.* Volume XII, Dar es Salaam, Tanzania. http://www.nbs.go.tz/nbs/takwimu/Population/REG_AND_DIST_PROJECTIONS.zip.

———. 2012. *Tanzania National Panel Survey Report—Wave 2, 2010–2011.* Dar es Salaam, Tanzania.

NBS (National Bureau of Statistics) and Macro International Inc. 1997. *Tanzania Demographic and Health Survey 1996.* Dar es Salaam, Tanzania.

NBS (National Bureau of Statistics) and ORC Macro. 2005. *Tanzania Demographic and Health Survey 2004–2005.* Dar es Salaam, Tanzania.

NBS (National Bureau of Statistics) and ICF Macro. 2011. *Tanzania Demographic and Health Survey 2010.* Dar es Salaam, Tanzania.

United Republic of Tanzania. 2005. *Poverty and Human Development Report 2005.* Research and Analysis Working Group, Dar es Salaam, Tanzania.

CHAPTER 3

Addressing Tanzania's Gender Inequality Challenge in Secondary Schools

Oyin Shyllon

Summary

Although little evidence exists of gender inequality in primary school enrollment in Tanzania, girls are less likely than boys to attend secondary schools. Gender parity in enrollment is found at the preprimary and primary school levels, but by the lower secondary level girls make up only 45 percent of the student population, declining further to 35 percent at the upper secondary level. The inability of girls to progress is not the result of a failure of girls to pass qualifying examinations, rather it is the results of a boy bias in household demand for secondary schooling in some regions of Tanzania. The gender parity index (GPI) measure ranges from 0.56 in Shinyanga region (a huge disparity in favor of boys) to 1.12 in Kilimanjaro region (the only region with a disparity in favor of girls).

Very few countries in Sub-Saharan Africa (SSA) have a stronger boy bias in the transition from the primary to the secondary level than is the case in Tanzania. The statistical difference in the out-of-school female population that would ensure parity between girls and boys in secondary schools is attributable to pregnant girls that do not enroll and the fact that more girls refuse to continue schooling because they and/or their parents believe they have achieved their desired level of schooling. The influence of the desired level of schooling on the continuation of girls is mostly applicable to girls aged 15–19. As girls get older, the other key contributors to their out-of-school status are, in order of importance, working at home or an office, early marriage, and affordability of the education. Pregnancy is of great importance to adolescent women (15–19 years) but begins to wane as an impediment as women get older.

Three factors seem to be responsible for the low female secondary participation, and public policy has a role to play in addressing them. First, imperfect information is available to students, parents, and communities on the benefits attributable to more schooling for girls in certain parts of Tanzania. Second, poverty combined with liquidity and credit market imperfections make the cost of secondary schooling prohibitive for poor families; indeed, past efforts at reducing user fees have been accompanied by rapid increases in student enrollment. Third, supply-side shortcomings with respect to accessibility (secondary schools are farther away from the home than primary schools), the absence of enough female teachers and adults as role models and mentors, and the lack of sufficient toilet facilities also deter higher rates of female secondary participation.

Conditional cash transfers (CCTs) targeting poor households have proven effective in many countries at bringing adolescent girls that are outside the education system back into school. CCTs can be designed to straddle the domains of addressing imperfect information and household affordability—two key barriers to female schooling—simultaneously. For CCTs to be effective, markets must work to provide higher private returns to education, and policies must be in place to supply schools and reduce the direct, indirect, and opportunity costs of schooling, which are high in Tanzania.

Introduction

Significant international experience points to the high benefits of young girls' education in terms of increased household health, better infant nutrition, higher agricultural productivity, higher household educational achievements, and lower fertility and population growth rates. Efforts to address gender inequalities in access and retention of girls at the secondary level not only contribute to the education of girls but also generate additional positive spillover effects on girls' learning, empowerment, and leadership and help to keep them free from gender-based violence.

Tanzania's policy makers are concerned about enrollment of girls in secondary education, female dropouts, high prevalence of early pregnancies, and very high adolescent female fertility rates (box 3.1). This chapter presents the challenges facing female secondary enrollment with a view to proposing suitable policy responses.

Gender Dimension of the Demand for Education Services

Few Tanzanian Children Make It Past Primary School
Tanzania's 2006 Integrated Labor Force Survey (ILFS) conducted by the National Bureau of Statistics (NBS) indicates that for the labor force cohort born between 1987 and 1991, the average number of years of schooling was six years. Although low, this is still a marked improvement when this cohort is compared with that born 40 years earlier between 1947 and 1951 with an average of 3.7 years of schooling.[1] This rapid increase is attributable to greater access to primary schooling, but access to postprimary education has remained low.

Box 3.1 Sumbawanga Parents Given Ultimatum to Send Girls to School

MPANDA District Commissioner (DC), Dr. Rajab Rutengwe, on Wednesday ordered a crackdown starting on Thursday of parents and the guardians who have not sent their daughters to school. Dr. Rutengwe said the order follows a report that 15 girls who excelled in their final Standard Seven Examinations last year have not yet reported to their respective schools. The schools opened in January this year. The DC has given the parents and guardians a 15-day ultimatum starting today to ensure that their children are sent to schools or face stern actions including legal measures. Visibly angry, the DC said that it is disgusting to witness that some parents as well as guardians do not see the importance of sending their children, mostly girls, to school despite government efforts to improve both primary and secondary education. Dr. Rutengwe issued the order at a public rally held at Ilembo Ward in Mpanda Township in the district. About 3,382 pupils were selected to join Form One early this year; out of them, 1,688 were girls and 1,694 were boys.

Source: The Daily News (Tanzania), March 8, 2012.

Improvement in access to primary schooling in Tanzania over a short period has been impressive, with primary net enrollment rates increasing from 59 percent in 2001 (URT 2001) to 84 percent in 2007 (URT 2007). Yet in 2007, as was the case in 2001, education participation drops rapidly following the completion of primary education.[2] Age-specific net enrollment rates fall from 89 percent at the age of 13, which is the official age of primary completion, although most children in their final year of primary schooling were 14 years of age, to 76 percent at the age of 15. By the age of 17, only one in every two children is in school.

Secondary Enrollment Is Low and Girls Are Less Likely to Be in Tanzanian Secondary Schools

This finding for Tanzania is consistent with global findings (World Bank 2011). For Tanzania, the enrollment rates for children aged 7–15 is relatively high, so that low enrollment is a phenomenon of secondary schooling (official age is 14–19) and not primary schooling (official age is 7–13). We also find that although girls slightly outnumber boys in primary schools, they are overwhelmingly outnumbered at the upper secondary level. According to the 2007 Household Budget Survey (HBS), the reduction in female participation commences at the age of 15, so that at that age one sees the commencement of a rapid disappearance of girls from the school system. Even when we consider more recent age-specific net attendance data from the 2010 Demographic and Health Survey (DHS) (URT 2010), we find that the disappearance of girls now starts much earlier at the age of 13 (table 3.1).

Table 3.1 Girls Stop Attending School as Early as 13 Years of Age

Age	Male NAR (%)	Female NAR (%)	Extent to which male NAR is higher[a] (%)
5	2	6	−4
6	22	30	−8
7	55	65	−10
8	74	76	−2
9	83	85	−2
10	87	90	−3
11	90	89	1
12	88	89	−1
13	84	81	3
14	77	66	11
15	65	57	8
16	55	47	8
17	47	41	6
18	40	27	13
19	37	20	17
20	27	10	17
21	17	7	10
22	14	3	11
23	11	4	7
24	8	3	5

Source: URT 2010.
Note: NAR = net attendance rate.
a. Measures the percentage point difference in male and female NARs.

Low Secondary Student Enrollment Is Due to a Lower Primary-to-Secondary Transition Rate in Tanzania for the Region

Remarkable progress has been made in secondary enrollment expansion in Tanzania in recent years with student enrollment rising from 675,672 in 2006 to 1,789,547 in 2011—an average annual increase of 21.5 percent (URT 2012). However, measured as new entrants to the first grade of secondary education in the current year as a proportion of pupil enrollment in the final grade of primary education in the previous year, the 41 percent transition rate for Tanzania in 2009 is one of the lowest in SSA: Only three of 32 reporting countries perform worse.[3]

Girls Are More Adversely Affected by Low Primary-to-Secondary Transitions

The level of female participation remains steady in the intermediate years for each level of schooling: preprimary, primary, lower secondary, and upper secondary. One finds, however, major swings in the transition years. For the preprimary and primary schooling years, we see an almost even split between the number of boys and girls in public and private school system in Tanzania. About 45 percent of the lower secondary enrollees are girls, whereas about 35 percent of the upper secondary enrollees are girls. This raises an important question: What happens at the transition from primary to lower secondary or lower secondary to upper secondary that inhibits the progression of as many girls as there are boys. To clarify the causes of this enrollment pattern, it is useful to consider examination pass rates at the completion of studies for each level of education. This will be useful in determining the extent to which girls perform more poorly than boys do and as such are unable to progress to higher levels of schooling.

Tanzania's Boy Bias in the Transition from Primary to Secondary Schooling Is One of the Worst in the Region

According to the 2012 World Development Report on Gender and Inequality (World Bank 2011, 107–8), at low levels of secondary enrollment, girls are less likely to be in school. Burundi, Mauritania, and Tanzania are the classic examples of this phenomenon in SSA. In these countries, not only do fewer of the children that make the final grade of primary schooling progress to the first year of secondary schooling but most of the casualties are girls. The percentage point difference between the male and female primary-to-secondary transition rates in these three countries is 10.5 percent, 7.3 percent, and 7.6 percent, respectively (figure 3.1).[4] For Tanzania, 37.1 percent of girls that make the final grade of

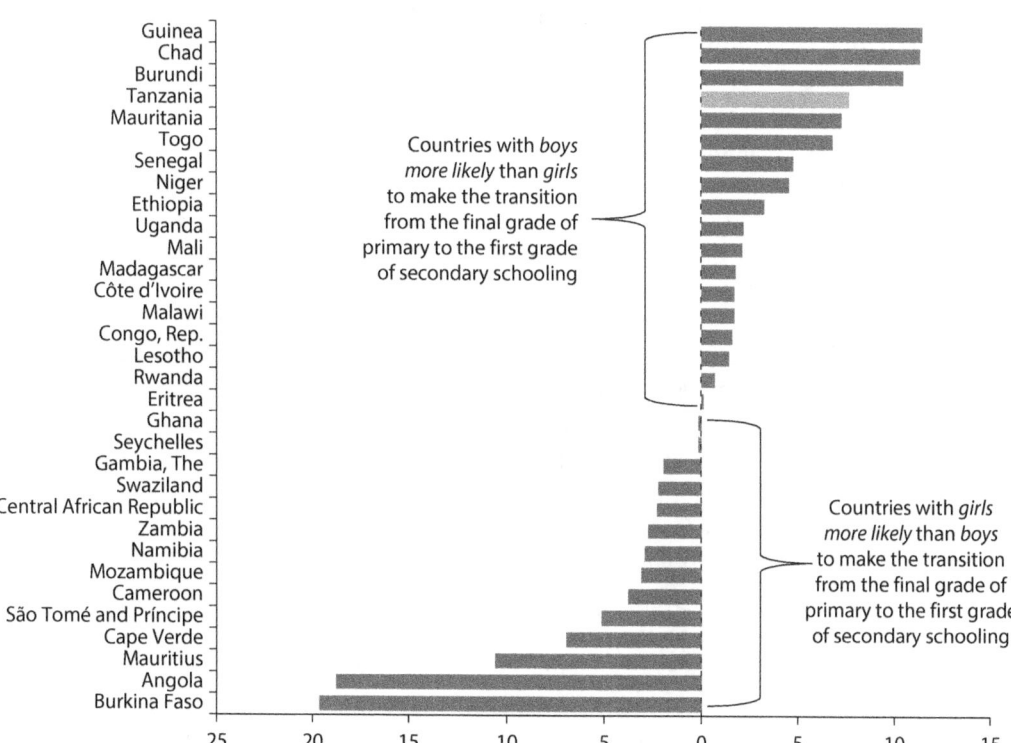

Figure 3.1 Few Countries Are Less Effective at Ensuring Girls Get to School

Source: World Bank 2012, based on the March 9, 2012, data update.
Note: Measures the percentage point difference in male and female transition rates (2008 or most recent year).

primary schooling become new entrants the following year in secondary schools, whereas 44.7 percent of boys that make the final grade of primary schooling become new entrants the following year in secondary schools.

The Plight of Girls with Respect to School Completion Gets Worse as We Move Progressively Upward in the Pretertiary Education Track

Measured by the percentage of children that reach the last year of each level of pretertiary education, known as the completion rate, Tanzania's girls make less progress compared with boys. The primary completion rate for girls is 52 percent, which is better than that for boys at 46 percent. The lower secondary completion rate for girls is 16 percent, which is worse than that for boys at 22 percent. This would suggest that about half of the boys that complete primary schooling end up completing lower secondary schooling, but less than a third of the girls that complete primary schooling end up completing lower secondary schooling. Even worse, the upper secondary completion rate for girls is 3 percent, whereas for boys it is 6 percent. Both rates are very low.

Next, we use estimates of educational attainment rather than school completion. We consider children aged 15–24 years, given evidence that the age group of concern for girls is those above 15 years, and we use a more recent survey data set. Unlike the school completion measure, educational attainment measures the highest level of education attained. The additional benefit of the attainment measure is that we are able to determine what proportion of children that do not complete each level of schooling fail to do so because of a failure to commence schooling or a failure to complete the cycle. We find evidence, similar to that on completion, to show that the girls that do pursue primary schooling do better at completing that level of schooling (71 percent) when compared with boys (60 percent). For boys in this age group, four out of every 11 had completed secondary schooling by the age of 24, whereas only three out of every 11 girls had succeeded in completing secondary schooling (figure 3.2).

Failure to Progress to Higher Levels of Education Is Not the Result of a Failure of Girls to Pass Qualifying Examinations

The starting point for the analysis of female progression through levels of education is a review of the evidence on pass rates from high-stakes examinations conducted in the final years of each level of education. In the final grade of primary education, known as Standard 7, children write the Primary School Leaving Examination (PSLE). At the time of data collection for the 2007 HBS, pass rates for boys and girls were identical. Specifically, the female pass rate was 78 percent in 2007, and the male pass rate was 79 percent. This implies that the low female progression into secondary education was not as a result of low female pass rates. By 2009, right around the time data collection for the 2010 DHS took place, the female pass rate had declined sharply to 43 percent, and the male pass rate was 55 percent. This lower female pass rate trend that started in 2009 continued in 2010 (female pass rate of 48 percent and male pass rate of 59 percent) and has

Figure 3.2 Among Youth, Primary Schooling Is the Norm for Girls with Boys More Successful at Progressing to Secondary Schooling

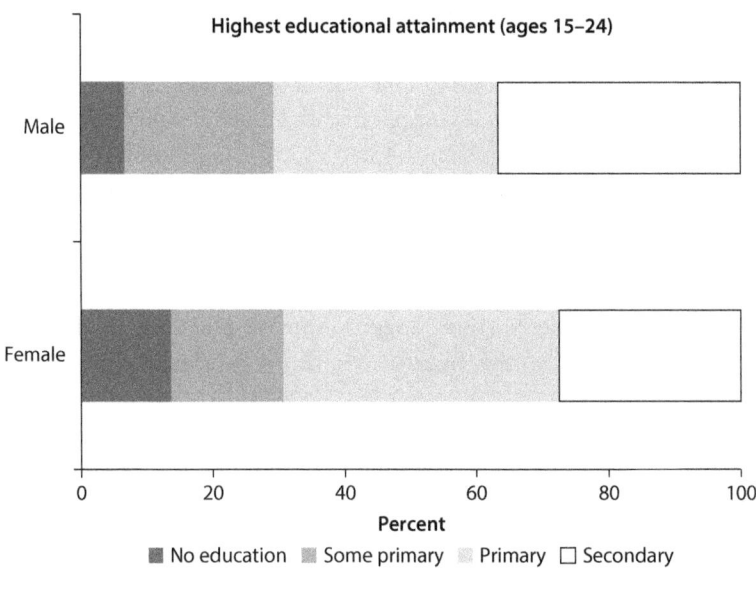

Source: URT 2010.

implications for interventions at the primary education level. The trend is also geographically widespread, with lower pass rates for girls than boys in 20 of the 21 regions.[5] Cohort effects and a history of variable examination pass rates explain the decline in pass rates.[6]

For the high-stakes examinations in the final grade of the lower secondary level, known as the Certificate of Secondary Education Examination, pass rates for boys was marginally better than that for girls in the years in which the 2007 HBS data were collected (for the 2006 and 2007 examinations). For the Advanced Certificate of Secondary Education Examination taken in the final grade of upper secondary schooling, however, pass rates for girls was marginally better than that for boys. These findings suggest that reasons other than academic success are responsible for the lack of progression to higher levels of education for girls.

The Failure of Girls to Progress from Primary to Secondary Schools Is a Result of a Boy Bias in Household Demand for Secondary Schooling in Some Regions of Tanzania

At the primary school level, enrollment for boys and girls is almost equal at both the national and regional levels (based on Education Management Information System [EMIS] data for the 2011 school year). The region with the smallest proportion of girls is Kilimanjaro, and the region with the largest proportion of girls is Dodoma. We measure the GPI as the ratio of female pupils to male pupils so that a GPI of 1 indicates parity in the enrollment of girls and boys, and a value less than 1 indicates disparity in favor of boys. For primary schooling, the GPI varies between 0.96 in Kilimanjaro region (fewer girls than boys) and 1.05 in Dodoma region (more girls than boys).

At the national level, 45 percent of the secondary pupil population are girls with a national GPI of 0.81. This national average is accompanied by sharply varying regional GPIs. The region with the largest proportion of boys is Shinyanga, where boys represent 64 percent of the secondary pupil population, and the region with the largest proportion of girls is Kilimanjaro, where girls represent 53 percent of the secondary pupil population. The GPI measure thus ranges from 0.56 in Shinyanga region (a huge disparity in favor of boys) to 1.12 in Kilimanjaro region (the only region with a disparity in favor of girls). These findings suggest that region-specific factors may be partly responsible for the failure of girls to proceed from primary to secondary school.

This section of the chapter has raised an important question: Why is it that households are less likely to have their female children attend secondary school as they are likely to have their male children despite the fact that (a) parents in all regions of Tanzania are just as likely to have female children attend primary school as they are likely to have their male children and (b) girls and boys had the same PSLE pass rates?

Causes of Nonattendance in and Dropping from School

The High Out-of-School Female Population Eligible for Secondary Education Is Attributable to Pregnant Girls and More Girls Completing Their Desired Level of Schooling

The official age for children in secondary schools in Tanzania is 14–19 years. However, the actual age of most secondary school goers in Tanzania is 13–21 years (URT 2012). For this age group, there is a 12 percentage point difference in school enrollment between boys and girls with 49.7 percent of girls enrolled and 61.4 percent of boys enrolled (table 3.2). The 2007 HBS obtained self-reported information on the reasons for nonenrollment for out-of-school children in this age group. The primary reason for boys (21.2 percent) and girls (28.6 percent) in this age group is based on the completion of their desired level of schooling. An additional 4.2 percent of girls were not enrolled because they were pregnant. To be sure, Tanzania's adolescent fertility rate of 130 births per thousand women aged 15–19 is one of the highest in the world.[7] This 12 percentage point difference in enrollment is equivalent to the proportion of girls that are out of school because they are pregnant and the additional share of girls (relative to boys) that have completed their desired level of schooling. The remaining boys (17.4 percent) and girls (17.5 percent) were out of school for a variety of reasons, including school accessibility (school is too far away), affordability (school is too expensive), employment, disinterest, sickness, failed examinations, marriage, and other unspecified reasons.

Table 3.2 More than Half of Tanzanian Females Aged 13–21 Are Not in School

	Male (%)	Female (%)	All (%)
Enrolled in school	61.4	49.7	55.3
Not enrolled (completed desired level of schooling)	21.2	28.6	25.1
Not enrolled (too far away)	0.9	0.3	0.6
Not enrolled (too expensive)	3.3	3.2	3.3
Not enrolled (working at home/in an office)	3.4	4.9	4.2
Not enrolled (not interested)	4.4	3.1	3.7
Not enrolled (sick)	1.2	1.3	1.3
Not enrolled (pregnancy)	0.0	4.2	2.4
Not enrolled (failed examination)	2.6	1.0	0.5
Not enrolled (got married)	0.3	2.7	2.6
Not enrolled (other)	1.2	1.0	1.1

Source: URT 2007.

The Influence of the Desired Level of Schooling on the Continuation of Girls in School Really Kicks in for Girls Aged 15–19

Only 6 percent of 14-year-old girls believe they should no longer be in school because they have achieved their desired level of schooling. Many 14-year-old girls are still in primary school. For those girls aged 20 years, more than half of them believe they have achieved their desired level of schooling and no longer need to continue schooling. As girls get older, the other key contributors to their out-of-school status are, in order of importance, working at home or an office, early marriage, and affordability, which all suggest high opportunity cost of schooling. Pregnancy is of great importance to adolescent women (aged 15–19 years) but begins to wane as an impediment to schooling subsequently.

Teen Pregnancy and Early Marriage Enforce Early Completion of Schooling for Women in Tanzania

All women between the ages of 15 and 25 who are pregnant do not enroll in school. Efforts to curtail early marriages are important for keeping girls in the school system because the majority of women between the ages of 15 and 25 that get married do not enroll in school. Data from the 2007 HBS indicate that 4 percent of married 16-year-old women are able to continue schooling whereas 62 percent of unmarried 16-year-olds enroll in school. The reduction in the rates of early marriages is strongly correlated with continued school progression for girls aged 15–19 years of age; subsequently, other factors begin to weigh more heavily on the decision and/or ability of girls to continue schooling.

A Shorter School-to-Work Transition for Women Encourages Early Completion of Schooling for Women in Tanzania

Women in Tanzania have a shorter school-to-work transition (Laderchi 2009). This is based on evidence from the 2006 ILFS. Consequently, and as Tanzanian women get older, an increasing proportion of them choose to stop schooling and

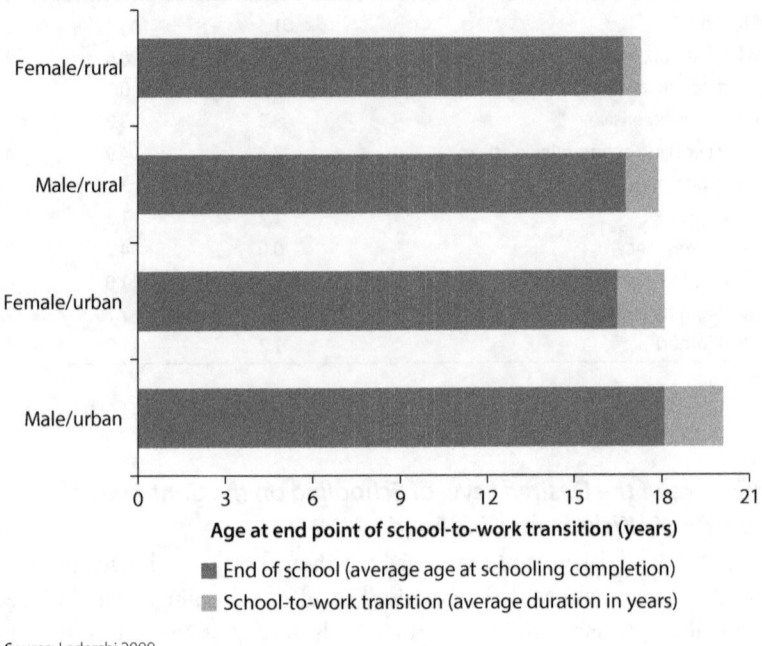

Figure 3.3 Young Women Leave Schooling Earlier Partly Because They Get Jobs Much More Quickly than Young Men

Source: Laderchi 2009.

pursue labor market opportunities. According to the 2006 ILFS, rural women have on average a seven-month school-to-work transition but urban women have an additional year for their job searches. This job search duration is shorter than that for men, which is 13 months for rural men and 24 months for urban men (figure 3.3). The ease of labor market entry for women relative to men is a contributor to their early exit from the school system. The fact that Tanzanian youth are much older than their peers in other countries by the time they complete secondary schooling facilitates the search for jobs given the high opportunity cost of continued schooling.

Low Returns to the Completion of Lower Secondary Schooling, Especially for Women, Discourages the Transition from Primary to Lower Secondary Schools

Affordability is a key deterrent to female progression from primary to secondary schools. Unlike the primary school level with free tuition public schools, public secondary schools in Tanzania require tuition fees from enrollees. The returns from incurring these and other costs for secondary schooling are low. Using an index of wages with the mean for uneducated females at 100, we find that the mean for women who complete lower secondary school is an 82 percent premium, which is higher than the mean for women who complete primary school at a premium of 50 percent (figure 3.4).

Figure 3.4 Young Women Leave Schooling Earlier Also Because They Get a Smaller Wage Premium from Staying Longer in School than Young Men

[Bar chart showing wage index (uneducated female = 100) by education level, comparing mean wage (male) and mean wage (female):
- Some or complete upper secondary: male ~1,250, female ~600
- Completed lower secondary: male ~200, female ~175
- Incomplete lower secondary: male ~125, female ~150
- Completed primary: male ~150, female ~125
- Incomplete primary: male ~125, female ~75
- No education: male ~125, female ~100]

Source: URT 2006.

Barriers, Remedies, and Drivers for Female Enrollment

Barriers to Female Secondary Enrollment

Imperfect Information, Inappropriate Supply-Side Services, and Household Liquidity Constraints Are Key Impediments in the Literature

Low levels of parental education, inhibiting cultural factors, high levels of adult female workforce participation, poverty, large household sizes, and poor school accessibility all have been identified in the literature as the factors responsible for a large out-of-school female population.[8] Four factors are at work: (1) information available to students, parents, and communities on the benefits attributable to more rather than less schooling is imperfect across regions; (2) girls fall victim to school-based violence, which serves as a deterrent to schooling; (3) household schooling affordability is low given poverty and low liquidity, as well as credit market constraints; and (4) education services and the school environment for girls may be inappropriate given supply-side shortcomings.

There Is Evidence of Information Barriers Preventing Higher Levels of Female Enrollment in Regions of Tanzania with Low Adult Female Literacy

A strong positive correlation is found between adult female literacy and female primary enrollment across the regions of Tanzania (figure 3.5). This supports the importance of parental education as a determinant of female schooling in Tanzania. Interventions are needed that break the cycle for girls with illiterate parents and offer opportunities to girls in regions, districts, and households where

Figure 3.5 Young Women Require Adult Female Role Models to Emulate

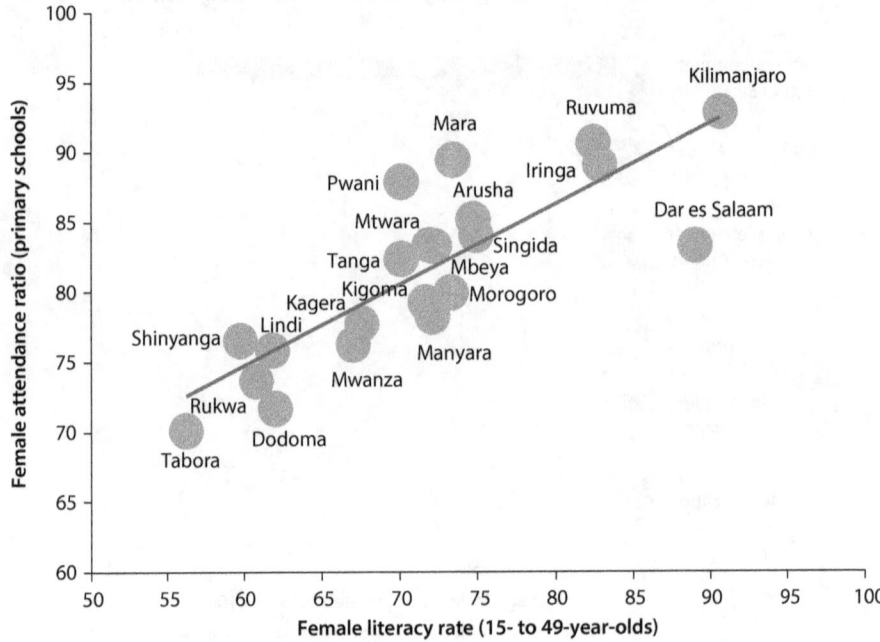

Source: URT 2010.

the benefits of female schooling are underappreciated. Schooling decisions, made by parents in these regions on behalf of their female children, do not fully reflect the societal benefits accruing from education: Female children with insufficient education impose a future tax burden on other citizens. The case for universal primary education as a good that governments should compel all their citizens to consume for their own benefit has already received wide acceptance, but the case to extend this meritorious argument to secondary school continuation in Tanzania needs to be made. Adolescent children in Tanzania may be unable to determine the benefits attributable to good-quality secondary education because they heavily discount the future over the present, making decisions without adequately considering the consequences. Evidence on high risk-taking behavior among Tanzanian youth is clearly demonstrated with respect to sexual intercourse, where only 39.7 percent of sexually active unmarried adolescent females aged 15–19 report using condoms even when the HIV/AIDS prevalence is high, compared with 57.6 percent of sexually active unmarried women aged 20–24.[9]

Household Liquidity Constraints Are a Key Impediment to Higher Levels of Female Enrollment in Tanzania

Measured as the percentage of the school-age population (7–13 for primary and 14–19 for secondary) that attends school, the 2010 net attendance rate (NAR) in Tanzania was 79.7 percent for primary education and 25.3 percent for secondary education (UTR 2010, 19–21). A strong negative correlation is found between

Figure 3.6 Young Women (and Men) from Poorer Households Need Financial Support

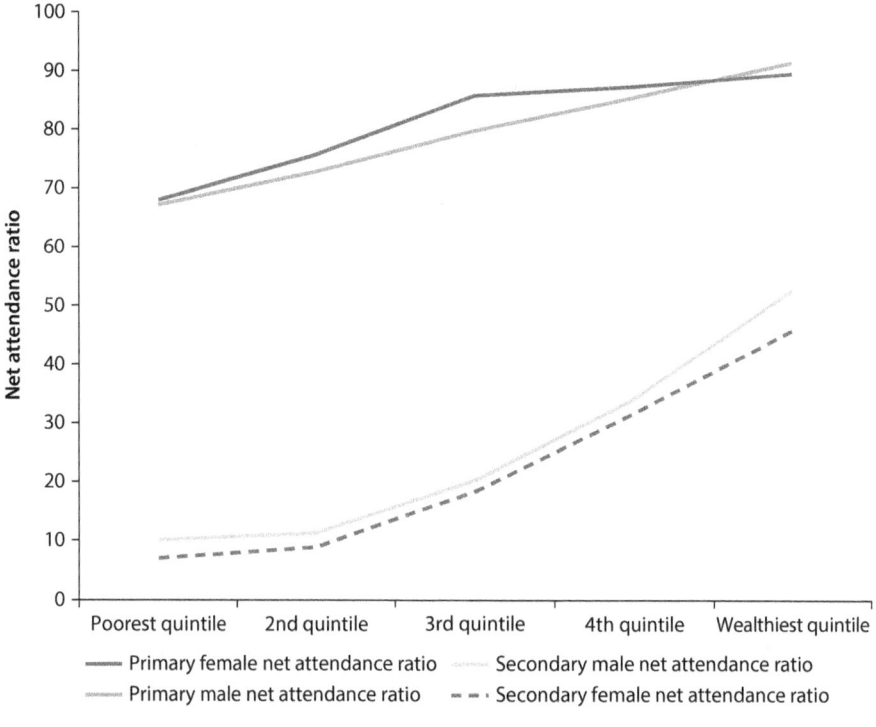

Source: URT 2010.

household poverty and NAR in Tanzania: Children from very poor households have very low NARs. In figure 3.6, we see that the gradient of the poverty-NAR curve is steeper at the secondary level. Interventions are needed that alleviate the plight of the poor: (a) through transfers that make schooling more affordable (with targeting implications) and/or (b) better cost control of secondary schooling.

Unavailability of Female-Friendly Supply-Side Services Is a Major Schooling Deterrent

Proximity of the school to the home is an important consideration for making the decision to enroll in school given the safety concerns of girls and their parents. There is cross-country evidence of a 10–20 percentage point increase in the likelihood of school-aged children to attend school if they live in a village with a primary school, with larger effects for girls (Filmer 1999). Tanzania has primary schools in every ward, and the mean distance to primary schools from the home in 2007 was 2.9 kilometers. The mean distance to secondary schools from the home was greater at 6.4 kilometers (figure 3.7). Interventions that address distance to school can go a long way to increase female secondary enrollment rates, which are lower than primary enrollment rates in part because adolescent boys and girls have to travel farther distances to make it to school. A randomized evaluation of the impact of village-based schools in Afghanistan found that

Figure 3.7 Young Women Need Secondary Schools Closer to Their Homes

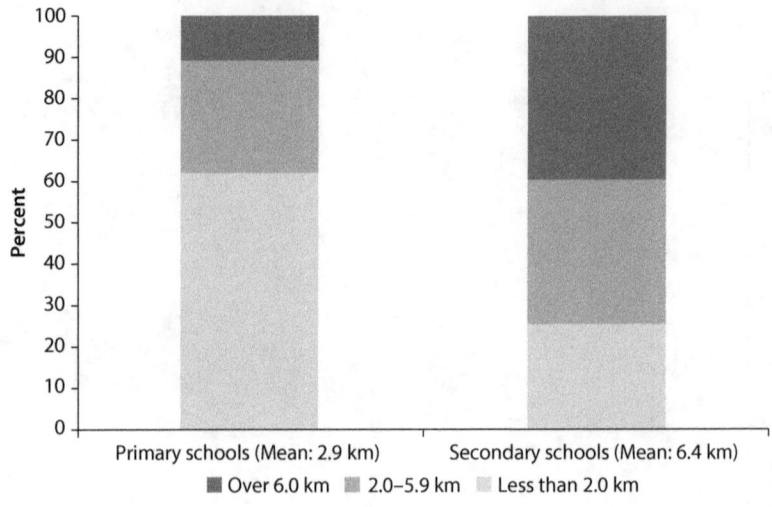

Source: URT 2007.
Note: km = kilometer.

reducing the distance to the closest primary school increased the enrollment of girls by 19 percentage points per mile compared with 13 percentage points per mile for boys (Burde and Linden 2009).

Evidence from a multilevel analysis linking household and district level data from 30 developing countries shows that the percentage of female teachers in a district is positively correlated with female but not male enrollment in primary schools (Huisman and Smits 2009). In Tanzania, female secondary school teachers represent 30 percent of the secondary teaching force. More male teachers than female teachers are found in every region of Tanzania. The lack of female teachers is the result of a vicious cycle, whereby very few girls complete lower secondary schooling and thus are qualified for teacher training, leading to few female teachers and role models (Kirk 2006). Further, conditions in hard-to-reach rural areas are not conducive to young unmarried female teachers with concerns about safety and cultural pressures to get married.

Tanzania has made good progress with respect to ensuring that boys and girls have separate toilet facilities in secondary schools. In each region of Tanzania, toilet facilities designated for girls represent between 44 percent and 52 percent of the existing toilet facilities in public secondary schools.[10] No robust evidence is available for or against the impact of single-sex toilets on female educational outcomes (Birdthistle et al. 2011). The practice of constructing an equal number of these facilities for boys and girls at the same time that there are many fewer girls than boys has led to a much better pupil-latrine ratio for girls (the national average is 31.9:1) than boys (the national average is 39.7:1). These ratios for boys and girls are worse than the existing service standard norms: Girls and boys alike have too few toilet facilities to make use of. The availability of too few toilets for girls may also explain low female secondary enrollment.

Remedies to Address the Barriers to Female Secondary Schooling

There Are Remedies for Information Barriers Affecting Female Schooling

An evaluation of the Strategies for Advancing Girls' Education program in Ghana after two years of implementation provided inconclusive quantitative evidence but strong qualitative evidence of the impact of peer support and mentoring on increased enrollment and reduced absenteeism of girls (Ofori-Bah, Kudzi, and Donney 2004). Sutherland-Addy (2002) reports that the community sensitization and mobilization component assisted communities in seeing themselves as being responsible for female education.

Curbing School-Based Violence Will Improve Female Schooling

A recent survey in Tanzania estimated the prevalence of violence among children and youth aged 13–24 that occurred before the age of 18 (URT 2011). According to the study, 52.6 percent of women that experienced physical violence before age 18 reported a teacher as perpetrator,[11] and 15.1 percent of women that were victims of sexual violence experienced it in school.[12] Measures to reduce school-based violence against girls will encourage female school participation.

There Is a History of Successfully Utilizing a Reduction in User Fees to Address Household Affordability Constraints

Reduction in user fees has been used to increase primary school enrollment in various countries including Tanzania. Tanzania's primary gross enrollment rate (GER) was 63.2 percent in 2000, and then the government introduced free primary tuition in October 2001, and by 2002, the primary GER had risen to 100.4.[13] The effect on the primary net enrollment rate (NER) was also significant across all wealth quintiles and was very progressive, with children in the poorer quintiles benefiting more than those in the wealthier quintiles. A 31 percentage point increase was seen in the NER for the poorest quintile from 2001 to 2007, compared with a 19 percentage point increase in the NER for the wealthiest quintile (figure 3.8). A similar reduction in user fees was implemented three years later for the secondary level with a 50 percent reduction in tuition fees. This was accompanied by a surge in enrollment that was less progressive. A 9 percentage point increase was reported in the NER for the poorest quintile from 2001 to 2007, compared with a 10 percentage point increase in the NER for the wealthiest quintile and 19 percentage point increase for the second wealthiest quintile.

School Feeding and Scholarships/Stipends Are Other Viable Options for Making Schooling Affordable That Are Effective at Increasing Female School Participation

The regressive outcome from the introduction of the reduction in user fees at the secondary level raises questions about alternative school affordability interventions that do not subsidize those that are able to pay. Further, any affordability intervention should be able to address the lack of female participation.

Figure 3.8 First Generation Reforms Targeted at Affordability Have Been Successful

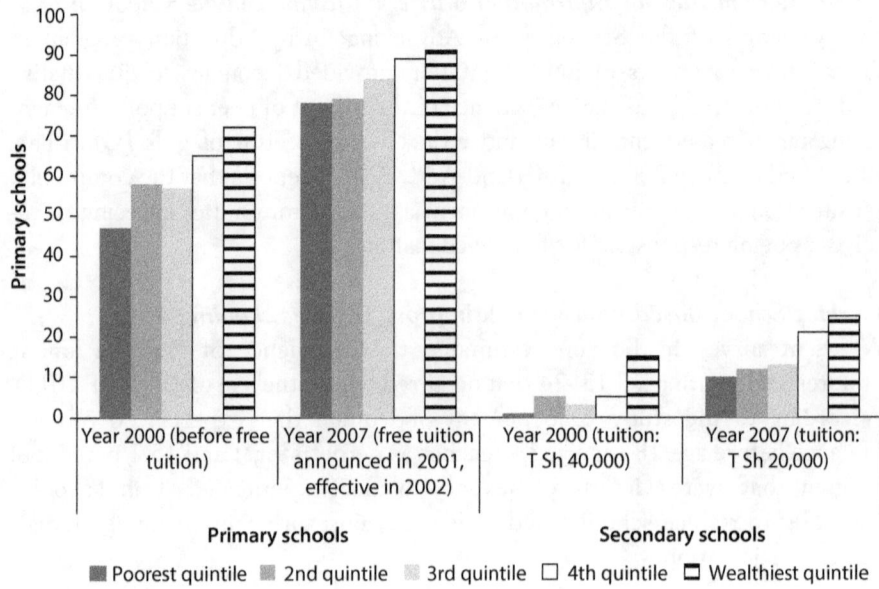

Sources: URT 2001, 2007.

An evaluation of the world's largest school feeding program, India's Mid-Day Meals program, found evidence that it increased female school participation by 15 percent in implementing schools (Drèze and Kingdon 2001). Presently no national school feeding program is found in Tanzania. Strong evidence also shows that cash and in-kind contributions to girls and/or families for the purpose of school attendance are more effective than for boys' schooling. Evidence exists of a 12 percentage point increase in female enrollment as a result of cash transfers under the Female Secondary Assistance Project in Bangladesh (Khandker, Pitt, and Fuwa 2003).

Various Facets of School Service Provision Can Be Improved to Attract More Female Students

Evidence from Chad reports that 80 percent of school enrollees in 179 villages were from the 8 percent of villages with schools located in them. Village enrollment rates dropped off sharply for satellite villages officially served by the local school with schools more than one kilometer away. Proportionally, girls' enrollment dropped off more quickly than boys' for distances of less than a kilometer (Lehman 2003). Reducing physical distances does affect access to school for girls.[14] Evidence indicates that the gender of school teachers matters for female school participation (Huisman and Smits 2009). Tanzania's secondary pupil teacher ratio is one of the lowest in SSA, and female teachers make up only 30 percent of the teaching force. Evidence from Bangladesh shows that female teachers increased the percentage of correct answers given by girls in secondary-level mathematics because the presence of female teachers is associated with more enlightened attitudes toward working women and more schooling (Asadullah and Chaudhury 2008).

A highly relevant consideration for Tanzania in the short term is the large pool of out-of-school girls. Opportunities for complementary education have been identified as a viable option from the accelerated learning program administered by the Bangladesh Rural Advancement Committee. According to Sukontamarn (2005), girls made up 63 percent of those enrolled in the flexible satellite schools with a 1 percent dropout rate and 90 percent transition rate to the traditional school track.

A Role for Conditional Cash Transfers
According to the 2012 World Development Report (World Bank 2011), the interaction of markets, institutions, and households creates low or high levels of female schooling. It then becomes important to consider the role of policy instruments to address each of, or a combination of, these and incentivize girls to enroll and complete schooling. CCTs target households and provide them with more stable incomes. They have proven effective in many countries at bringing adolescent girls who are outside the school system back into the school system. This intervention can be designed to straddle the domains of addressing imperfect information and household affordability—two key barriers to female schooling—simultaneously. For CCTs to be effective markets, an adequate supply of good-quality and female-friendly services are needed as well as a wage premium that offsets the full opportunity cost of additional years of schooling for girls. Also, policies must be in place to reduce the direct, indirect, and opportunity cost of schooling. In this regard, it is important to note that the opportunity cost of secondary school completion in Tanzania is very high because adolescents and youth have to wait as much as three years longer to complete secondary schooling compared with their peers in other SSA countries.

Notes

1. Author's calculations as outlined in the Project Appraisal Document for the World Bank's assistance to the government of Tanzania's Secondary Education Development Program II (SEDP II); see p. 82.
2. These net enrollment estimates are based on survey data and differ from estimates provided by administrative sources (EMIS). The discrepancy between survey and administrative data is discussed in chapter 2.
3. Tanzania's Secondary Education Development Program II (SEDP II) is designed, in part, to address the low transition rate problem by ensuring an annual average 6 percent increase in secondary enrollment.
4. Male (female) primary-to-secondary transition rate is measured as new male entrants to the first grade of secondary education in the current year as a proportion of male (female) pupils enrolled in the final grade of primary education in the previous year.
5. Kilimanjaro region is the exception with pass rates of 54 and 49 percent for girls and boys, respectively.

6. The reasons for and implications of declining pass rates for both boys and girls are discussed in chapter 7.
7. According to 2009 World Development Indicators, only 10 countries had a higher adolescent fertility rate: Niger (202), the Democratic Republic of the Congo (189), Mali (179), Angola (162), Chad (154), Guinea (148), Zambia (143), Uganda (141), Mozambique (139), and Liberia (135).
8. For a recent discussion on this see Duman (2010).
9. Tanzania DHS Report (2004), p. 69.
10. Although data on the availability of separate toilet units for boys and girls exist, no data are available on the functionality of existing facilities. Even more toilet facilities for girls are found in the private school system.
11. Physical is defined as being punched, whipped, or kicked. The statistic is available on page 46 of the report.
12. The statistic is available on page 52 of the report. There is a discussion of this in World Bank (2011, p. 295).
13. In addition to free tuition fees, the requirement for school uniforms became noncompulsory. Neighboring Kenya and Uganda are examples of such countries. In Kenya, primary GER was 87.6 in 2002, rising to 104.0 in 2003 after the introduction of free tuition in January 2003. In Uganda, primary GER was 74.3 in 1995, rising to 128.9 in 2000 after the introduction of free tuition in January 1997.
14. Cultural distance (the drop-off as children leave their community for another for school) and time distance (obstacles such as mountains and rivers impact travel time) are other aspects of distance that are identified as relevant for consideration to improve female enrollment (Lehman 2003).

References

Asadullah, M. N., and N. Chaudhury. 2008. "Holy Alliances: Public Subsidies, Islamic High Schools, and Female Schooling in Bangladesh." In *Girl's Education in the 21st Century: Gender Equality, Empowerment and Growth*, edited by M. Tembon and L. Fort. Washington, DC: World Bank.

Birdthistle, I., K. Dickson, L. Javidi, and M. Freeman. 2011. "What Impact Does the Provision of Separate Toilets for Girls at Schools Have on Their Primary and Secondary School Enrolment, Attendance and Completion? A Systematic Review of the Evidence." EPPI-Centre, Social Science Research Unit, Institute of Education, University of London, London.

Burde, D., and L. L. Linden. 2009. "The Effect of Proximity on School Enrollment: Evidence from a Randomized Controlled Trial in Afghanistan." http://sticerd.lse.ac.uk/seminarpapers/dg11052009.pdf.

Dréze, J., and G. Kingdon. 2001. "School Participation in Rural India." *Review of Development Economics* 5 (1): 1–24.

Duman, A. 2010. "Female Education Inequality in Turkey: Factors Affecting Girls' Schooling Decisions." *International Journal of Education Economics and Development* 1 (3): 243–58.

Filmer, D. 1999. "The Structure of Social Disparities in Education: Gender and Wealth." Policy Research Report on Gender and Development, Working Paper Series 5, World Bank, Washington, DC.

Huisman, J., and J. Smits. 2009. "Effects of Household and District-Level Factors on Primary School Enrollment in 30 Developing Countries." *World Development* 37 (1): 179–93.

Khandker, S., M. Pitt, and N. Fuwa. 2003. "Subsidy to Promote Girls' Secondary Education: The Female Stipend Program in Bangladesh." Unpublished manuscript.

Kirk, J. 2006. *The Impact of Women Teachers on Girls' Education*. Bangkok: United Nations Educational, Scientific, and Cultural Organization. http://unesdoc.unesco.org/images/0014/001459/145990e.pdf.

Laderchi, C. 2009. "Transitions and Informality: Improving Young People's Opportunities in Tanzania's Urban Labor Markets." World Bank Policy Note, World Bank, Washington, DC.

Lehman, D. 2003. "Bringing the School to the Children: Shortening the Path to EFA." World Bank, Washington, DC.

Ofori-Bah, A., A. Kudzi, and T. Donney. 2004. *Evaluation of the Community Mobilization Component of Strategies for Advancing Girls Education (SAGE)*. Bureau for African Division of U.S. Agency for International Development (USAID) and Management Systems International (MSI), Washington, DC.

Sukontamarn, P. 2005. "The Entry of NGO Schools and Girls' Educational Outcomes in Bangladesh." Political Economy and Public Policy Series, Suntory and Toyota International Centres for Economics and Related Disciplines, London School of Economics, London.

Sutherland-Addy, E. 2002. *Impact Assessment Study of the Girls' Education Programme in Ghana*. UNICEF-Ghana, Accra.

Tanzania DHS Report (2004).

URT (United Republic of Tanzania). 2001. *Household Budget Survey*. National Bureau of Statistics, Dar es Salaam, Tanzania.

———. 2006. *Integrated Labor Force Survey*. National Bureau of Statistics, Dar es Salaam, Tanzania.

———. 2007. *Household Budget Survey*. National Bureau of Statistics, Dar es Salaam, Tanzania.

———. 2010. *Tanzania's Demographic and Health Survey*. National Bureau of Statistics, Dar es Salaam, Tanzania.

———. 2011. *Violence against Children in Tanzania: Findings from a National Survey 2009*. Dar es Salaam, Tanzania: URT.

———. 2012. "Education Management Information System (EMIS) Database." Ministry of Education and Vocational Training.

World Bank. 2011. *Gender Inequality and Development: World Development Report 2012*. Washington, DC: World Bank.

———. 2012. "Education Statistics Database." World Bank, Washington, DC.

CHAPTER 4

Assessing Literacy and Numeracy in Tanzania's Primary Schools: The Uwezo Approach

Suleman Sumra, Sara Ruto, and Rakesh Rajani

Summary

Since 2009, Uwezo, an initiative of Twaweza (http://www.twaweza.org), has implemented large-scale nationally representative household surveys to assess basic literary and numeracy competencies of school-aged children across Kenya, Tanzania, and Uganda and to answer a simple question: Are all our children learning?[1] The initiative is based on the premise that information can increase awareness, which in turn has the potential to harness agency and evoke action. This holds especially when information is presented in a way in which people can see its immediate link with their own life and well-being. Use of robustly generated evidence is therefore the entry point used for engagement in educational discourse. Uwezo has a basic literacy and numeracy pivot, through use of national assessments conducted by citizens and citizen groups. Citizens are viewed not simply as consumers, but also as generators of knowledge. Additional to this is the understanding that the "data will not speak for itself." Heavy investment has been made to communicate, in simple and understandable formats, to key audiences, particularly policy makers and implementers but also ordinary citizens, the bulk of whom are parents.

The 2011 Uwezo tests show that children in Tanzania are not learning nearly as well as they ought to. Every child in Standard 3 and above should master Standard 2–level competencies. However, in fact only three out of 10 Standard 3 pupils are able to do read a Standard 2–level Kiswahili story or perform Standard 2–level numeracy operations. Results are even worse for English, where only one in 10 Standard 3 students masters Standard 2–level literacy competencies. Moreover, vast differences are found across districts, indicating that although overall learning outcomes are poor, some schools and districts are doing much better than others, despite facing similar constraints.

To improve the quality of education in Tanzania, the chapter argues that the discussion ought to move away from a narrow focus on resources and educational inputs to an assessment of educational achievements and a discussion about the types of interventions that are appropriate to promote better learning outcomes. This should be coupled with an emphasis on rigorous empirical analysis and a culture of innovation, testing, and learning from what works elsewhere.

Introduction

The Kiswahili term "Uwezo" is a powerful word. Depending on the context used, it can mean "capability," "power," "strength." It can be used to share feelings of energy, of being confident, of feeling empowered. Uwezo espouses core values and competencies that an education system ought to offer.

Over time, the education system in Tanzania has been under scrutiny in the effort to ensure that the system serves all, shares nationally accepted values, and offers skills and competencies that better the individual for his or her own as well as national socioeconomic development. The efforts have borne fruit. Arguably, compared with its East African neighbors, the sense of nationhood is strongest in Tanzania. Access to basic education has largely been met. Indeed, some children successfully go through the system and are skilled citizens. Unfortunately, a significant number do not even complete the primary school cycle. Among those who do, many nonetheless leave school semiliterate, seminumerate, and semiskilled. It is this concern that makes Uwezo pose the simple question "Are all our children learning?" in the ways envisioned in the national objectives of education.

Citizen-Led Assessment: The Key Tenets

Social change needs to be informed and interpreted through rigorous analysis. Education reforms in East Africa have often failed to gain traction because of a tendency to analyze them in isolated, apolitical terms, and to throw technocratic solutions at what are essentially political and institutional problems. The Uwezo design is adapted from Pratham (http://www.pratham.org)—an independent civil society organization in India—that developed an innovative methodology to produce the Annual Status of Education Reports (ASER; see http://www.asercentre.org). ASER is a household-based nationwide assessment that measures ability in basic literacy and numeracy among children between ages six and 16 years; it was started in India in 2005 and has been adapted for use in Pakistan (since 2009); Kenya, Tanzania, and Uganda (2009); Mali (2011); and Senegal (2012). In India and Pakistan, the exercise is called ASER (which means "Impact"); in East Africa, it is called "Uwezo" (which means "Capability"). The Malian effort has been named "Beekungo" (meaning "We are in it together"), and in Senegal, it is called "Jangandoo" (meaning "Learn together"). In 2011, these citizen-based large-scale assessments covered more than one million children in South Asia and Sub-Saharan Africa.

Uwezo has retained many of the ASER attributes. First, it is based on the measurement of actual literacy (reading and comprehension) and arithmetic levels, rather than perceptions of reported behavior. Second, it involves a very large, scientifically derived sample that allows for an unprecedented level of regional disaggregation and comparison. Third, the survey is conducted at a household level and reaches children that are both in and out of school. Fourth, the research design is so simple that it can be easily understood and implemented, in a relatively short time frame, and with minimum error. Fifth, the survey is conducted by strategically recruited citizen volunteers, which makes it possible to go to scale, keep costs reasonable, and, perhaps most importantly, plant the seeds for continued public debate, follow-up, and action.

The singular focus on basic literacy and numeracy, together with the international attention to early grade reading and numeracy seems to be bearing fruit. Previously, the tradition in Tanzania was to pay attention to "quality" when results of national state-controlled Primary School Leaving Examinations (PSLEs) were released. Today, judging by media reports and conversations with citizens, we find a heightened consciousness on the poor state of learning and the essence of refocusing on competencies. Uwezo uses the annual learning assessment report to catalyze countrywide debate and create pressure for policy change from the bottom up.

To align operation across the three East Africa countries in which Uwezo operates, as well as over the years, operations are guided by the Uwezo Standards manual.[2] The generation of information on levels of numeracy and literacy among children involves in-depth processes in the areas listed below.

Test Development

The creation of tests for use in the national assessments is guided by the Test Development Framework, which stipulates the guidelines, process, and specifications for the tests that would ensure comparability across the tests samples and over the years. The tests are pegged at the Tanzanian curriculum for Standard 2 and are developed, pretested, revised, and finalized by a panel of subject experts drawn from the Tanzania Institute of Education, the University of Dar es Salaam, and the ranks of public primary school teachers (see Uwezo 2011a for further information on the test tools).

Sampling

Just as important as creating valid tests is creating a representative sample that allows the evidence to be generalized. The census frame is used as the basis of sampling. The first Tanzania assessment in 2010 started small and was based on 38 randomly selected districts. However, all subsequent assessments have been nationwide, covering the 133 districts. Sampling up to the enumeration area (EA) level is conducted by the National Bureau of Statistics (NBS), and sampling of the households (HH) is undertaken by the district coordinators using simple listings upon which an nth number is calculated to give 20 randomly selected

HHs. This provides a sample of 600 (20 HH × 30 EAs) HHs within every district, and 79,800 sampled HHs throughout the country.

Partner Recruitment

A survey on such a scale is possible only with a decentralized approach. Partner organizations, most of whom are civil society organizations, are recruited based on a set of criteria. Nearly all of the district coordinators from the first annual assessment returned for the second year, adding experience and expertise. These partners, in turn, recruit two volunteers, preferably a man and woman, from the sampled EAs, giving a total of 7,980 volunteers. The volunteers, who are the front line of Uwezo, conducted the assessment of more than 128,000 children in 2011.

Training

Given the participatory nature of Uwezo in relying on partners and volunteers to conduct the assessment, proper training becomes essential. A cascading training model is used in which master trainers, who have fully been immersed in the Uwezo process and philosophy, train district coordinators, who thereafter train the volunteers. Training combines both theory and practical exercises, and the primary training document is the trainers and volunteers manual.

The Assessment

Finally, after the test development, sampling, partner recruitment, and training, comes the main Uwezo event, the national assessment, which encompasses visits to the (a) village chairperson to collect data on the EA/village characteristics, (b) primary school to collect school data, and (c) HHs to collect household-level data and test the children aged 7–16 years to gauge their abilities in basic literacy and numeracy.[3] Table 4.1 presents the statistics at a glance.

Findings

This section presents findings under three main subheadings: evidence in literacy and numeracy, emerging factors, and conditions of learning in the schools. Uwezo 1 refers to evidence generated from the first annual national assessment of 2010, and Uwezo 2 refers to the 2011 assessment.[4]

Table 4.1 Coverage of the Uwezo 1 (2010) and Uwezo 2 (2011) in Tanzania

Date	Round	Districts	Percent	Schools	Villages	Households	Children
May 2010	Uwezo 1	38	32	1,010	1,077	18,952	37,683
May/April 2011	Uwezo 2	119	100	3,709	3,825	59,992	114,761

Sources: Uwezo 2010 and 2011a data.
Note: All cells (excluding date, round, percent) refer to the number of units sampled and retained in the data set after cleaning; the percent column refers to the proportion of districts in the sample frame out of all districts in the country; the number of schools sampled is slightly smaller than the number of enumeration areas (villages) because not all enumeration areas contained a school.

Evidence on Literacy and Numeracy Levels

A child in Standard 3 in Tanzania is expected to pass the Uwezo tests, which are set on the basis of the curriculum expectations at the Standard 2 level. The evidence generated from the Uwezo 1 and Uwezo 2 have consistently confirmed the low learning levels across Tanzania as discussed below. The biggest difference from the first assessment to the second is that the numeracy results have slightly improved. Whether this is a one-time occurrence or the beginning of a trend would need to be studied more closely in future assessments. Figure 4.1 plots the two-year results in English, Kiswahili, and numeracy. It is instructive to note that even as children reach the end of the primary school level, many still do have Standard 2 level competencies in reading and doing simple arithmetic.

Kiswahili Literacy Levels

Every child in Standard 3 and above should have been able to read and understand the Standard 2–level story contained in the Uwezo test. The results of the assessment, however, show something quite different (figure 4.2): Only about three in 10 Standard 3 pupils can read a Standard 2 story. Literacy improves gradually as children progress to higher levels, but the competency levels are still wanting. As many as 24 percent of Standard 7 pupils can neither read a basic story in Kiswahili nor read words or recognize syllables.

If the purpose of reading is to comprehend, or "reading to learn," then the Uwezo results point to a disturbing trend. Many had trouble explaining what

Figure 4.1 Performance by Class and Subject (2010–11)

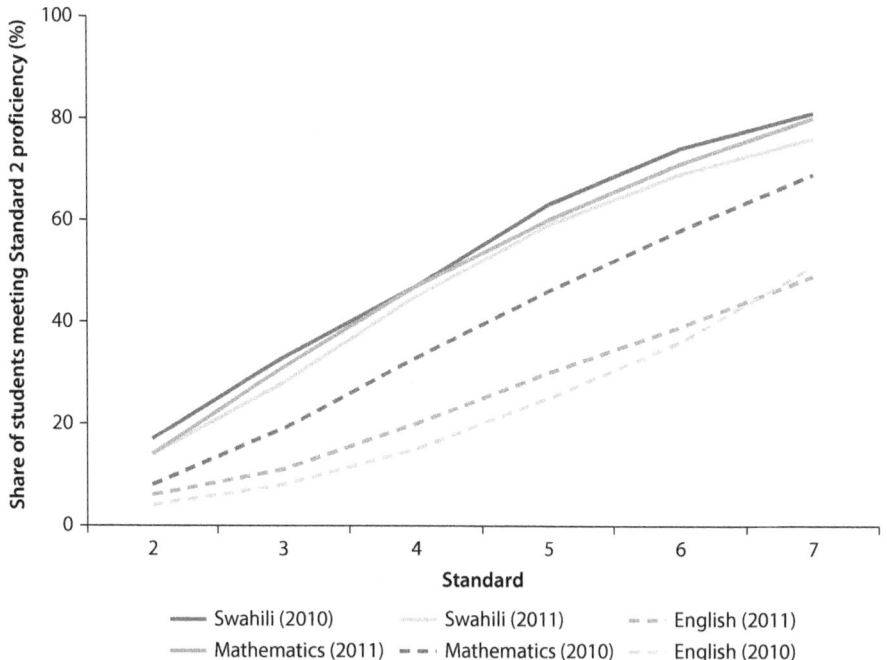

Sources: Uwezo 2010 and 2011a data.

Figure 4.2 Kiswahili Reading Levels by Class, 2011

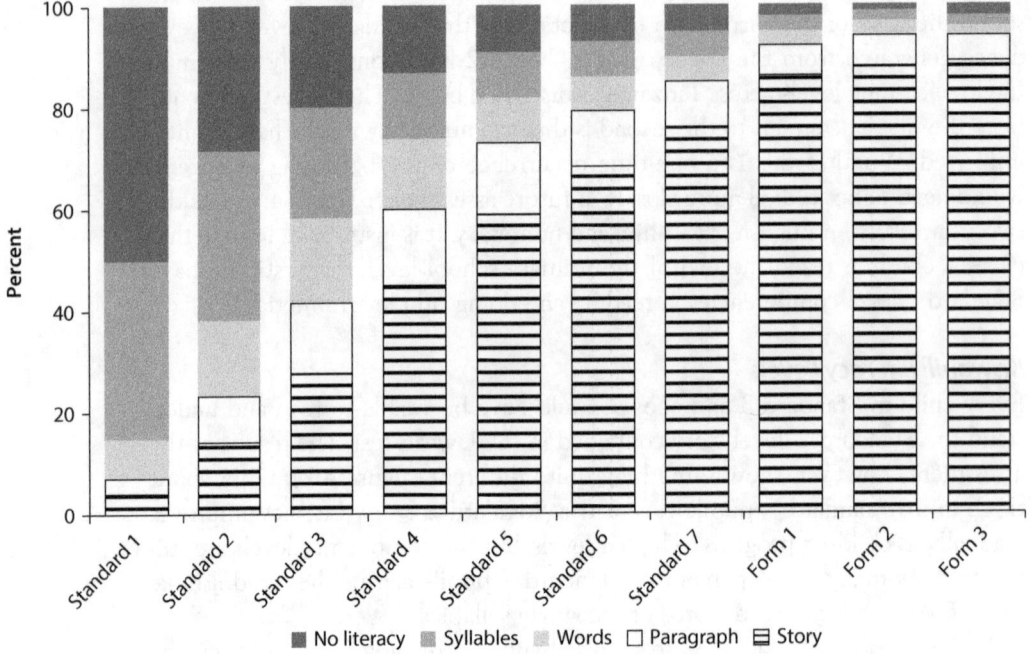

Source: Uwezo 2011a data.
Note: The graph shows the highest level achieved by the students.

they had just read. Even in Standard 7, only about half of the pupils who could read the story were then able to answer both of the comprehension questions that followed.

Results of Kiswahili literacy levels are surprising because it is the national language of the country and Kiswahili is used as a language of instruction from preprimary levels. Figure 4.2 shows furthermore the reading levels of the key components tested in Uwezo: ability to recognize letters and sounds and read a word, paragraph, and story.

Although regional variations abound in the Kiswahili performance, the gender differences are minimal. Girls and boys perform equally well in Kiswahili literacy. In each standard and form, the difference in Kiswahili literacy between girls and boys is relatively minor, with girls performing slightly better than boys. This finding mirrors Uwezo 1 evidence. Furthermore, girls and boys are about equally likely to be enrolled in school. Among 7- to 16-year-olds, 89 percent of girls are enrolled, compared with 87 percent of boys.

The regional variations in Kiswahili literacy are, however, more acute. Nationally, about three in 10 Standard 3 pupils are able to read the basic Kiswahili story. By district, this ranges from seven in 10 in Rombo down to fewer than one in 10 in Tarime. The urban districts generally outperform the districts in more rural regions. In addition to Rombo, Arusha, and Kibaha Urban, districts in which more than half of the Standard 3 pupils could read Kiswahili include Iringa Urban, Mufindi, Bukoba Urban, Tanga, and Morogoro Urban. On the other hand, the four districts in which fewer than one in 10 Standard 3 pupils could read Kiswahili (Rungwe, Meatu, Tandahimba, and Mbozi) are typically rural districts.

English Literacy Levels

If the Kiswahili results are poor, then the performance in English is critical. Only one in 10 Standard 3 pupils can read a Standard 2 story. Although pupils in later standards perform better, even the majority of Standard 7 pupils are unable to read the Standard 2 English story. Far fewer students were able to read the English story than the Kiswahili story. Those that could read it, however, were more likely to be able to comprehend the questions than those that read the Kiswahili story: Even in Standard 1, of the pupils who could read the story, most could then answer the questions as well. The reason for this difference may be that Kiswahili is much more familiar to pupils, so they may be able to read words even if they do not fully understand them. With English, however, those that are able to read the words are likely to have studied the language and may be more likely to know the meanings. Also, as per the curriculum stipulations for Grade 2, the vocabulary in the English stories was simpler than the Kiswahili stories. Figure 4.3 illustrates the reading levels by class.

Figure 4.3 English Reading Levels by Class, 2011

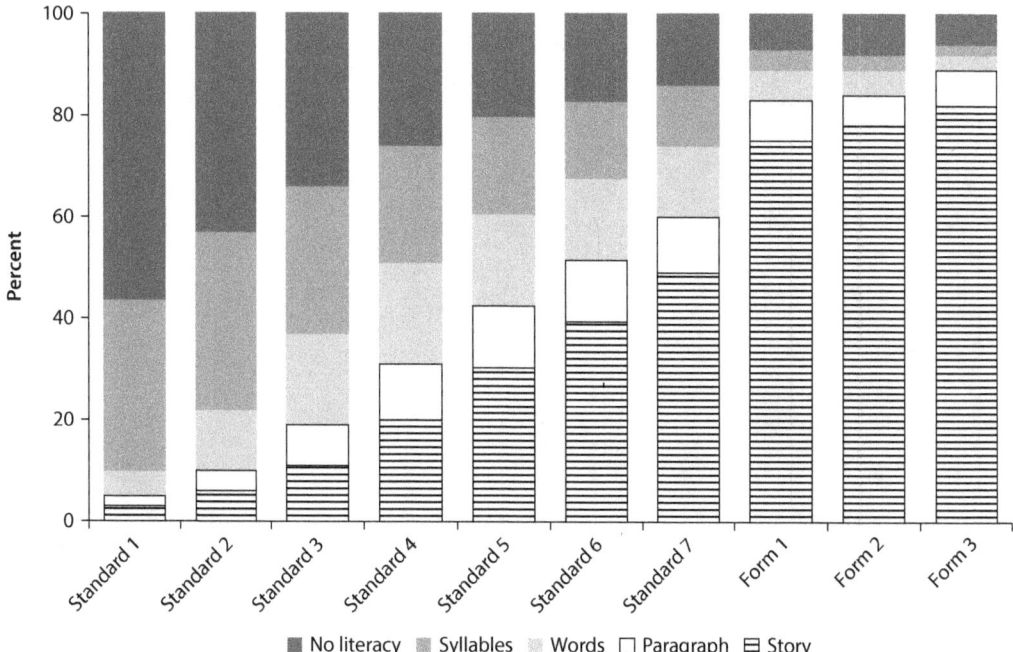

Source: Uwezo 2011a data.
Note: The graph shows the highest level achieved by the students.

No gender disparities were discerned in the English language reading abilities. However, distinct regional variations were seen, although most districts were united in their low reading levels. The highest performing district, Arusha, had fewer than four in 10 children able to read the story. Standard 3 pupils perform best in English in Arusha, Kigoma Urban, and Iringa Urban. Other districts performing relatively well include Bukoba Urban and Tanga. At the other end, hardly any Standard 3 pupils were able to read English in Tandahimba, Musoma Rural, Meatu, and Rungwe. Although the overall levels are lower, the pattern of performance across Tanzania is similar to Kiswahili literacy.

Numeracy Levels

In addition to literacy, numeracy is a fundamental skill expected of all children. As with literacy, however, not all children are learning numeracy skills as early as they should: Only three in 10 Standard 3 pupils can add, subtract, and multiply. As detailed in figure 4.4, multiplication was the most difficult category for children, as expected. By Standard 7, eight in 10 pupils are able to pass all levels.

As with English and Kiswahili, almost no gender gap is found with regard to numeracy: Girls and boys perform equally well in numeracy. Of the differences that do exist, boys tend to do just a bit better than girls in most numeracy standards, whereas girls did a bit better than boys in both literacy categories.

Figure 4.4 Numeracy Levels by Class, 2011

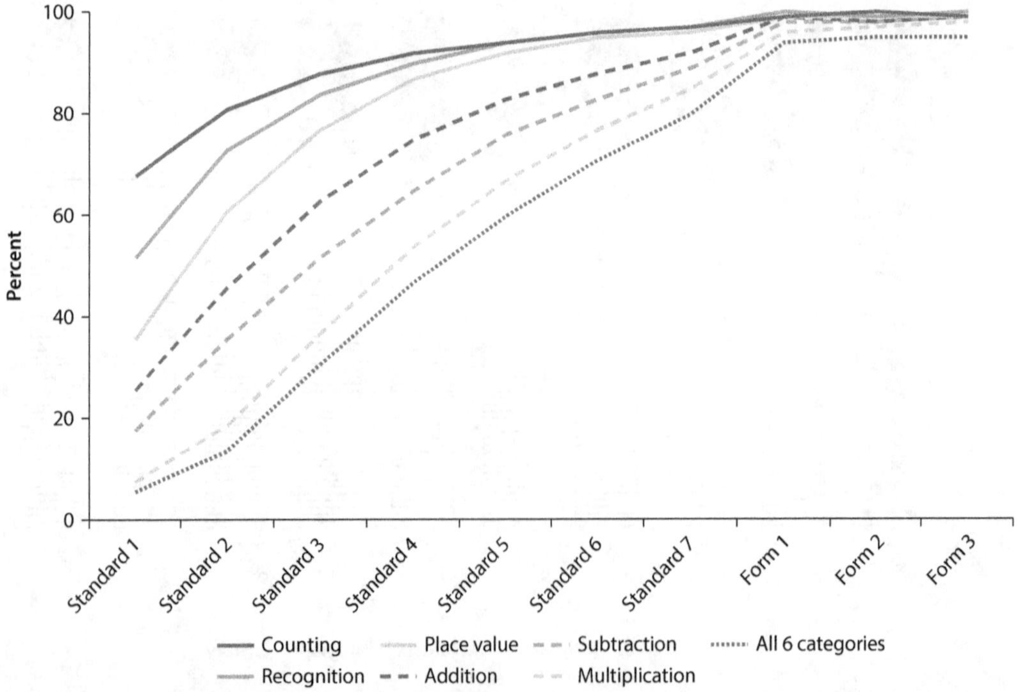

Source: Uwezo 2011a data.

The difference is, however, not significant, but the regional variations are more distinct. At the national level, about three in 10 Standard 3 pupils are able to perform Standard 2 level operations. The highest performing district is Tanga, in which six in 10 pupils were able to complete the assessment. Standard 3 pupils perform best in numeracy in Tanga, Kibaha Urban, and Mbulu. Tunduru and Kibondo were the lowest performing districts: Fewer than one in 10 Standard 3 pupils there were able to add, subtract, and multiply at a Standard 2 level.

Factors Influencing Performance in Literacy and Numeracy

This section lays out some of the factors that are linked to performance in literacy and numeracy. Mere correlations cannot prove causality, but nevertheless, the results show interesting associations. Throughout this section and unless otherwise noted, performance is measured as the percentage of children who are proficient at the Standard 2 level curriculum, that is, those that successfully completed the assessment in all three subjects.[5]

Enrollment: Pupils in Private Schools Perform Better than in Public Schools

Nearly nine in 10 children between the ages of 7 and 16 are enrolled in school, with the vast majority enrolled in government schools. Children between 9 and 13 are especially likely to be enrolled. At the same time, it is the youngest and oldest children who are most likely to be enrolled in private school, although only by a small margin.

Although there are not many private school students, those children who are in private school have an advantage over those in public school. Among children 10 and younger, not much difference is found between being enrolled in a public school and not being enrolled at all, in terms of being able to pass the Uwezo test. Beginning at age 11, however, children enrolled in public school do better than those not enrolled but perform worse than their counterparts in private school. Of course, these results mirror not only differences in the quality of education delivered in public and private schools, but also selection effects, because children in private schools are more likely to come from wealthier families (figure 4.5).

Early Start: Pupils with Preprimary Education Demonstrate a Head Start

Nearly three out of four children throughout Tanzania are enrolled in preprimary school. Pupils in lower standards are slightly more likely to have attended preprimary school than pupils in higher standards, which suggests that preprimary enrollment is becoming more common. A clear association is found between attending preprimary school and later success in literacy and numeracy. Pupils that have been in preprimary school perform better than those who have not. The gap closes in secondary school but never quite disappears. Again, these results reflect not only the positive effects of preprimary education per se but also selection effects, whereby families with higher levels of income and/or greater interest in education are more likely to send their children to preprimary school.

Figure 4.5 Performance by Schooling Status

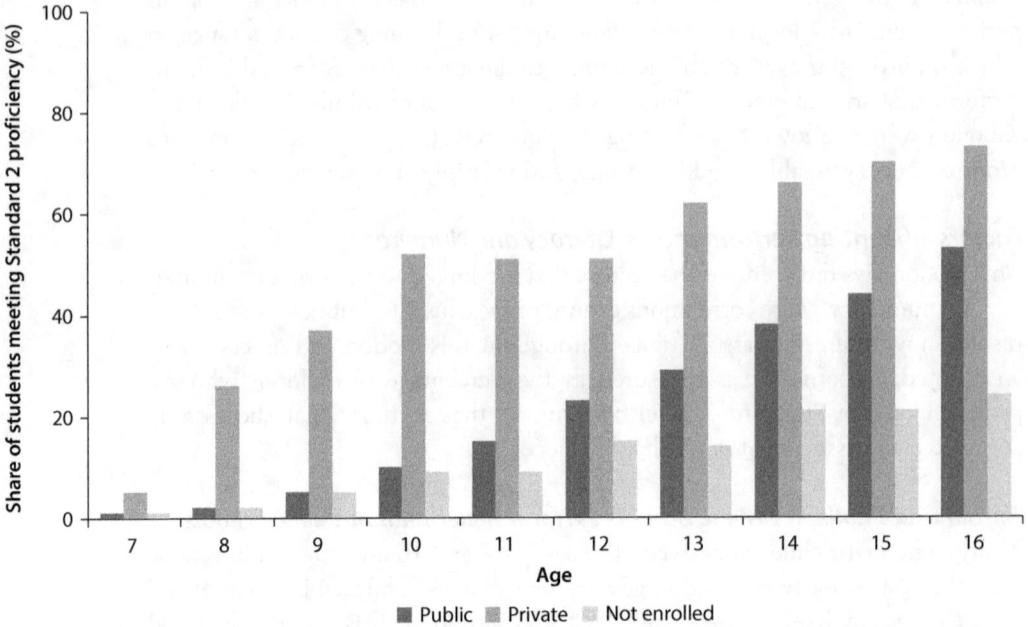

Source: Uwezo 2011a data.

Home Language: Kiswahili Speakers Perform Better

Although Kiswahili is the most common language spoken in Tanzania and is the language of instruction in primary school, it is not always the first language spoken at home. More than one in three HHs in the Uwezo assessment reported speaking a language other than Kiswahili at home. Children whose home language is Kiswahili registered better performance in all three subjects. The gap between the two groups diminishes in secondary school (see figure 4.6).

Parental Education: Children Whose Parents Have Secondary-Level Schooling Perform Better

About eight out of 10 pupils have at least one parent who went as far as primary school as a child. As observed during Uwezo 1, parental education is related to their children's competency level in literacy and numeracy. As table 4.2 shows, more than six out of 10 Standard 7 pupils whose parents both attended secondary school are proficient at the Standard 2 level, compared with just three in 10 students whose parents did not attend any school.

Location: Urban-Based Learners Prosper

About three in four children live in rural locations, but it is their peers in urban locations who tend to perform best in literacy and numeracy. In Standard 3, for example, urban students are twice as likely to meet proficiency standards in all three subjects compared with rural-based learners.

Figure 4.6 Performance by Language Spoken at Home

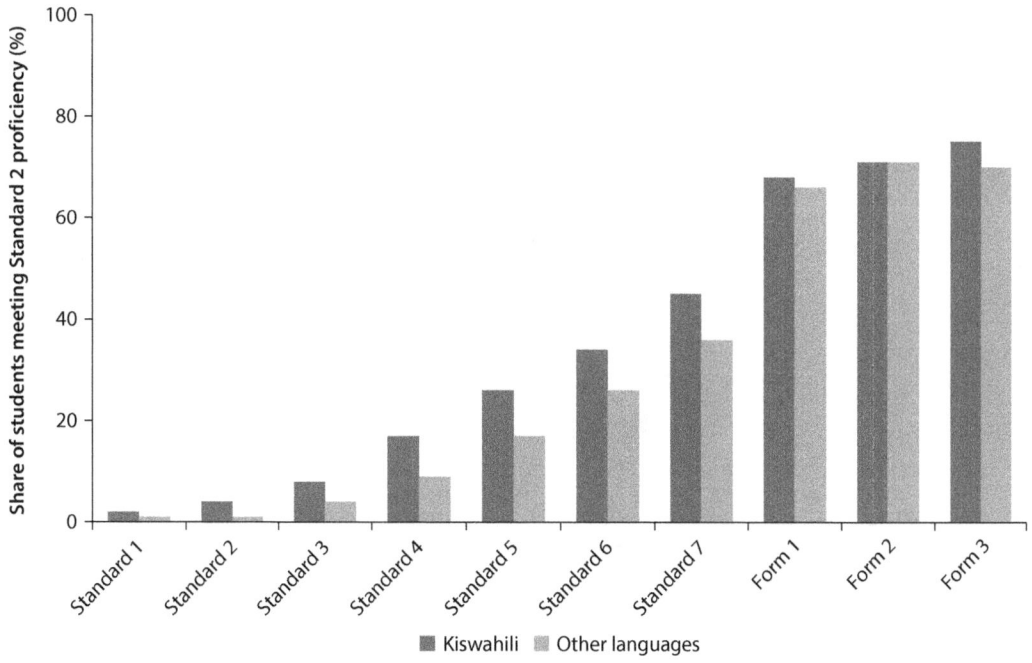

Source: Uwezo 2011a data.

Table 4.2 Percentage of Standard 7 Pupils Meeting Standard 2 Proficiency by Parents' Schooling Levels
Percent

	No primary school	Primary school	Secondary school	Postsecondary education
Parents' education	33	33	..	..
	31	42	54	..
	..	58	64	..
	..	68	..	..

Source: Uwezo 2011a data.
Note: .. = negligible (e.g., inadequate to be representative).

Urban secondary school pupils tend to perform better than rural pupils as well. Further, children from urban locations are a good deal more likely to attend secondary school than children from rural locations. About four in 10 secondary school pupils are from urban areas, compared with about two in 10 primary school pupils (see figure 4.7).

Beyond the urban-rural distinction, the 133 districts varied substantially from each other in terms of children's performance. For Standard 7 pupils, the highest performing district in Standard 2 proficiency across all subjects was Iringa

Figure 4.7 Percentage of Pupils Meeting Standard 2 Proficiency by Location

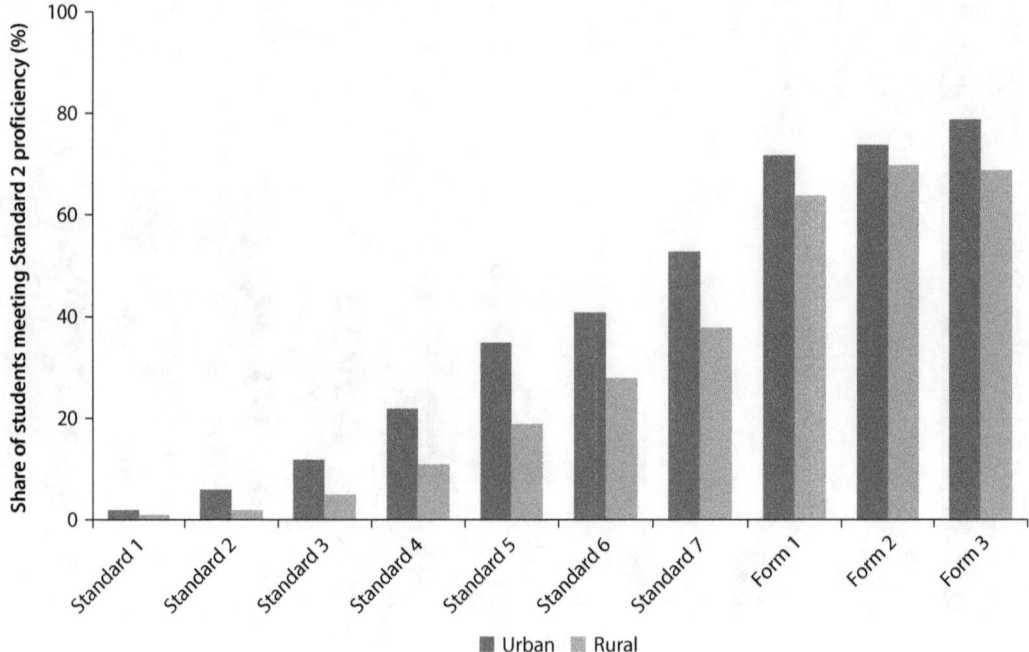

Source: Uwezo 2011a data.

Urban, followed by Bukoba Urban and Arusha. On the other end, Kibondo, Tandahimba, and Rorya were among the lowest performing. Temeke scored highest in Kiswahili literacy among Standard 7 students, with nearly all pupils able to read the story. Similarly, nearly all Standard 7 pupils in Arusha were able to complete the math assessment. The highest performing district in English literacy was Bukoba Urban: Nearly nine in 10 Standard 7 pupils were able to read the English story.

The School Environment

Although the actual assessments are undertaken at home, schools that belong to the sampled EAs are also visited. In Uwezo 2 (2011), about 3,700 schools were visited, compared with just more than 1,000 schools in Uwezo 1 (2010). The following section presents general characteristics of schools visited in 2011.

Teacher Attendance

Across Tanzania, four out of five teachers were in school on the day of the survey. Somewhat more women than men were found among the ranks of teachers: The average school had 12 teachers, five men and seven women. However, three out of four head teachers surveyed were men. Perfect attendance among teachers was relatively rare: Only about one in 10 schools visited had all of their teachers at work on that particular day (see figure 4.8).

Libraries

Slightly more than one out of four primary schools in the Uwezo survey had a library. Furthermore, whether or not the school had a library varied considerably by district. At least 90 percent of the visited schools in Meatu, Missungwi, Chato, and Geita had libraries, compared with none of the schools visited in Lindi Rural, Mkinga, or Muheza (see figure 4.9).

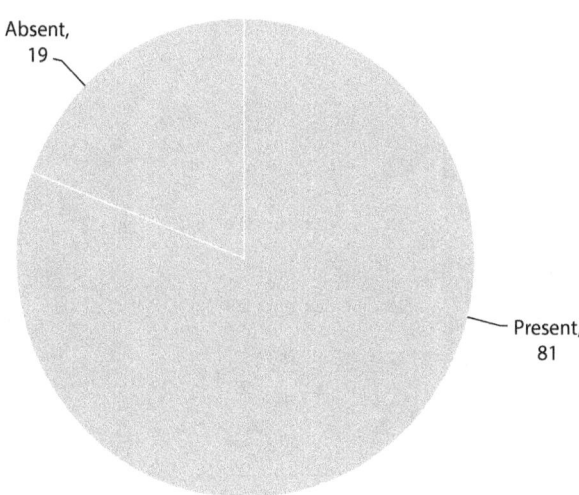

Figure 4.8 Average Teacher Attendance
Percent

Absent, 19
Present, 81

Source: Uwezo 2011a data.

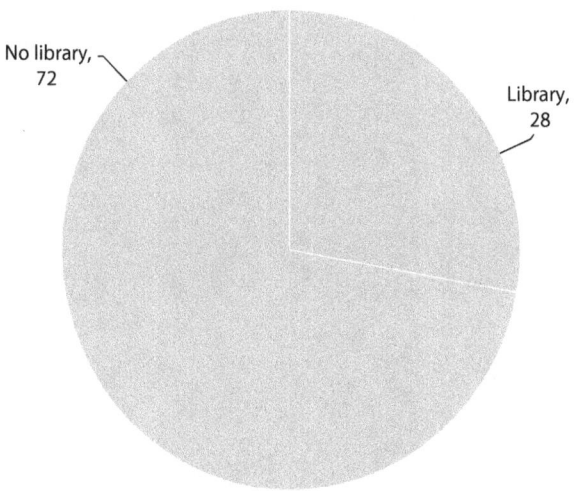

Figure 4.9 School Libraries
Percent

No library, 72
Library, 28

Source: Uwezo 2011a data.

Toilet Pits

A basic facility that each school ought to have is a toilet. For girls, and especially those experiencing their menses, the adequacy of the sanitation can become a factor in their daily attendance. In the 3,700 schools visited by Uwezo 2, an average of nearly 80 children shared a single toilet.

Combining the Factors

All of the factors detailed have some relationship with children's learning. The relationship is especially noticeable when the factors are combined. This is illustrated in the student profiles in figure 4.10, which show the likelihood for

Figure 4.10 Student Profile

Student A in Standard 7	Student B in Standard 7	Student C in Standard 7
Home: Kibondo	Home: Ukerewe	Home: Mbulu
Parents' highest education: none	Parents' highest education: primary school	Parents' highest education: primary school
Wealth index: low	Wealth index: medium	Wealth index: low
Home language: local	Home language: Kiswahili	Home language: local
Preprimary: yes	Preprimary: yes	Preprimary: no
Likelihood of completing all Standard 2 assessments:	Likelihood of completing all Standard 2 assessments:	Likelihood of completing all Standard 2 assessments:
9%	29%	52%

Student D in Standard 7	Student E in Standard 7	Student F in Standard 7
Home: Iramba	Home: Ngara	Home: Bukoba Urban
Parents' highest education: secondary school	Parents' highest education: none	Parents' highest education: postsecondary
Wealth index: low	Wealth index: high	Wealth index: medium
Home language: Kiswahili	Home language: local	Home language: Kiswahili
Preprimary: yes	Preprimary: yes	Preprimary: yes
Likelihood of completing all Standard 2 assessments:	Likelihood of completing all Standard 2 assessments:	Likelihood of completing all Standard 2 assessments:
60%	72%	95%

a student in Standard 7 to complete all Standard 2 assessments for students living in different regions and with specific characteristics. Bukoba performs higher than Kibondo in general, but the difference is exaggerated even further when looking at educated parents in Bukoba Urban and uneducated parents in Kibondo. Mbulu generally performs a bit higher than Iramba, but certain children in Iramba will have an advantage over those in Mbulu depending on other factors.

Communicating with Key Actors

Uwezo places great emphasis on communication of findings and in fostering informed public debate about the situation and what can be done about it (see Uwezo 2011b for further details).

Uwezo's communication involves the following, interlinked forms:

- Communities involved in the household assessment survey are given instant feedback and provided with copies of the assessment tool for their own use. Various efforts are also made to reach the wider public through different communication means, such as mass media (for example, radio, television, and mobile telephony) or piggybacking on existing networks (for example, religious organizations and the popular culture).
- National reports of survey findings are distributed across the country using the district partners, and disaggregated data by district is provided at local levels.
- A few selected materials are developed and targeted to key actors (such as ministry officials, members of parliament, and teachers) as may be appropriate in the local sociopolitical context.

The information is shared in popular formats (such as short fliers, calendars, and popular story books), and Uwezo seeks to promote two-way communication and public debate. Differences among districts, including examples of both successes and failures, are highlighted to foster comparison and learning. The approach is to both inform and raise debate and to stimulate citizen feedback. Emphasis is placed on raising questions rather than quickly jumping to solutions and on a practical and shared agency, that is, what each citizen and policy actor can do to make a difference.

Critically, in Uwezo's theory of change, the citizen focus is important in at least three regards. First, much can be done to improve literacy and numeracy by parents, children, teachers, and other ordinary citizens, even within existing constraints. Second, citizen engagement is essential to creating the public pressure needed to hold leaders and service providers to account, at both local and national levels. Third, the citizen focus creates for greater sustainability by diversifying interest, ownership, and follow-up among people who are directly affected by the poor state of learning, rather than becoming dependent on a few elite individuals.

It is anticipated that Uwezo's second- and third-stage interventions will create conditions that lead to a range of initiatives by other actors. At the local level, the conduct of the assessments and immediate feedback of information has the potential to motivate parents, children, and some teachers to take practical actions that enhance learning. Nationwide, the broad sharing of findings and ensuing debate in the media will puncture the easy conflation of enrollment and classrooms with education, creating public pressure for action. The idea is that the broad public concern and among influential key actors will compel ministries of education and other government leaders to prioritize the issue of learning and take appropriate actions. This pressure may be reinforced by other parties—such as members of parliaments, think tanks, teachers' unions, civil society organizations, editors—choosing to "run with the findings" in their own ways and promoting their own related agendas. Furthermore, the targeted materials mentioned above will provide key actors with specific evidence or options of what they can do, and in this way equip them to better respond to public demand.

Teachers need to be at the heart of any education reform, and even more so when it is related to quality. Teachers unions have become more active in recent years, and they represent increasingly actors for organizing and reaching teachers. At the same time, however, the emphasis to date has been on working conditions and payments, rather than on quality issues. Uwezo believes there is a key opportunity to link teachers' welfare with "standards" and quality, including possibly developing a "compact" in which teachers are promised better conditions in return for greater, learning-centered performance. Borrowing from the experience of other (lawyers, engineers) professional associations, and in concert with initiatives such as Twaweza, Uwezo will explore ways to involve teachers' unions along these lines.

Overall, it is hoped that this dynamic will lead to policy and programmatic changes, principally among government ministries and their key educational agencies, as well as teaching practice and parental follow-up of children's work. Some impacts on private schools are also anticipated, through school owners, managers, teachers, and parents responding to the need to focus on learning.

What Comes Next?

The Uwezo initiative began in 2009 with the purpose of promoting literacy and numeracy among children in Tanzania and other East African countries. To do so, it was necessary to first establish basic competency levels. The second Annual Learning Assessment shows powerfully that children are not learning nearly as well as they ought to be doing. But cautious signs of improvement are also seen: The fact that more and more children are going to preprimary schools gives optimism that literacy and numeracy levels may improve in the future.

We propose the following five considerations as a way of thinking and approaching the challenge as opposed to claims of a "magic solution":

- *Do not do more of the same.* In the face of poor results, politicians, education managers, and nongovernmental organizations often call for *more* to be done,

or *more resources* to be invested in the same interventions, when in fact the key problem may be the choice of interventions rather than lack of resources.
- *Insist on rigorous evidence.* Too many policies and budgets are determined on the basis of past practice, ideological preference, or political whim. Policy makers and school administrators alike would do better to examine the evidence for the effectiveness of different interventions so as to develop a more informed sense of what works.
- *Focus on learning outcomes instead of educational inputs.* Among the public and policy makers alike, education is often characterized in terms of physical inputs such as classrooms, desks, and books, as well as human inputs such as numbers of qualified teachers and enrolled pupils. Although these aspects can no doubt contribute, the ultimate measure of success should be how well children can read and write, perform basic numerical operations, and the like.
- *Learn from what works.* Although overall results are poor, some schools and districts do better than others despite facing similar constraints. Their success may be explained by historical and income advantages in part, but other factors of success may be at work regarding management of institutions, collective action, and innovation that others could emulate.
- *Experiment and test out new ideas.* The basic mode of classroom pedagogy today in most schools has not changed much for decades. It may be worthwhile to consciously create a culture and room for "disruptive" ideas and technologies and test whether innovations and different approaches work better than the status quo.

These five considerations are more about a way of thinking and approaching a problem than about proffering any specific solution. Perhaps that is the key point. Indeed, when an enormously expanded schooling infrastructure continues to yield such poor results, the fundamental challenge may be less about identifying a policy or technocratic fix, or setting up a new project or raising funds, but rather more a reflection of the failure of educational imagination and innovation. If Uwezo's findings can stimulate educational leaders and the public alike, including teachers and parents, to pause and contemplate whether we are doing the right thing, and what works and how to scale it up, Uwezo will have done a large part of its job.

Notes

1. We wish to acknowledge the contribution of Brad Gunton to earlier versions of this chapter. We further appreciate contributions from Youdi Schipper and Sam Jones on reviewing the data and providing quality assurance.
2. See http://www.uwezo.net/standards-2/.
3. Some children included in the survey were not administered the test scores or did not answer certain tests. Given the potentially selective pattern of nonresponse, missing test scores where imputed to ensure that the results are representative of the entire school-age population. In the Uwezo (2011a) data set, between 2 and 3 percent of (weighted) observation had to be imputed, but its impact on the results is marginal.

4. This chapter was written before the public release of the cleaned data sets in 2013. As a result, some minor differences are seen between results presented here and those from the public release. This is also why the 2012 data are not presented.
5. Standard 2 proficiency hence means that the students were able to read a story in Kiswahili and English and were proficient in all the numeracy categories.

References

Uwezo. 2010. *Are Our Children Learning? Annual Learning Assessment Report*. Dar es Salaam, Tanzania.

———. 2011a. *Are Our Children Learning? Annual Learning Assessment Report*. Dar es Salaam, Tanzania.

———. 2011b. "Improving Learning Outcomes in East Africa 2009–2013." Strategy Update 30 September, Uwezo, Nairobi.

CHAPTER 5

An Educational Service Delivery Scorecard for Tanzania

Waly Wane and Isis Gaddis

Summary

Africa faces daunting human development challenges. On a consideration of current trends, most countries in the region are off track on many Millennium Development Goals. However, a look beneath this aggregate record reveals that much progress has taken place in many countries, although often from a low base, and that examples can be identified of extraordinary progress in a short time. If successes could be quickly scaled up, and if problems could be ironed out based on evidence of what works and what does not, Africa could reach the goals—if not by 2015, then in the not-too-distant future.

To accelerate progress toward the Millennium Development Goals, governments, donors, and nongovernmental organizations in low- and middle-income countries (LMICs) have committed increased resources to improve service delivery. However, budget allocations alone are poor indicators of the true quality of services or of value for money in countries with weak institutions. Moreover, when the service delivery failures are systematic, relying exclusively on the public sector to address them may not be realistic. Empowering citizens and civil society actors is necessary to put pressure on governments to improve performance. For this to work, citizens must have access to information on service delivery performance. The Service Delivery Indicators (SDI) project is an attempt to provide such information to the public in Africa.

The indicators, which were piloted in Senegal and Tanzania, document poor service delivery in the Tanzanian education sector in terms of school inputs and infrastructure, teachers' effort and knowledge, and school funding. Most schools appear to be overcrowded (with an average of 74 enrolled children per classroom) and only a tiny minority provide basic infrastructure facilities. Teacher absenteeism—from the school and from the classroom—is widespread. The average student in primary school is taught just over two hours per day, less than half of the scheduled time. Moreover, many teachers lack basic knowledge of the primary curriculum. The results also show considerable leakage of funds along the supply chain, because 37 percent of resources from the capitation grant do not reach the schools. Finally, consistent correlations are found between the quality of service delivery (as measured by the various indicators) and learning achievements of fourth-grade students, suggesting that improvements in service delivery could potentially go a long way in enhancing the quality of education and raising learning outcomes.

Introduction

There is no robust, standardized set of indicators to measure the quality of services as experienced by citizens in Africa. Existing indicators tend to be fragmented and focus on either final outcomes or final inputs, rather than on the underlying systems that help generate the outcomes or make use of the inputs. No set of indicators is available for measuring constraints associated with service delivery and the behavior of front-line providers, both of which have a direct impact on the quality of services citizens are able to access. Without consistent and accurate information on the quality of services, it is difficult for citizens or politicians (the principal) to assess how service providers (the agent) are performing and to take corrective action.

This chapter portrays the SDI project, which provides a set of metrics to benchmark the performance of schools and health clinics in Africa. The indicators can be used to track progress within and across countries to increase public accountability and good governance. Ultimately, the goal is to help policy makers, citizens, service providers, donors, and other stakeholders enhance the quality of services and improve development outcomes.

The Service Delivery Indicators Project

The perspective adopted by the indicators is that of citizens accessing a service. The indicators can be viewed as a service delivery report card on education and health care. However, instead of using citizens' perceptions to assess performance, the indicators assemble objective and quantitative information from a survey of front-line service delivery units, using modules from the Public Expenditure Tracking Survey (PETS), Quantitative Service Delivery Survey (QSDS), Staff Absence Survey (SAS), and observational studies (see also box 5.1).

The SDI project takes as its starting point the literature on how to boost education and health outcomes in low- and middle-income countries. This literature shows robust evidence that the type of individuals attracted to specific tasks at different levels of the service delivery hierarchy, as well as the set of incentives they face to actually exert effort, are positively and significantly related to education and health outcomes. In addition, conditional on providers exerting effort, increased resource flows can have beneficial effects. Therefore, the proposed indicators focus predominantly on measures that capture the outcome of these efforts, both by the front-line service providers and by higher-level authorities

Box 5.1 Microlevel Survey Instruments for Measuring Resource Flows and Service Delivery

Over the past decade, microlevel survey instruments, such as Public Expenditure Tracking Surveys (PETSs), Quantitative Service Delivery Surveys (QSDSs), Staff Absence Surveys (SASs), and observational studies have proven to be powerful tools for identifying bottlenecks, inefficiencies, and other problems in service delivery.

PETSs trace the flow of public resources from the budget to the intended end users through the administrative structure, as a means of ascertaining the extent to which the actual spending on services is consistent with budget allocations. QSDSs examine inputs, outputs, and incentives at the facility level, as well as provider behavior, to assess performance and efficiency of service delivery. SASs focus on the availability of teachers and health practitioners on the front line and identify problems with their incentives. Observational studies aim to measure the quality of services, proxied for by the level of effort exerted by service providers.

In the Ugandan education sector, for example, Reinikka and Svensson (2004, 2005, 2006) use PETSs to study leakage of funds and the impact of a public information campaign on the leakage rates, enrollment levels, and learning outcomes. They find a large reduction in resource leakage, increased enrollments, and some improved test scores in response to the campaign. Using QSDS, the same authors (2010) explore what motivates religious not-for-profit health care providers. They use a change in financing of not-for-profit health care providers in Uganda to test two different theories of organizational behavior (profit maker versus altruistic). They show that financial aid leads to more laboratory testing, lower user charges, and increased utilization, but to no increase in staff remuneration. The findings are consistent with the view that the not-for-profit health care providers are intrinsically motivated to serve (poor) people and that these preferences matter quantitatively.

Chaudhury et al. (2006) use the SAS approach to measure absence rates in education and health services. They report results from surveys in which enumerators made unannounced visits to primary schools and health clinics in Bangladesh, Ecuador, India, Indonesia, Peru, and Uganda, and recorded whether they found teachers and health workers at the facilities. Averaging across the countries, about 19 percent of teachers and 35 percent of health workers were absent. However, the survey focused only on whether providers were present at the facilities, not whether they were actually working, and so even these figures may present too favorable a picture. For example, in India, one-quarter of government primary school teachers were absent from school, but only about one-half of the teachers were actually teaching when enumerators arrived at the schools.

---

entrusted with the task of ensuring that schools and clinics are receiving proper support. The choice of indicators avoids the need to make strong structural assumptions about the link between inputs, behavior, and outcomes. Although the data collection focuses on front-line providers, the indicators will not only mirror how the service delivery unit itself is performing, it will also indicate the efficacy of the entire health and education system. We do not maintain that we can directly measure the incentives and constraints that influence performance, but we argue that we can, at best, use microdata to measure the outcomes of these incentives and constraints. Because health and education services are largely a government responsibility in most African countries, and many public resources have gone into these sectors, the SDI pilot focuses on public providers. However, it would be relatively straightforward to expand the indicators to include nongovernmental service providers.

To evaluate the feasibility of the proposed indicators, pilot surveys in primary education and health care were implemented in Senegal and Tanzania in 2010. The results from the pilot studies demonstrate that the indicators methodology is capable of providing the necessary information to construct harmonized indicators on the quality of service delivery, as experienced by the citizen, using a single set of instruments at a single point of collection (the facility). However, although collecting this information from front-line service providers is feasible, it is also demanding, both financially and logistically. The decision to scale up the project should hence weigh the benefits—having comparable and powerful data on the quality of service delivery—with the costs.

The Analytical Underpinnings of the Service Delivery Indicators

Service Delivery Outcomes and Perspective of the Indicators

Service delivery outcomes are determined by the relationships of accountability between policy makers, service providers, and citizens (figure 5.1). Education and health outcomes are the result of the interaction between various actors in the multistep service delivery system and depend on the characteristics and behavior of individuals and households. Although delivery of quality health care and education is contingent foremost on what happens in clinics and in classrooms, a combination of several basic elements have to be present for quality

Figure 5.1 The Relationships of Accountability among Citizens, Service Providers, and Policy Makers

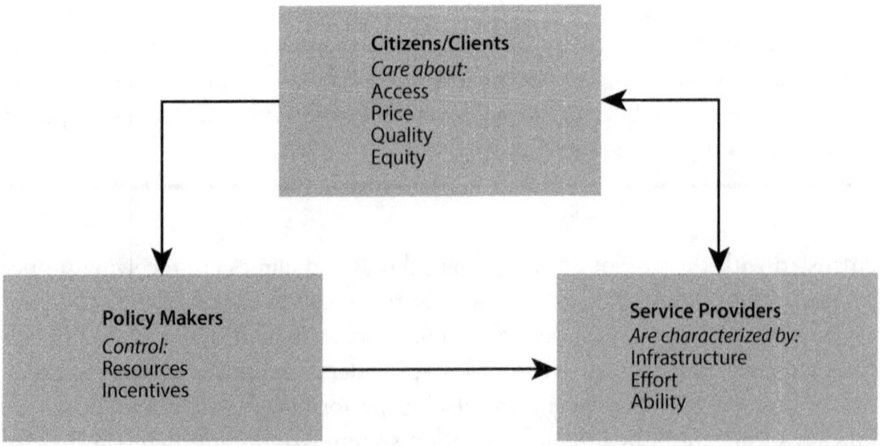

Citizens/Clients
Care about:
Access
Price
Quality
Equity

Policy Makers
Control:
Resources
Incentives

Service Providers
Are characterized by:
Infrastructure
Effort
Ability

Source: Based on the accountability framework in the *World Development Report 2004* (World Bank 2003).

services to be accessible and produced by teachers and health personnel at the front line, which depend on the overall service delivery system and supply chain. Adequate financing, infrastructure, human resources, material, and equipment need to be made available, while the institutions and governance structure provide incentives for the service providers to perform.

Indicator Categories and the Selection Criteria

Many data sets are available in both education and health, which measure inputs, outcomes, and outputs in the service delivery process, mostly from a household perspective. Although providing a wealth of information, existing data sources (such as Demographic and Health Surveys and Living Standard Measurement Surveys) cover only a subsample of countries and are, in many cases, outdated. We propose that all the data required for the SDI should be collected through one standard instrument administered in all countries.

Given the quantitative and micro focus, we have essentially two options for collecting the data necessary for the indicators. We could either take beneficiaries or service providers as the unit of observation. We argue that the most cost-effective option is to focus on service providers. Obviously, this choice will, to some extent, restrict what type of data we can collect and what indicators we can create.

Our proposed choice of indicators takes as its starting point the recent literature on the economics of education and health. This literature stresses the importance of provider behavior and competence in the delivery of health and education services. Conditional on service providers exerting effort, some evidence also suggests that the provision of physical resources and infrastructure has important effects on the quality of service delivery (see also box 5.2).[1]

Box 5.2 Service Delivery Production Function

Consider a service delivery production function, f, which maps physical inputs, x, the effort put in by the service provider, e, as well as his or her type (or knowledge), θ, to deliver quality services into individual-level outcomes, y. The effort variable e could be thought of as multidimensional and thus include effort (broadly defined) of other actors in the service delivery system. We can think of type as the characteristic (knowledge) of the individuals who select into specific task. Of course, outcomes of this production process are affected not just by the service delivery unit, but also by the actions and behaviors of households, which we denote by ε. We can therefore write

$$y = f(x, e, \theta) + \varepsilon. \qquad (1)$$

To assess the quality of services provided, one should ideally measure $f(x, e, \theta)$. Of course, it is notoriously difficult to measure all the arguments that enter the production and would involve a huge data collection effort. A more feasible approach is therefore to focus instead on proxies of the arguments that, to a first-order approximation, have the largest effects.

The sometimes weak relationship between resources and outcomes documented in the literature has been associated with deficiencies in the incentive structure of school and health systems. Indeed, most service delivery systems in developing countries present front-line providers with a set of incentives that negate the impact of pure resource-based policies. Therefore, although resources alone appear to have a limited impact on the quality of education and health in developing countries, it is possible that inputs are complementary to changes in incentives, and so coupling improvements in both may have large and significant impacts (see Hanushek and Woessman 2007). As noted by Duflo, Dupas, and Kremer (2009), the fact that budgets have not kept pace with enrollment, leading to large student-teacher ratios, overstretched physical infrastructure, insufficient number of textbooks, and the like, is problematic. However, simply increasing the level of resources might not address the quality deficit in education and health without also taking providers' incentives into account.

Three sets of indicators are proposed in this chapter. The first attempts to measure availability of key infrastructure and inputs at the front-line service provider level. The second attempts to measure effort and knowledge of service providers at the front-line level. The third attempts to proxy for effort, broadly defined, higher up in the service delivery chain. Providing countries with detailed and comparable data on these important dimensions of service delivery is one of the main innovations of the SDI project.[2]

In addition, it is important that the selected indicators are (1) quantitative (to avoid problems of perception biases that limit both cross-country and longitudinal comparisons)[3]; (2) cardinal in nature (to allow within and cross-country comparisons); (3) robust (in the sense that the methodology used to construct the indicators can be verified and readily replicated); (4) actionable; and (5) cost effective.

Table 5.1 lists the simple indicators that have been identified to create a scorecard for the education sector.

Table 5.1 Indicators in an Education Service Delivery Report Card

At the school: Inputs and infrastructure
Infrastructure (electricity, water, sanitation)
Children per classroom
Student-teacher ratio
Textbooks per student
Teachers: Effort and knowledge
Absence rate
Time children are in school being taught
Share of teachers with minimum knowledge
Funding: Effort in the supply chain
Education expenditures reaching primary school
Delays in salaries

Implementation of the Service Delivery Survey

The SDI were piloted in Tanzania in the summer of 2010. The main objective of the pilots was to test the survey instruments in the field and to verify that robust indicators of service delivery quality could be collected with a single facility-level instrument in different settings. Research on Poverty Alleviation (REPOA), a think tank with significant experience in carrying out facility surveys, handled the SDI fieldwork.

The sample was designed to provide estimates for each of the key indicators, broken down by urban and rural location. To achieve this purpose in a cost-effective manner, a stratified multistage random sampling design was employed. Given the budget constraint, roughly 180 public primary schools were surveyed, of which 132 were in rural areas versus 48 urban schools. In terms of geographic coverage, 20 districts were included in the survey. The sample frame employed consisted of the most recent list of all public primary schools, including information on the size of the population they serve. Map 5.1 illustrates the sampling areas.

Map 5.1 Map of the Sampling Areas

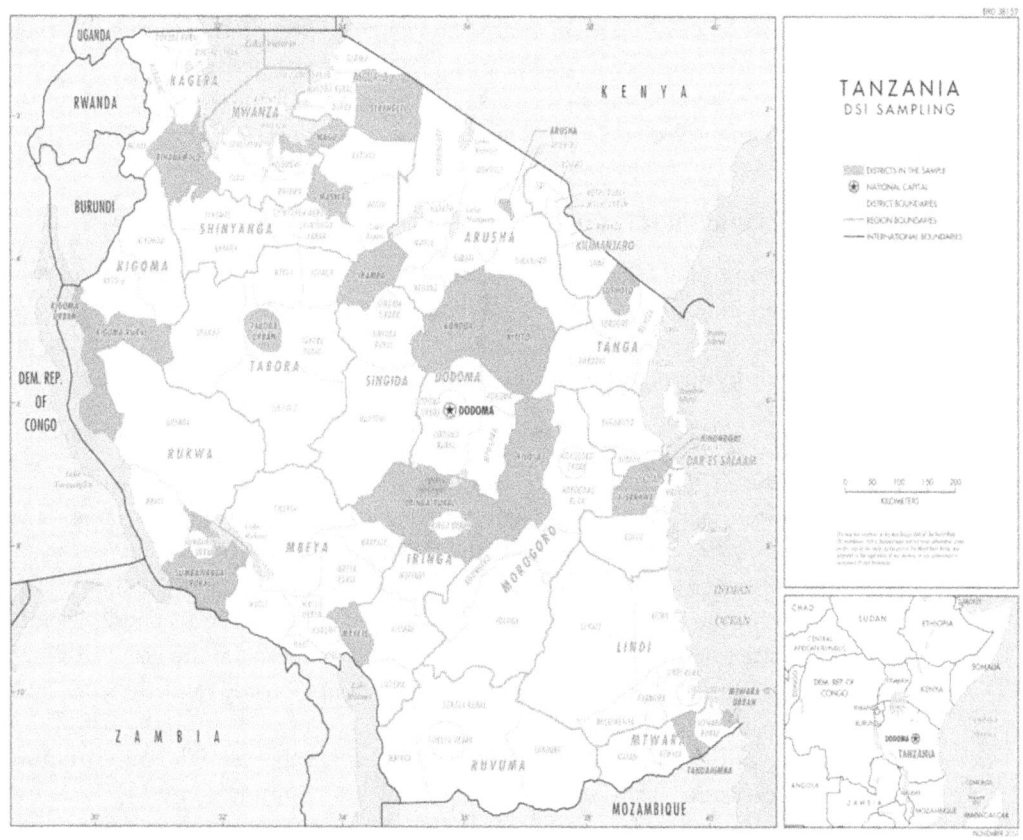

The survey used a sector-specific questionnaire with several modules, all of which were administered at the facility level. The questionnaires built on previous similar questionnaires based on international good practice for PETS, QSDS, SAS, and observational surveys. All instruments went through a pretest and the final questionnaires were translated into Swahili.

The questionnaire has six modules as follows:

- *Module 1:* This module is administered to the principal, the head teacher, or most senior teacher in the school. It collects self-reported and administrative data on school characteristics, students, teachers, and resource flows.
- *Module 2:* This module is administered to (a maximum of) 10 teachers randomly selected from the list of all teachers. Its main purpose is to collect information on delays in the receipt of wages.
- *Module 3:* This module is administered to the same 10 teachers as in module 2. It is used to measure teacher absenteeism. The teachers are interviewed one week after the first visit to the school; however, this time around the visit is unannounced.
- *Module 4:* This is a classroom observation module. Two different Grade 4 lessons in either language or mathematics are observed. Each observation lasts 40 minutes.
- *Module 5:* This module consists of a test for the teachers. All (maximum is 10) Grade 3–4 teachers in mathematics and language were tested to measure their knowledge in these two subject areas as well as basic pedagogy.
- *Module 6:* A test in mathematics and language is administered one-on-one to 10 randomly selected Grade 4 students to measure learning achievement.

Indicators and Pilot Results

This section presents the findings of the pilot surveys in education for Tanzania. For selected indicators, the findings from Senegal are also shown for the sake of comparison. The results are presented for the country as a whole along with the breakdowns by rural and urban locations.[4]

At the School
Infrastructure (Electricity, Water, Sanitation)
Schools often lack basic infrastructure, particularly schools in rural areas. The indicator *Infrastructure* accounts for the three basic infrastructure services: availability of electricity (in the classrooms), clean water (in the school), and improved sanitation (in the school). The data are derived from the head teacher questionnaire and measure the availability of the service at the time of the visit. Although these data are self-reported, the quality of the data is good, and the biases are likely to be minimal (table 5.2).

Results for Senegal and Tanzania are reported in table 5.2. The infrastructure indicator measures if the school has access to basic infrastructure (= 1), that is, access to electricity, clean water, and improved sanitation, or if it lacks one or

An Educational Service Delivery Scorecard for Tanzania

Table 5.2 Infrastructure in Tanzania (Percentage of Schools with Electricity, Water, and Sanitation)

	All	Rural	Urban
Senegal	17	8	55
	(3)	(2)	(8)
Tanzania	3	2	8
	(1)	(1)	(8)

Note: Weighted mean with standard errors adjusted for weighting and clustering in parentheses (all in percent); 180 observations for Tanzania, of which 45 are urban schools; and 151 observations for Senegal, of which 61 are urban schools.

Table 5.3 Average Number of Children per Classroom in Tanzania

	All	Rural	Urban
Number of children	74.1	70.5	92.5
	(5.3)	(5.3)	(12.6)

Note: Weighted mean with standard errors adjusted for weighting and clustering in parentheses; 180 observations for Tanzania, of which 45 are urban schools.

more of them (= 0). The gap between Senegal and Tanzania is large and significant. On average, only 3 percent of the schools in Tanzania have access to the three basic infrastructure services, electricity being the key constraint. This compares with 17 percent in Senegal.

Looking at the rural-urban breakdown, it is worth noting the significant difference between rural and urban schools in Senegal, whereas the infrastructure availability in Tanzania is poor in both urban and rural areas.

Children per Classroom

The indicator *Children per Classroom* is measured as the ratio of the number of primary school children to available classrooms. The source for the data is the school enrollment list (for students) and reported classrooms (by the headmaster). Our assessment is that the quality of the data is good, although the enrollment lists may not always be up-to-date.[5]

With an average of more than 74 students per classroom, Tanzania's public schools appear overcrowded (table 5.3).[6] It is interesting to note that the average urban primary school has 20 more students per classroom than its rural counterpart and is thus significantly more crowded.

Student-Teacher Ratio

Teacher shortage is a problem in many developing countries, especially in poor and rural areas. The indicator *Student-Teacher Ratio* is measured as the average number of students per teacher. The data on teachers are from the head teacher questionnaire and codes all teachers listed to be teaching. Our assessment is that the quality of the data is good, although the enrollment lists may not always be up-to-date, as noted. Table 5.4 reports the results.

Table 5.4 Student-Teacher Ratio

Sample	All	Rural	Urban
Senegal	28.7	28.0	31.9
	(0.8)	(1.0)	(1.7)
Tanzania	48.7	50.6	39.1
	(2.2)	(2.5)	(3.1)

Note: Weighted mean with standard errors adjusted for weighting and clustering in parentheses; 180 observations for Tanzania, of which 45 are urban schools; and 151 observations for Senegal, of which 61 are urban schools.

Table 5.5 Textbooks per Student

	All	Rural	Urban
Tanzania	0.94	0.95	0.90
	(0.08)	(0.09)	(0.17)

Note: Sample is all books. Weighted mean with standard errors adjusted for weighting and clustering in parentheses; 179 (164 for language books) observations for Tanzania, of which 44 (43) are urban schools.

The student-teacher ratio is significantly higher in Tanzania than in Senegal. Although the difference between the urban areas of both countries is small, the Tanzanian schools in rural areas have significantly higher student-teacher ratios than the Senegalese schools in rural areas.

Textbooks per Student

Lack of basic education material may also be an important constraint for learning faced by children and teachers in many developing countries. The indicator *Textbooks per Student* is measured as the overall number of textbooks available within primary schools per student. Not all schools could report breakdowns of books per grade and subject. In this case, data on the reported total number of books (for a grade) are used.[7] Measurement errors in the number of books are likely to be an issue, although the enumerators were asked to verify the reports using school records (if available). The results reported in table 5.5 show few differences between urban and rural areas in Tanzania.

Teachers

Absence Rate

In many countries, highly centralized personnel systems, inadequate incentives, and weak local accountability have resulted in high levels of staff absence. The indicator *Absence Rate* is measured as the share of teachers not in school as observed during one unannounced visit.[8]

For cross-country comparisons, we believe the data are of good quality. However, because the information is based on one unannounced visit only, the estimate for each school is likely to be imprecisely measured. By averaging across schools, however, these measurement error problems are likely to be less of a concern.

Table 5.6 Absence Rate (Percentage of Teachers Not in School)

Sample	All	Rural	Urban
Tanzania	23	20	36
	(2)	(2)	(4)

Note: Weighted mean with standard errors adjusted for weighting and clustering in parentheses (all in percent); 180 observations for Tanzania, of which 45 are urban schools.

Table 5.7 Absence Rate from Classroom (Percentage of Time Teachers Not in the Classroom)

Sample	All	Rural	Urban
Tanzania	53	50	68
	(3)	(2)	(5)

Note: Weighted mean with standard errors adjusted for weighting and clustering in parentheses (all in percent); 179 observations for Tanzania, of which 45 are urban schools.

About one in four teachers is absent from school on any given school day (table 5.6). Interestingly, the absence rate in urban schools in Tanzania is significantly higher than in rural schools. Even if at school, however, the teachers may not be in the classroom. As a complementary indicator, it is important to also consider absence from the classroom.[9] The findings presented in table 5.7 are striking. Altogether the teachers are absent from the classroom more than half of the time—either because they are not in school in the first place, or, if they are in school, because they are not in the classroom during the scheduled teaching hours. Again, absenteeism is significantly higher in urban schools than in rural schools.

Time Children in School Are Being Taught

The SAS, together with classroom observation, can also be used to measure the indicator *Time Children in School Are Being Taught*. To this end, we start by calculating the scheduled hours of teaching. We then adjust the scheduled time for the time teachers are absent from the classroom on average. Finally, from the classroom observation, it is possible to measure to what extent the teacher is actually teaching when he or she is in the classroom. Specifically, the enumerator recorded every five minutes (for a total of 15 minutes) if the teacher remained in the classroom to teach, or if he or she is engaged in nonteaching activities.[10]

As the information is based on one unannounced visit and a short observational period, the estimate for each school is likely to be imprecisely measured. By taking an average across many schools, however, one can arrive at an accurate estimate of the mean number of hours children are being taught. The results capture the lower bound of the estimate if, as seems reasonable, the classroom observations are biased upward because of Hawthorne effects (whereby teachers spend longer hours in the classroom because they are under scrutiny).

On average, students in primary schools in Tanzania are taught two hours a day, and even 40 minutes less in urban areas. Students get about one hour more

Table 5.8 Time Children in School Are Being Taught per Day

Sample	All	Rural	Urban
Senegal	3 hr 15 min	3 hr 17 min	3 hr 8 min
	(10 min)	(12 min)	(10 min)
Tanzania	2 hr 4 min	2 hr 11 min	1 hr 24 min
	(10 min)	(10 min)	(18 min)

Note: Weighted mean with standard errors adjusted for weighting and clustering in parentheses; 173 observations for Tanzania, of which 43 are urban schools; and 146 observations for Senegal, of which 60 are urban schools.

of effective teaching in Senegal, and this difference is significant. The difference between urban and rural areas is significant in Tanzania, but not in Senegal. The scheduled teaching time is 5 hours and 12 minutes in Tanzania, and 4 hours and 36 minutes in Senegal (table 5.8).

Because the scheduled time differs across grades, a more accurate measure would be to look at the time children in a given grade, who are at school, are being taught. These estimates, however, are similar to those of the pooled findings reported in table 5.8.

Share of Teachers with Minimum Knowledge

Having teachers doing their job, however, may not be enough if the teachers' competence (ability and knowledge) is inadequate, a major problem in several LMICs. To assess this issue, up to 10 teachers per school were administered a basic test of knowledge. The teacher test consisted of two parts: mathematics and English. Current teachers of Grade 4 students and those teachers who taught the current Grade 4 students in the previous year were tested. The test comprised material from both lower and upper primary school in language and mathematics. The test was administered en masse.

The test consisted of a number of different tasks ranging from a simple spelling task (involving four questions) to a more challenging vocabulary test (involving 13 questions) in languages and from adding double digits (one question) to solving a complex logic problem (involving two questions) in mathematics (table 5.9).

Although it is a matter of debate what constitutes minimum knowledge for a Grade 3 and 4 teacher, a fairly conservative measure is that the teacher demonstrates mastery of the particular curriculum he or she teaches. Our suggested measure for the indicator *Share of Teachers with Minimum Knowledge* attempts to capture this. In the basic knowledge test, 14 questions were related to the lower primary curriculum on the language test, and five questions were related to the primary mathematics curriculum. We define mastery of the primary curriculum as answering all of these questions correctly and derive then the share of teachers that correctly manages to do so. To be precise, for the language section, we derive the share of language teachers who were able to answer all questions correctly. For the mathematics section, we derive the share of mathematics teachers who were able to answer all the questions correctly.[11] Of course, the content of the

Table 5.9 Share of Teachers with Minimum Knowledge in Tanzania
Percent

	All	Rural	Urban
Language	11	13	5
	(3)	(4)	(4)
Mathematics	75	75	74
	(3)	(4)	(6)

Note: Dependent variable is share of teachers that managed to complete all questions on the primary language and primary mathematics curriculum, respectively. Weighted mean with standard errors adjusted for weighting and clustering in parentheses (all in percent); 504 observations from 180 schools in Tanzania (260 English teachers and 244 mathematics teachers), of which 152 (45 schools) are from urban areas.

Table 5.10 Share of Teachers Answering Correctly on Specific Questions
Percent

	Senegal	Tanzania
Noun identification	39	51
	(5)	(4)
Subtraction of two double-digit numbers	90	90
	(2)	(3)
Division of two fractions	26	66
	(4)	(4)

Note: For identifying a noun, the teacher was given a word and asked to identify which parts of speech a particular word belonged to from a given set of options. For the mathematics question, the teacher was asked to subtract two double-digit numbers (i.e., 87−32) and divide two fractions (3/4 / 5/8). The division test was not part of the minimum knowledge test in table 5.9. Weighted mean with standard errors adjusted for weighting and clustering in parentheses (all in percent); 504 observations from 180 schools in Tanzania (260 English teachers and 244 mathematics teachers), of which 152 (45 schools) are from urban areas; and 248 observations from 151 schools in Senegal (the teachers in Senegal taught both subjects), of which 133 (61 schools) are urban schools.

lower primary curriculum may vary slightly across countries. We here define lower primary curriculum as all the questions that test basic competencies, that is, those that were included in the student test.

As is evident from table 5.9, only one in 10 teachers in Tanzania manages to complete all the questions on the primary language curriculum.[12] For mathematics, the picture is less bleak, with three out of four teachers managing to complete all questions on the primary mathematics curriculum. No significant differences are found between urban and rural schools.

Another way to assess teachers' knowledge is to analyze the results on specific questions (table 5.10). Strikingly, five out of 10 teachers could not identify a noun in Tanzania (six out of 10 in Senegal), and one in 10 teachers failed to correctly subtract double-digit numbers in both countries. With the exception of the noun task, again no significant difference is found between urban and rural schools.

Funding
Education Expenditures Reaching Primary Schools

The indicator *Education Expenditures Reaching Primary Schools* assesses the amount of resources available for services to students at the school. It is measured as the recurrent expenditure (wage and nonwage) reaching the primary schools per primary school student in U.S. dollars (at 2005 purchasing power parity [PPP]) per year. Unlike the other indicators, this indicator is not a school-specific indicator. Instead, we calculate the amount reached per surveyed school, and then use the sample weights to estimate the population (of all schools) in aggregate.[13]

Measuring effective education expenditures reaching primary schools is a challenging task, because resource systems and flows differ across countries. To fully account for the flow of resources reaching the schools from all government sources and programs, schools need to have up-to-date and comprehensive records of inflows. This is not the case in many schools, likely causing us to misinterpret, at least in some cases, poor records for lack of resources reaching the school.

The amount of recurrent funds (wage and nonwage) reaching primary schools is lower in Tanzania than in Senegal (per primary school student). In Senegal, rural and urban schools receive about the same amount in financial and in-kind support, whereas rural schools in Tanzania, on average, receive more than their urban counterparts (figure 5.2).

The estimates in figure 5.2 are driven both by budget decisions at the central level and the efficiency with which budgeted resources are made available to primary schools. For Tanzania, we can derive an estimate of the latter effect, that is, the efficiency of the supply chain, by estimating resource leakage in one of the support programs for primary schools, the capitation grant program.[14] The capitation grant is based on the number of pupils attending school and is mainly intended for books and school supplies. As table 5.11 indicates, leakage, defined as the share of resources intended for schools, but not received by them,

Figure 5.2 Education Expenditures (per Student) Reaching Primary Schools
US$ at 2005 PPP per year

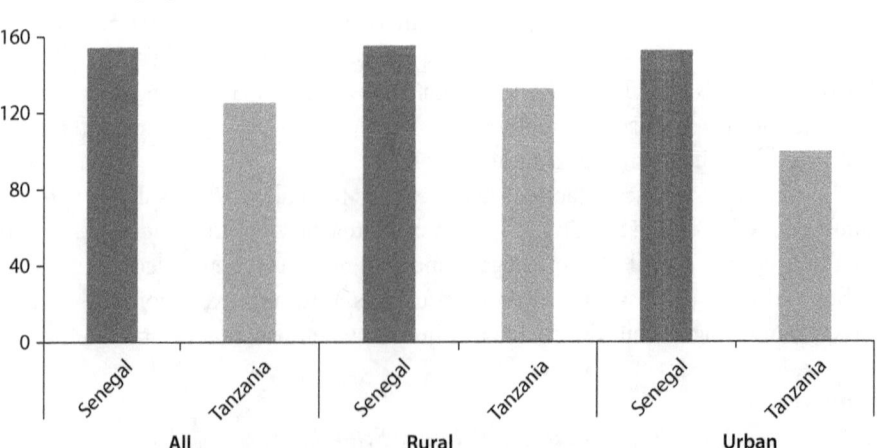

Note: The estimates are based on data from 180 observations for Tanzania, of which 45 are urban schools, and 151 observations for Senegal, of which 61 are urban schools. PPP = purchasing power parity.

Table 5.11 Leakage of Capitation Grant (Percentage of Intended Resources Not Received by the Schools)

Sample	All	Rural	Urban
Tanzania	37	36	41
	(3)	(3)	(2)

Note: Weighted mean with standard errors adjusted for weighting and clustering in parentheses (all in percent); 173 observations of schools in Tanzania, of which 41 are urban schools.

Table 5.12 Delays in Salaries (Percentage of Teachers Whose Salary Is Overdue More than Two Months)

Sample	All	Rural	Urban
Tanzania	2	2	0.6
	(0.5)	(0.5)	(0.4)

Note: Weighted mean with standard errors adjusted for weighting and clustering in parentheses (all in percent); 174 observations of schools in Tanzania, of which 43 are urban schools.

represents 37 percent of the capitation grant budget. Leakage is higher, but not significantly so, in urban areas. Such high levels of resource leakage could potentially have serious consequences for service quality.

Delays in Salaries

The indicator *Delays in Salaries*, which may have an adverse effect on staff morale and therefore on the quality of service, is measured as the proportion of teachers whose salary has been overdue for more than two months. The data are collected directly from teachers at the school and we believe the data are of good quality. Table 5.12 reports the results.

Significant delays in salaries do not appear to be a common problem in Tanzania, where only about 2 percent of the teaching staff reports more than two months delay in salary, and this happens almost exclusively in rural schools.

Learning Outcomes: Test Scores in Education

To avoid making structural assumptions about the link between inputs, performance, and outcomes, we do not suggest that outcomes should be part of the SDI survey. However, it may make sense to report separately on outcomes when the various subindicators and the potential aggregate index are presented. In health, measures are found for many countries at the national level, such as under-five mortality rates, but no indicator that can be linked directly to the service quality of individual facilities. Quantity outcomes in education are also available (various measures of flows and stock of schooling) for a large subset of countries. However, on quality, there are no comparable data available, at least not for multiple countries. Thus, student learning achievement has been collected as part of the survey in education.

Available evidence indicates that the level of learning tends to be very low in Africa. For instance, assessments of the reading capacity among Grade 6 students in 12 eastern and southern African countries indicate that less than 25 percent of the children in 10 of the 12 countries tested reached the desirable level of reading literacy (SACMEQ 2000–02). As part of this survey, learning outcomes were measured by student scores on a mathematics and language test.

We test younger cohorts partly because we have very little data on their achievement, partly because the Southern and Eastern Africa Consortium for Monitoring Educational Quality (SACMEQ) already tests students in higher grades, partly because the sample of children in school becomes more and more self-selective as we go higher up due to high dropout rates, and partly because we know that cognitive ability is most malleable at younger ages (see Cunha and Heckman 2007).

For the pilots, the student test consisted of two parts: language (English and French, respectively, in Tanzania and Senegal) and mathematics. Students in fourth grade were tested on material for grades 1, 2, 3, and 4. The test was designed as a one-on-one test with enumerators reading out instructions to students in their mother tongue. This was done so as to build up a differentiated picture of students' cognitive skills. Results of the Grade 4 student test are presented in table 5.13.

Tanzanian students scored on average 43 percent in the language section and 39 percent in the mathematics section. Senegalese students performed significantly better on both sections of the test, with an average score of 50 percent in the language part and of 45 percent in mathematics.[15] The difference on the language test is at least partly due to the fact that teaching takes place in French from Grade 1 onward in Senegal, whereas English is only introduced as the medium of instruction in Grade 3 in Tanzania. As expected, rural schools score significantly worse than urban schools.

Although the mean score is an important statistic, it is also an estimate that by itself is not easy to interpret. Tables 5.14 and 5.15 depict a breakdown of the results on specific questions for Tanzania. As is evident, reading ability in English is low. Only 6 percent of students in Tanzania are able to read a sentence.[16] In mathematics, 83 percent of Tanzanian students can add two single digits.

The SDI are a measure of inputs (including effort), not of final outcomes. Nevertheless, in the final instance, we should be interested in inputs, not in and

Table 5.13 Average Score on Student Test in Tanzania
Percent

	All	Rural	Urban
Language	43	41	52
	(2)	(2)	(3)
Mathematics	39	38	48
	(2)	(2)	(3)

Note: Weighted mean with standard errors adjusted for weighting and clustering in parentheses (all in percent); 1,787 observations from 180 schools in Tanzania, of which 449 (45 schools) are from urban areas.

An Educational Service Delivery Scorecard for Tanzania

Table 5.14 Language: Percentage of Students Who Can Read a Sentence (in English)

	All	Rural	Urban
Tanzania	6	6	10
	(1)	(1)	(3)

Note: Weighted mean with standard errors adjusted for weighting and clustering in parentheses (all in percent); 1,787 observations from 180 schools in Tanzania, of which 449 (45 schools) are from urban areas. Test scores are averaged at the school level.

Table 5.15 Mathematics: Percentage of Students Who Can Add Two Single Digits

Sample	All	Rural	Urban
Tanzania	83	81	93
	(2)	(3)	(2)

Note: Weighted mean with standard errors adjusted for weighting and clustering in parentheses (all in percent); 1,787 observations from 180 schools in Tanzania, of which 449 (45 schools) are from urban areas. Test scores are averaged at the school level.

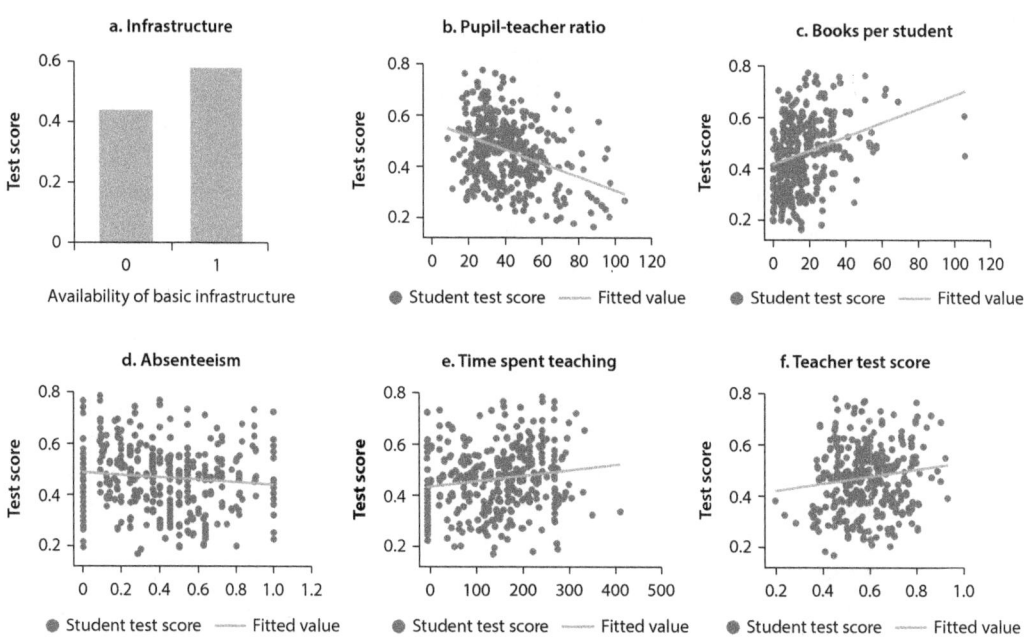

Figure 5.3 Relationship between Student Performance and the Education Service Delivery Indicators

of themselves, but only in as far as they deliver the outcomes we care about. Given that we have collected outcome data in education, we can also check whether our input measures are in some way related to outcomes. Of course, these are mere correlations that cannot be interpreted causally, but we still believe that it is interesting to examine how our indicators correlate with educational achievement. Figure 5.3 depicts unconditional correlations between student achievement (of Grade 4 students) and the education indicators, where the data from Senegal and Tanzania are pooled. Interestingly, and across the board, the indicators are related to student knowledge, with all the correlations having the expected sign.[17]

Lessons Learned, Trade-Offs, and Policy Recommendations for Scale-Up

The pilot of the SDI project in Senegal and Tanzania demonstrates that this methodology is capable, through a single set of instruments and at a single point of collection, to provide information to construct a set of indices for benchmarking service delivery performance in education (and health) in Africa. The survey instruments used in the pilots can, with some modifications, be employed when scaling up the project. In what follows, we outline some of the important issues that have arisen during the pilot phase and the trade-offs that would need to be considered when the project is scaled up. We focus on those issues that are of particular relevance for the education sector.

Sample Size and Sample Strategy

To be credible, the indicators must be representative of the population in question. To determine the required sample size, one faces a number of issues. First, the sample size depends on the sampling technique used.[18] Second, when the mean outcome (with specified precision) is required not only for the population as a whole, but also for certain subpopulations, one needs to draw a much larger sample. In the end, the choice one has to make to get precise estimates for the total population, or for subdivisions, be it urban-rural or districts and provinces, comes down to a trade-off between the cost and value of the indicators based on their planned use. Third, the sample size requirement will differ across the indicators. The easiest way to address this problem is to specify the margin of error for the indicator that is the most vital. The desired standard of precision for the remaining indicators will then probably have to be relaxed. Finally, as the required sample size depends on the variance of the indicator in question, and seeing that variance is country specific, one cannot determine a precise number for the sample size that holds for all countries. In practice, however, this may be less of a concern. For practical reasons, it is probably better to set a reasonable sample size, adjust the standard of precision for the indicators accordingly, and focus on minimizing nonsampling errors.

Measuring Outcomes

The indicators are designed primarily to measure inputs, including effort, in the service delivery production function. In the final instance, it is outcomes that we care about. The question is whether the SDI should seek to collect data on outcomes where such data do not exist, and where doing so would be feasible and cost effective.

Our pilot has shown that it is possible to test for learning outcomes in the two countries by administering homogeneous instruments. If this project were to be scaled up to all of Africa, the task of creating test instruments for students and teachers becomes more daunting. There are two avenues: First, one could try to find the smallest common denominator of all the curricula in Africa and write a test on the basis of this. This is the strategy currently followed by SACMEQ. This is a process that takes several weeks to months in the first instance, involving education experts from every country. An alternative route would be to administer a curriculum-independent test in all countries. This may be especially appropriate for mathematics, where general agreement exists on what constitutes core skills.

In terms of which subjects to test, our experience from the pilot has perhaps raised questions about the correct way to test, across countries, for language skills, and this would be even more so the case if one were to test language skills in many countries. Students start with foreign languages at different ages, and this may compromise comparability. Therefore, testing in the local vernacular may be more appropriate, but of course this requires the development of different instruments for each country. Alternatively, the test could focus on mathematics only.

We believe that it is very beneficial to test early. The self-selection in terms of students is much less severe at early ages, so we observe a much more accurate picture of the state of learning in schools than at higher grades, and, as demonstrated by the current state of research, we can identify simply no substitute for early childhood learning.

Finally, one would have to decide how to test. We decided to test children one-on-one and, where possible, give instructions orally in a child's first language precisely to take into account the fact that reading ability may be low. This is time intensive, and the sample of children we can test is accordingly small. Still, we think that the added accuracy is well worthwhile, and that for testing young children, it is surely the optimal method.

Overall, then, it may be a worthwhile addition to collect data on outcomes as well as inputs. At the very minimum, this could be done by a simple reading test (in the local language perhaps) and a set of mathematics questions, which would not require a synthesis of a large number of curricula.

Notes

1. For overview papers, see Glewwe et al. (2011); Hanushek (2003); and Krishnaratne, White, and Carpenter (2013). Case and Deaton (1999) show, using a natural experiment in South Africa, that increases in school resources (as measured by the student-teacher ratio) raises academic achievement among black students. Duflo (2001) finds that a school construction policy in Indonesia was effective in increasing the quantity of education. Banerjee et al. (2000) find, using a randomized evaluation in India, that provision of additional teachers in nonformal education centers increases school participation of girls. However, a series of randomized evaluations in Kenya indicate that the only effect of textbooks on outcomes was among the better students

(Glewwe and Kremer 2006; Glewwe, Kremer, and Moulin 2002). Further evidence from natural experiments and randomized evaluations also indicate some potential positive effect of school resources on outcomes, but not uniformly positive (Duflo 2001; Glewwe and Kremer 2006).

2. The suggested indicators for education and health are partly based on an initial list of 50 PETS and QSDS indicators devised as part of the project "Harmonization of Public Expenditure Tracking Surveys (PETS) and Quantitative Service delivery Surveys (QSDS) at the World Bank" (Gauthier 2008). That initial list, which covers a wide range of variables characterizing public expenditure and service delivery, was streamlined using this project's criteria and conceptual framework.

3. See, for instance, Olken (2009).

4. Sampling weights are taken into account when deriving the estimates. Standard errors are adjusted for clustering.

5. Enrollment numbers may suffer from overreporting biases if schools have incentives to report higher enrollment figures in order to attract more funds.

6. Although 74 enrolled students per classroom appears very high, the average number of actual students per classroom is often significantly lower due to student absenteeism. The pilot SDI project data used in this chapter collected information only on the number of enrolled students, but the revised SDI methodology also includes actual student counts.

7. The number of subjects (and potentially therefore also the number of books) may differ across countries, and so it would make sense to (also) report disaggregated estimates for the numbers of mathematics and language books per student. However, records of books per grade and subject were not available for enough schools in the two samples.

8. In the first (announced) visit, 10 teachers were randomly selected from the list of all teachers. The whereabouts of these 10 teachers are checked upon during the second, unannounced, visit.

9. This indicator is also derived using data from the unannounced visit, because the enumerators were also asked to verify if teachers present in the school were actually in the classroom.

10. Teaching is defined very broadly, including interacting with students, correcting or grading students' work, asking questions, testing, using the blackboard, and having students working on a specific task.

11. We tested all the teachers in both language and mathematics. However, *all* test statistics we report are based on teachers in their respective subjects only.

12. With a somewhat more lenient definition of answering 90 percent or more questions correctly (for language), the numbers jump to 63 percent and 38 percent in Senegal and Tanzania, respectively.

13. The source for the number of primary school children, broken down by rural and urban location, is Ministry of Education and Vocational Training (2010) for Tanzania. Quantities and values of in-kind items were collected as part of the survey. In cases where values of in-kind items were missing, average unit cost was inferred using information from other surveyed schools.

14. Leakage is not included in the indicators, since we can only measure it for the subset of resources that are allocated by a fixed rule, and not those that are based on bureaucratic discretion.

15. The test consisted of a number of different tasks ranging from a simple task testing knowledge of the alphabet (involving three questions) to a more challenging reading comprehension test (involving three questions) in languages and from adding two single digits (one question) to solving a more difficult sequence problem (one question) in mathematics. Just as for the teacher test, the average test scores are calculated by first calculating the score on each task (given a score between 0 and 100 percent) and then reporting the mean of the score on all tasks in the language section and in the mathematics section, respectively. Because more complex tasks in the language section tended to involve more questions, this way of aggregation gives a higher score than simply adding up the score on each question and dividing by the total possible score.
16. In Tanzania, the reading task consisted of reading a sentence with 11 words. We have defined the percentage of students who can read a sentence correctly as those who can read all words correctly. With a somewhat more lenient definition of being able to read all but one word, the number rises to 11 percent.
17. Results are similar when running a regression of student test scores separately on each indicator, a country dummy and a rural-urban dummy.
18. Partly to reduce costs, but also to generate statistics for population subgroups, a multistage sampling procedure is to be recommended. In general, stratification would tend to increase sampling precision, whereas clustering will tend to reduce sampling precision.

References

Banerjee, Abhijit, Suraj Jacob, and Michael Kremer with Jenny Lanjouw and Peter Lanjouw. 2000. "Promoting School Participation in Rural Rajasthan: Results from Some Prospective Trials." Unpublished, Massachusetts Institute of Technology, Cambridge, MA.

Case, Anne, and Angus Deaton. 1999. "School Inputs and Educational Outcomes in South Africa." *Quarterly Journal of Economics* 114 (3): 1047–85.

Chaudhury, Nazmul, Jeffrey Hammer, Michael Kremer, Karthik Muralidharan, and Halsey Rogers. 2006. "Missing in Action: Teacher and Health Worker Absence in Developing Countries." *Journal of Economic Perspectives* 20 (1): 91–116.

Cunha, Flavio, and James Heckman. 2007. "The Technology of Skill Formation." *American Economic Review* 97 (2): 31–47.

Duflo, Esther. 2001. "Schooling and Labor Market Consequences of School Construction in Indonesia: Evidence from an Unusual Policy Experiment." *American Economic Review* 91 (4): 795–814.

Duflo, Esther, Pascaline Dupas, and Michael Kremer. 2009. "Additional Resources versus Organizational Changes in Education: Experimental Evidence from Kenya." Mimeo, Massachusetts Institute of Technology, Cambridge, MA.

Gauthier, Bernard. 2008. "Harmonizing and Improving the Efficiency of PETS/QSDS." Unpublished, World Bank, Washington, DC.

Glewwe, Paul, Eric Hanushek, Sarah Humpage, and Renato Ravina. 2011. "School Resources and Educational Outcomes in Developing Countries: A Review of the Literature from 1990 to 2010." Working Paper 17554, National Bureau of Economic Research, Cambridge, MA.

Glewwe, Paul, and Michael Kremer. 2006. "Schools, Teachers, and Education Outcomes in Developing Countries." In *Handbook on the Economics of Education*, edited by E. Hanushek and F. Welch, 945–1017, Amsterdam: North-Holland.

Glewwe, Paul, Michael Kremer, and Sylvie Moulin. 2002. "Textbooks and Test Scores: Evidence from a Randomized Evaluation in Kenya." Development Research Group, World Bank, Washington, DC.

Hanushek, Eric. 2003. "The Failure of Input-Based Schooling Policies." *Economic Journal* 113 (February): F64–98.

Hanushek, Eric, and Ludger Woessman. 2007. "The Role of Education Quality for Economic Growth." Policy Research Working Paper Series 4122, World Bank, Washington, DC.

Krishnaratne, Shari, Howard White, and Ella Carpenter. 2013. "Quality Education for All Children? What Works in Education in Developing Countries." Working Paper 20, International Initiative for Impact Evaluation (3ie), New Delhi.

Ministry of Education and Vocational Training. 2010. "Basic Statistics in Education—National." United Republic of Tanzania, Dar es Salaam, Tanzania.

Olken, Ben. 2009. "Corruption Perceptions vs. Corruption Reality." *Journal of Public Economics* 93 (7–8): 950–64.

Reinikka, Ritva, and Jakob Svensson. 2004. "Local Capture: Evidence from a Central Government Transfer Program in Uganda." *Quarterly Journal of Economics* 119 (2): 679–705.

———. 2005. "Fighting Corruption to Improve Schooling: Evidence from a Newspaper Campaign in Uganda." *Journal of the European Economic Association* 3 (2–3): 259–67.

———. 2006. "How Corruption Affects Service Delivery and What Can Be Done about It." In *International Handbook on the Economics of Corruption*, edited by Susan Rose Ackerman, 441–46. Northampton, MA: Edward Elgar.

———. 2010. "Working for God? Evidence from a Change in Financing of Nonprofit Health Care Providers in Uganda." *Journal of the European Economic Association* 8 (6): 1159–78.

SACMEQ. 2000–02. "Southern and Eastern Africa Consortium for Monitoring Educational Quality." http://www.sacmeq.org.

World Bank. 2003. *World Development Report 2004: Making Services Work for Poor People*. Washington, DC: World Bank.

CHAPTER 6

Education Finance and Spending in Tanzania: Challenges and Opportunities

Oyin Shyllon and Arun R. Joshi

Summary

The education sector receives the largest share of public resources of all sectors in Tanzania, and allocations to the sector increased in nominal and real terms between 2007–08 and 2011–12. Private education spending is constrained by low levels of affordability. It has been complemented by public education spending, which has been partially effective in ensuring that children from poor households are able to participate in the education system. This success is, however, largely limited to the primary education level, with continued low participation for households in the bottom three quintiles at the secondary and postsecondary levels.

In recent history, the secondary education level has been the mainstream education track that has suffered the most from intrasector resource allocations. Its share of mainstream allocations was as low as 13 percent as recently as 2008–09 and 2009–10, climbing to a modest 21 percent in the 2011–12 budget. At the same time, the secondary-level student achievements have declined. Despite the dearth of research on the reasons for poor student achievement at the secondary level, studies on the primary education level provide insights on the nonfinance-related key challenges: teacher knowledge and level of effort. Incentive mechanisms that elicit desired selection into the teaching profession as well as time on task are urgently needed.

The higher education system is experiencing unprecedented growth in the demand-side financing requirement. Political will has been expressed to support students at the higher education level, but reform of the current loan scheme is imperative to sustain the student support system. The loan scheme is expensive to operate, with real costs as high as 14.1 percent for 2009–10, while loans were issued at zero interest repayment rates (Shyllon 2011). Access to loans for those in the bottom income quintiles was nonexistent because of weaknesses in the means-testing process. Repayment rates were extremely low in part because loan repayments were not income contingent.

Misalignments are also found in resource allocations with respect to geographical equity and national strategies. A subset of districts receives very little resources for teaching and learning materials for both primary and secondary education; this is in addition to certain districts with chronic teacher and facility shortages.

Introduction

This chapter first documents the extent of public and private education spending in Tanzania, with a focus on differences across the income distribution. It then proceeds to further examine public education spending patterns to identify areas of misalignments in resource allocation with respect to enrollment trends, sector strategies, and equity objectives, drawing on international evidence from countries with successful education reforms at similar levels of development.

Education Finance in Tanzania

Sources of Education Finance

Three primary sources of education finance are found in Tanzania: private resources of households; domestic government revenue; and external sources from multilateral organizations, bilateral agencies, international nongovernmental organizations, international religious institutions, and individuals.

Tuition Fee Structure

State-provided preprimary and primary education in Tanzania is tuition free, and tuition costs for state-provided secondary education is T Sh 20,000 per student. Nevertheless, Tanzanian households report spending considerable sums of money for the education of children at the preprimary, primary, and secondary levels, in part because parents who send their children to private schools cover the full cost of education but also because parents incur other levies and costs to educate their children through the public system. Tuition and instructional costs at public higher education training institutions (HETIs) were between T Sh 1.11 million and T Sh 4.29 million in 2010–11, but they were between T Sh 1.27 million and T Sh 5.067 million for private HETIs (table 6.1).

Household Education Finance

Education spending was, on average, 3.3 percent of household purchases in the 2007 Household Budget Survey (HBS). Given high levels of poverty, the largest use of household financial resources was for the purchase of food (49.3 percent). Tanzania is a largely agrarian nation, with food purchases representing only 68 percent of food consumption. Purchases of nondurable items for household maintenance including fuels and transportation (which together represent

Table 6.1 Tuition and Instructional Costs of Higher Education in 2010–11
T Sh

	Fee paying (public HETI)	Fee paying (private HETI)
Registration fee[a]	250,000	250,000
Student union subscription	10,000	10,000
Medical insurance	100,000	100,000
Tuition fees	550,000–1,820,000	650,000–3,650,000
Books and stationery	200,000	200,000
Field practical training (for eligible students)	200,000–1,260,000	130,000–1,540,000
Special faculty requirement (for eligible students)	5,300–650,000	50,000–500,000
Research (final year students)	Up to 100,000	Up to 100,000
Actual min-max	1,110,000–4,290,000	1,270,000–5,067,000

Source: Shyllon 2011.
Note: HETI = higher education training institutions.
a. The registration fee at one university is assumed to be representative of most universities in Tanzania.

44 percent of nondurable purchases) take up the second largest share of household resources (35 percent). As a result, after purchases of food and items for household maintenance, the share of household disposable income allocated to education is 21 percent. Despite this high share of spending, an annual mean spending of about T Sh 3,702 per capita (in 2007) combined with the postprimary fee structure would put affordability at these levels beyond that of the average Tanzanian.

Contributions to Education Finance

Using data from the 2007 HBS and the 2007–08 budget outturn data from Tanzania's Ministry of Finance, we find that the government of Tanzania was responsible for 75 percent of finances directed toward the education sector, whereas private financing of education in Tanzania accounted for 18 percent of spending. Direct foreign (donor) resources accounted for 7 percent of education finance.[1] Rapid enrollment expansions at all levels of education over the past decade has increased pressures on the public purse to come through with needed resources for high-quality education given limited affordability for households using private resources.

Private and Public Education Spending

Private Education Spending in Tanzania

Wealthier households spend more on education but also receive more in absolute terms from the government. Wealthier households spend more private resources on education than their poorer counterparts. In 2007, private education spending for households in the wealthiest quintile was 53 percent of total private spending, whereas households in the poorest wealth quintile contributed 6 percent of total private spending. Public education spending does not completely resolve the cash constraint of poorer households. To be sure, households in the poorest quintile benefited the least (16 percent) from public education spending. Households in the second, third, fourth, and wealthiest quintiles benefited more at 17 percent, 21 percent, 19 percent, and 27 percent, respectively. Given that public spending was 357 percent of private spending, the total education spending profile by wealth quintile more closely resembled the public education spending profile by wealth quintile. Private spending on education, in nominal shilling terms, for the poorest quintile was T Sh 15 billion and increased for the wealthier quintiles to T Sh 26 billion, T Sh 31 billion, T Sh 49 billion, and T Sh 136 billion. Similarly, nominal public spending on education for the poorest quintile was T Sh 188 billion and increased for the wealthier quintiles to T Sh 199 billion, T Sh 246 billion, T Sh 233 billion, and T Sh 316 billion (figure 6.1). These suggest a disproportionate benefit to wealthier households.

Benefits to the wealthier households are induced by low postprimary participation for poorer households. Private spending on education as a share of total spending on education for households in the bottom income quintile was 8 percent. The share for households in the higher income quintiles increased to 11 percent, 11 percent, 18 percent, and 30 percent (figure 6.1). The inconsistency between lower private spending shares for poorer quintile households and lower resource benefit for these households is explained by a lack of participation by the poorer households at the secondary and, particularly, tertiary education levels with higher cost structures.

The government of Tanzania plays an important role in education financing. Private returns to education are high in Tanzania, and marginal returns to

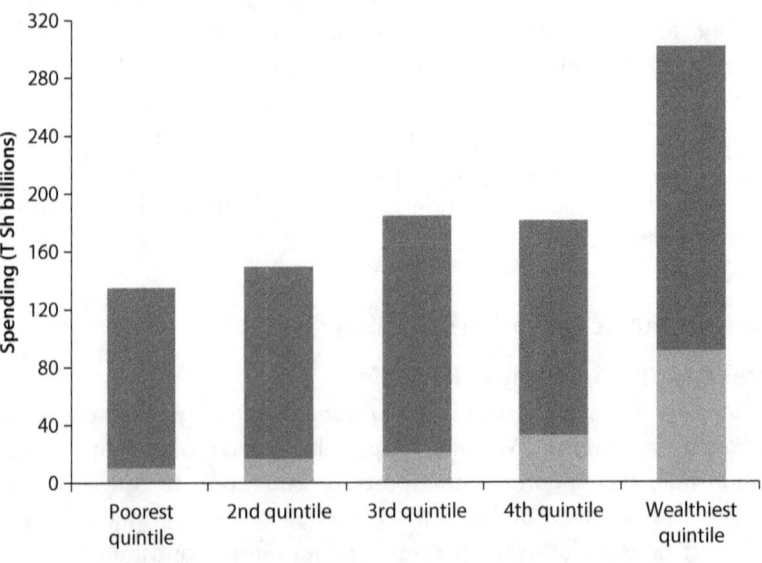

Figure 6.1 Private and Public Spending on Education in Tanzania, by Quintile

Sources: Hoogeveen and Ruhinduka 2009; URT 2007.

Table 6.2 Participation in Levels of Education by Quintile
Percent

	Preprimary/adult/ nonformal	Primary	Lower secondary	Upper secondary	Higher	Total
Poorest	16.0	22.0	7.1	6.9	0	19.0
2nd quintile	16.9	21.8	12.1	0	0	19.6
3rd quintile	21.9	21.2	19.4	13.3	0	20.7
4th quintile	24.6	19.7	29.6	17.3	10.2	21.4
Wealthiest	20.7	15.3	31.8	62.5	89.8	19.3
Total	100.0	100.0	100.0	100.0	100.0	100.0

Source: Based on 2009 National Panel Survey.

schooling increase with number of years of schooling.[2] Despite returns increasing as the level of education increases, participation by the poor declines as the level of education increases, with no higher education participation by individuals in the poorer quintiles (table 6.2). A high return together with low enrollment (or attendance) rates is compatible with some form of liquidity or credit market constraint in access to education. The key to first best reforms is to ensure that public spending is used to subsidize the poor without displacing private education spending by wealthier households.

Tanzania has showed great capacity to expand primary education access to poorer households. Doing so at the secondary and tertiary levels, however, increases the need for public education spending and the pressure on public resources.

Public Education Spending in Tanzania

Real education spending has increased in the last five years but has fluctuated relative to gross domestic product (GDP) and the national budget. Real recurrent education spending increased consistently at an average annual rate of 10.5 percent. Most of this increase was attributable to the increase in the personnel emoluments (PE) component of recurrent spending, which increased at an annual average rate of 13.4 percent over the period in contrast with the other charges component of public education recurrent spending, which fluctuated. Although education spending increased in nominal and real terms from 2007–08 to 2011–12, the education sector budget as a share of GDP fluctuated between 4.8 percent and 5.8 percent (table 6.3). This is attributable to fluctuations in the government's share of national output. For example, the government's share of the national output was 27 percent in 2010–11 but was projected to be 31 percent in 2011–12 (URT 2011). By extension, education spending as a share of the total government budget has also fluctuated between 17.9 percent and 21.3 percent.

Real investment in development projects experienced four years of sustained declines. Real development spending declined from 2007–08 to 2010–11 before an upsurge attributable to the World Bank–supported Secondary Education

Table 6.3 Sustained Increases in Nominal and Real Growth in Public Education Spending

Selected indicators of education spending	2007–08 actual	2008–09 actual	2009–10 actual	2010–11 actual	2011–12 budget
Nominal education spending in (T Sh billions)	1,109.9	1,317.8	1,462.9	1,783.8	2,285.4
Real education spending in (T Sh billions, in 2007–08 prices)	1,109.9	1,178.7	1,184.2	1,349.5	1,615.8
Nominal education spending per capita (T Sh)	27,025	31,178	33,611	39,780	49,447
Real education spending per capita (T Sh, in 2007–08 prices)	27,025	27,887	27,207	30,094	34,960
Education spending as a share of government spending (%)	21.3	19.3	17.9	18.9	18.1
Education spending as a share of GDP (%)	4.9	5.0	4.8	5.2	5.8
Education wage bill (PE) as share of total education spending (%)	53.8	60.4	61.1	64.0	61.0
Development spending as a share of total education spending (%)	15.1	9.5	8.4	7.2	12.9
Recurring spending as a share of total education spending (%)	84.9	90.5	91.6	92.8	87.1
Share of decentralized spending in education spending (%)	45.4	49.9	59.4	60.8	64.2
Nominal growth in spending (%)	N/A	18.7	11.0	21.9	28.1
Real growth in spending (%)	N/A	6.2	0.5	14.0	19.7
Nominal education spending in ($ millions)	923.3	1,042.6	1,094.2	1,196.4	1,302.2
Nominal education spending per capita ($)	22.5	24.7	25.1	26.7	28.2

Source: URT 2012a.
Note: GDP = gross domestic product; PE = personnel emoluments.

Development Program II (SEDP II) and Science and Technology in Higher Education Development Project (STHEP) government programs in the 2011–12 budget (figure 6.2).

Trends in Public Education Spending

Analysis of Development and Recurrent Public Spending

Development spending experienced a resurgence in 2011–12 as a result of SEDP II and STHEP. Development spending was set to rise at an annual rate of 131.4 percent from the level of actual spending in 2010–11 to budgeted spending in 2011–12 (table 6.4). The very rapid increase in planned development spending reflected planned investments attributable to the rehabilitation and construction of secondary school buildings to meet the requirements of SEDP II as well as the execution of civil works projects as required by the STHEP. This explains the surge in development spending for the secondary and higher education subsectors to T Sh 211.8 billion, which represented 72 percent of the T Sh 295 billion development budget for 2011–12. Real development spending at the

Figure 6.2 Recurring and Development Spending on Education, 2007–12

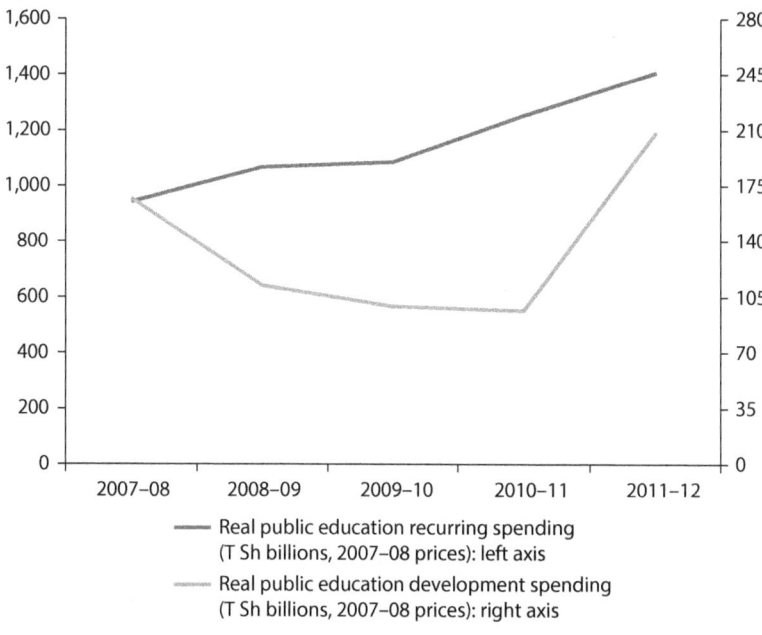

— Real public education recurring spending
(T Sh billions, 2007–08 prices): left axis
— Real public education development spending
(T Sh billions, 2007–08 prices): right axis

Source: URT 2011.

Table 6.4 Growth in Recurrent Spending, 2007–12
T Sh billions

	2007–08 actual	2008–09 actual	2009–10 actual	2010–11 actual	2011–12 budget
Development	167.2	125.3	122.6	127.6	295.1
Personnel emoluments	597.5	922.6	894.0	1,141.1	1,395.1
Other recurring charges	345.2	270.0	446.3	515.1	595.2
Total spending/budget	1,109.9	1,317.8	1,462.9	1,783.8	2,285.4

Source: URT 2012a.

secondary and higher education levels increased sharply from the 2010–11 level. However, real development spending on secondary education remained lower than the spending in 2007–08 so that the path to meet the infrastructure needs of SEDP II is a slow one. Numerous infrastructure projects emerged at technical training institutions (TTIs) from only three in 2007–08, which led to a real increase in spending by more than 600 percent. Most of this spending was expected to be absorbed by the Tanzania Law School construction project, which accounted for 46 percent of the T Sh 10.5 billion in 2010–11 and was expected to require 75 percent of the T Sh 15.1 billion planned for TTIs in 2011–12.

Rapid increase in the number of teachers has increased recurrent education spending. Planned recurrent spending increased 20.2 percent in nominal terms from the actual level of spending in 2010–11 to budgeted spending in 2011–12.

This was consistent with the need to deploy newly recruited teachers (and the consequent wage and training costs) to meet growing enrollments across districts for pretertiary education. To improve low pupil-teacher ratios, the number of teachers in public secondary school increased from 15,911 in 2007 to 39,934 in 2011 (BEST 2011). The average annual nominal increase in the PE component of recurrent spending was 23.6 percent between 2007–08 and 2011–12, but the average annual nominal increase in the other charges component of recurrent spending was 14.6 percent for the same period. These general increases over the five-year period nonetheless mask within each period nominal and real fluctuations between increases and decreases.

Analysis of Public Spending by Level of Education

The practice of increased allocations for higher education and reductions for the primary and/or secondary levels was replaced in 2010–11 by increased allocations for secondary education at the expense of primary and higher education. The share of planned education spending channeled toward primary education declined from 65 to 70 percent in the late 1990s, to about 47 percent of actual spending in 2010–11 and even further to 46 percent of the 2011–12 budget (figure 6.3). The share for secondary education increased markedly from 14 percent in 2007–08 to 21 percent of the 2011–12 budget in large part because of the injection of finances for SEDP II (2010–15). The higher education subsector declined

Figure 6.3 Distribution of Public Spending on Education

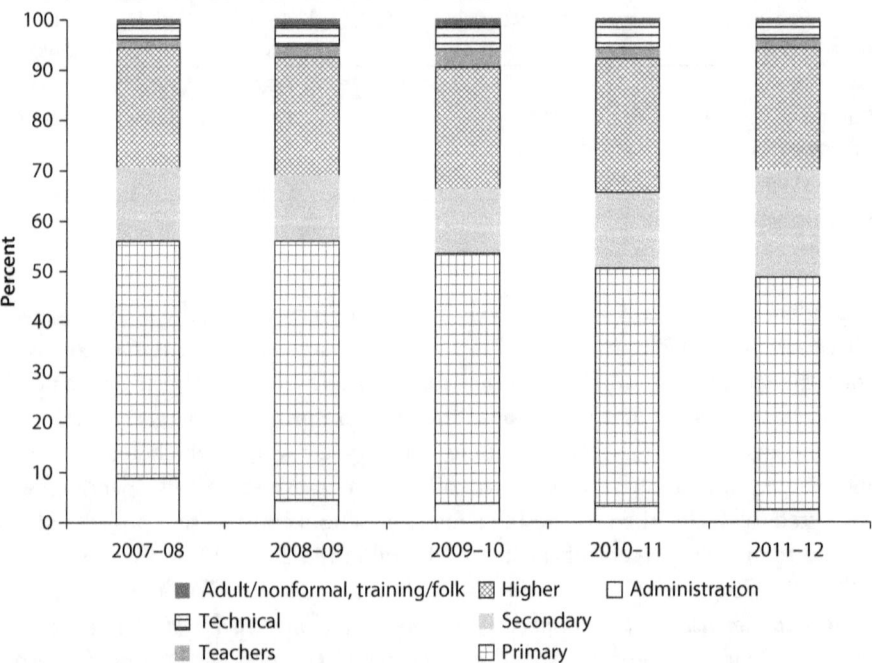

Source: URT 2011.

from an unusually high share of 27 percent in 2010–11 to the norm of 24 percent in the 2011–12 budget.

The share of total primary spending is trending downward, but the share of primary recurrent spending is stable. The share of planned recurrent education spending channeled toward primary education remained stable at between 49 percent and 54 percent over the five-year period. The share was 50 percent for the 2011–12 budget with the recurrent primary education budget increasing by 22 percent from its value in 2010–11. The reason for the decline in total primary education spending is a T Sh 64 billion surge in both the secondary and higher education development budgets representing annual increases of 191 percent and 121 percent, respectively. This combined increase of T Sh 128 billion accounted for 76 percent of the T Sh 168 billion increase in the education development budget (table 6.5). Education infrastructure support for the STHEP and SEDP II projects are geared to meet the demands that have arisen from the annual increase in student numbers with lower secondary and higher education student enrollment increasing 177 percent and 307 percent, respectively, from 2007 to 2011 (figure 6.5). Enrollment at the primary education level is more stable. Hence, the allocation of resources for recurrent spending provides a better representation of the long-term equilibrium allocation across education subsectors.

The education sector has made progress in aligning the budget with the needs of secondary education. Spending in 2010–11 and the budget for 2011–12 increased funding to the secondary education subsector. Secondary education enrollment expanded rapidly in Tanzania, as student numbers increased at 21.5 percent per annum from 675,672 in 2006 to 1,789,547 in 2011. In 2009–10, secondary education spending was only 53 percent of spending at the higher education level (table 6.6). Also, the secondary education subsector share of the budget shrank from 14.46 percent in 2007–08 to 12.96 in 2008–09 and further to 12.82 percent in 2009–10 (figure 6.3). In 2010–11, there was a 34.5 percent real increase in secondary spending, but before that, secondary spending declined in real terms in the previous two years by 0.6 percent in 2009–10 and 4.9 percent

Table 6.5 Development Projects for Secondary and Higher Education
T Sh millions

	2007–08 actual	2008–09 actual	2009–10 actual	2010–11 actual	2011–12 budget
Administration	11,378.5	19,236.4	8,221.8	6,205.0	6,441.0
Primary	47,510.4	33,886.7	32,672.6	23,789.6	55,725.7
Secondary	68,341.5	23,392.7	20,200.0	33,597.8	97,689.2
Higher	35,147.9	36,769.7	47,182.2	50,254.0	114,112.1
Teachers	596.2	533.4	437.2	998.4	1,168.7
Technical training institutions	1,740.1	4,334.4	6,211.1	10,544.2	15,127.6
Adult/nonformal, training/folk	2,496.4	7,125.3	7,708.9	2,174.3	4,867.1
Total	167,211.1	125,278.5	122,633.8	127,563.3	295,131.5

Source: URT 2012a.

Table 6.6 Slower Relative Growth in Tertiary Education Is Required
T Sh millions

	2007–08 actual	2008–09 actual	2009–10 actual	2010–11 actual	2011–12 budget
Administration	97,375.4	58,576.1	53,634.6	55,469.1	56,244.6
Primary	524,181.5	677,493.4	727,498.2	842,516.3	1,052,114.5
Secondary	160,537.6	170,763.2	187,594.2	269,923.3	486,672.0
Higher	265,708.0	309,829.4	352,868.8	472,877.2	555,298.5
Teachers	18,151.6	31,864.9	53,620.8	38,984.2	41,597.0
Technical training institutions	33,189.3	50,576.7	65,368.6	89,035.8	74,201.4
Adult/nonformal, training/folk	10,708.5	18,723.7	22,346.4	14,999.3	19,255.6
Total	1,109,851.9	1,317,827.3	1,462,931.5	1,783,805.2	2,285,383.6

Source: URT 2012a.

in 2008–09. In the 2011–12 budget, a sharper real increase of about 68.5 percent was included, so that the allocation to secondary education has substantially caught up with higher education as a share of the budget (88 percent of higher education spending compared with 53 percent in 2009–10). This funding increase could allow improvement in secondary student achievement if sustained in the long term.[3]

All components of tertiary education—higher education, teacher education, and technical education—are experiencing declines from recent subsector shares and/or nominal values. Despite the rapid increase in development spending for the higher education level by 127 percent from the actual level of spending in 2010–11 to budgeted spending in 2011–12 (table 6.5), the share of planned total education spending channeled toward higher education declined from an actual of 27 percent in 2010–11 to 24 percent in 2011–12. This decline was the result of slow growth in recurring higher education spending of 4 percent from actual spending in 2010–11 to budgeted spending in 2011–12. For TTIs, development spending increased 43 percent, but recurring spending plummeted by 25 percent over the same period. The total budget allocation for teacher education in 2011–12 was lower than the recurring portion of spending on teacher education of in 2009–10 (table 6.6).

Structural Imbalances in Public Education Spending Patterns

Spending Patterns in the Traditional Education Track

Measured by the level of recurrent spending for the student population in public preprimary, primary, lower secondary, upper secondary, or higher education, Tanzania has made some progress over the three-year period 2007–10 with respect to its education spending profile. Three key features emerge: (1) spending patterns for the preprimary and higher education subsectors remain largely unchanged; (2) most of the changes identified in spending relate to redistribution from primary education toward secondary education; and (3) the higher education subsector spending profile is on an unsustainable path.

Figure 6.4 Mismatch between Enrollment Levels and Public Education Spending

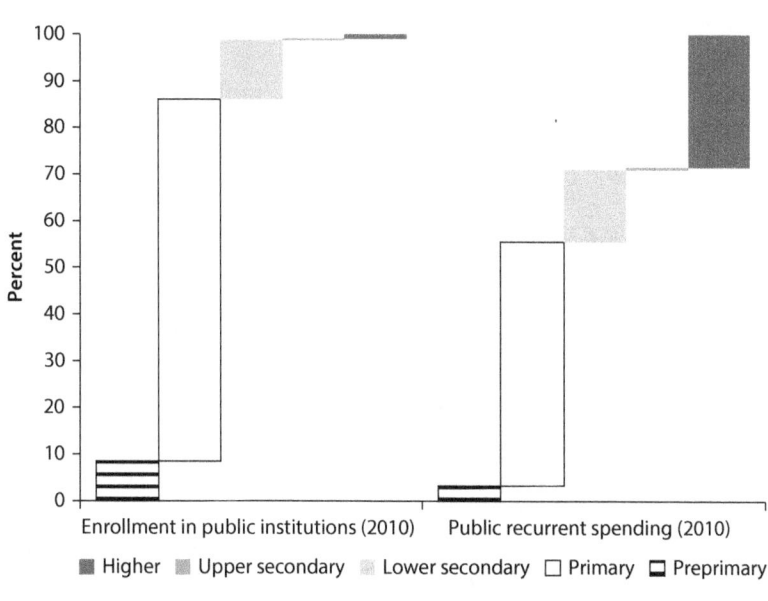

Sources: URT 2012a, 2012b.

Stability is seen in spending patterns relative to the size of the preprimary and higher education levels. The profile of the preprimary, primary, lower secondary, upper secondary, or higher education levels over the period 2007–10 shows consistency in spending shares relative to total enrollment shares only at the bottom and top of the education structure (figure 6.4). We find that in 2010, as was the case in 2007, 8 percent of the enrollment in all five levels of education was attributable to the preprimary level, whereas recurrent spending at this level was about 3 percent of the public recurrent education spending. Similarly, higher education enrollees made up 1 percent of public school enrollment for these levels of education and 29 percent of public recurrent education spending.

For the intermediate levels of education, the share of student enrollment has demonstrated more instability. In 2007, student enrollment as a share of total student enrollment in the traditional track public school system for the primary and lower secondary levels was 83 percent and 8 percent, respectively. These students benefited from 56 percent and 11 percent of public education spending, respectively. By 2010, the share of lower secondary student enrollment had risen by 5 percentage points, but that for primary education had declined by 5 percentage points (figure 6.4). This has been accompanied by a 4 percentage point shift in public resource spending away from primary education and toward lower secondary education.

Public education costs rise with the level of education. At the preprimary and primary levels, spending shares are lower than enrollment shares, whereas at the postprimary level, spending shares are higher than enrollment shares. The most disproportionate allocation is at the higher education level with 1 percent of enrollees benefiting from 29 percent of resources.

We see a redistribution of additional education resources away from primary enrollees and toward secondary enrollees. The 8.2 million children enrolled in public primary schools in 2007 represented 83 percent of the public enrollment in all five levels of education and benefited from 56 percent of recurrent public education spending. Recently, enrollment growth rates have proceeded at a much faster pace in other levels of education compared with the primary level (figure 6.5).[4] Following this, large relative reductions in spending by the public primary school system have emerged despite increases in the student population. Almost 8.3 million children were enrolled in public primary schools in 2010, representing 78 percent of the public enrollment in all five levels of the traditional education track and benefiting from 52 percent of recurrent public education spending. Although the share of public enrollment in primary schools has fallen, the actual number of students enrolled has increased by 1 percent from 8,235,432 to 8,267,026. Also, the public primary school system is budgeted to receive in 2011–12 twice the amount of resources (in nominal terms) it received in 2007–08. The path of nominal spending increases for the primary education level is similar to that for the higher education level and the secondary level before 2010–11. The large increase in

Figure 6.5 Student Enrollment

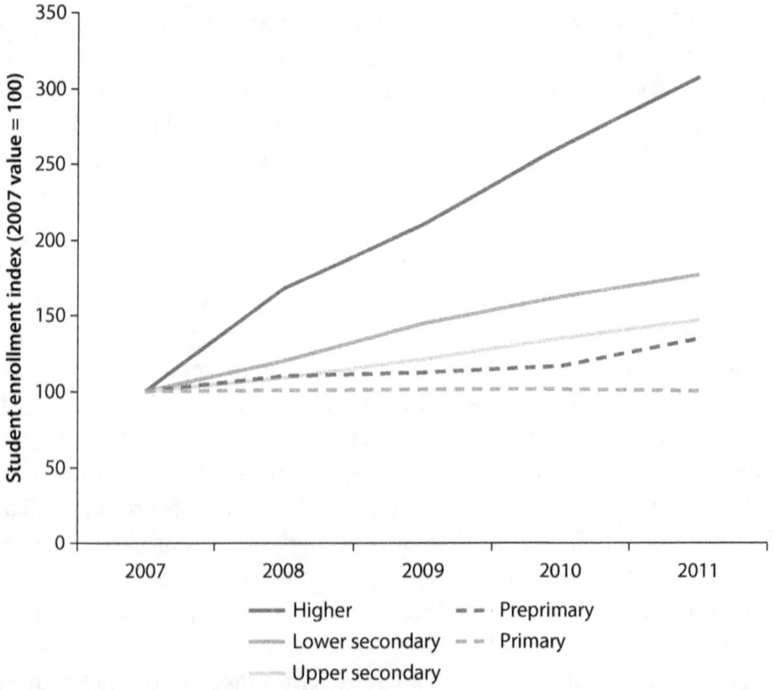

Source: URT 2012b.

secondary recurrent spending reflects the need to catch up with previous levels of severe underfunding. As a result, the 4 percentage point drop in public recurrent primary spending has been channeled toward the secondary education level. In 2007, secondary enrollees made up 8 percent of public school enrollment in the traditional track receiving 11 percent of public recurrent resources. This has grown to 13 percent of enrollees in the traditional track receiving 16 percent of public recurrent resources.

The rapid increase in higher education enrollment is accompanied by a rapid increase in higher education spending for the Student Loan scheme. To achieve its "education, knowledge and skills development" objective, the government of Tanzania provides supply-side and demand-side financing support to the higher education system. Supply-side recurrent financing resources are designed to provide teacher incentives that ensure an adequately motivated teaching force, and to tackle the issues of pedagogy and curriculum and their links with labor market needs. The number of HETIs receiving government supply-side subventions increased from 18 HETIs in 1994–95 to 26 HETIs in 2009–10.[5] With more recent rapid enrollment expansion, government transfers to HETIs for recurrent spending items increased at an annual average rate of 20 percent between 2007–08 and 2010–11. For 2010–11, a sharp movement was seen away from, more or less, splitting resources evenly between supply-side subventions and demand side subsidies, in favor of increased demand-side subsidies (figure 6.6).

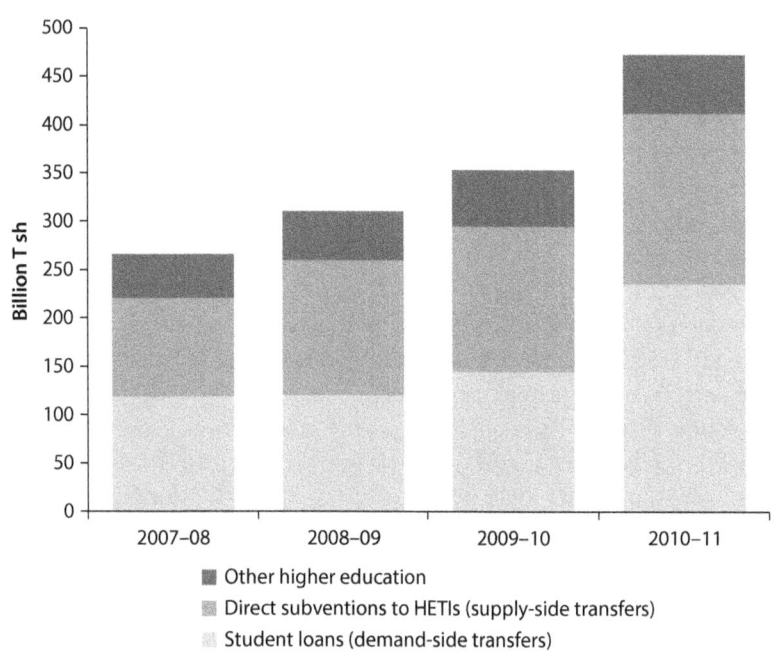

Figure 6.6 Funding Sources for Higher Education

■ Other higher education
■ Direct subventions to HETIs (supply-side transfers)
■ Student loans (demand-side transfers)

Sources: URT 2010a, 2012a.
Note: HETI = higher education training institution.

A risk exists of reduction in the quality of higher education, with the rapidly expanding system stretching public resources thinly and the Tanzania Commission for Universities uncovering more instances of student enrollment beyond existing capacity at HETIs.

Cost-sharing mechanisms for Tanzania's student support system have been designed to ensure that the private cost of education is affordable at the point of use to encourage participation across income quintiles. Yet no participation is found by those in the bottom three income quintiles. Despite the increased contributions expected from students and their families, government demand-side financing support continues to increase in real and nominal terms. Government support (through grants and subsidized student loans) to parents and students for higher education increased 68 percent in the two-year period between 2007–08 and 2009–10. Before 2005–06, part of this transfer was a grant to students, but beginning in 2005–06, all transfers were provided through student loans with zero interest rates.[6]

The fiscal sustainability of Tanzania's higher education student loan scheme is at risk given projected increases in student enrollment. Increasing enrollment at the secondary level has increased secondary education graduates with student enrollment in Form 1 for mainland Tanzania rising slowly from 53,698 in 1995 to 99,744 in 2003 (this is the cohort that was expected to commence higher education in 2009) and then very rapidly to 524,784 in 2009.[7] Using dropout, repetition, and examination pass rates from 2009–10, cohort survival analysis reveals that for every cohort of students that commence the first year of secondary education, only 17 percent will become eligible for higher education.[8] If this cohort survival rate is sustained, the number of "new" secondary school graduates sufficiently qualified to pursue higher education will rise from 25,073 in 2010–11 to 89,213 in 2014–15 (figure 6.7). Given the high cost of financing higher education, a severe strain will be placed on public resources because additional budget outlays will be required for the higher education level.

Scheme sustainability is also at risk because of high rates of loan default. To ensure that students do not use funds for purposes other than education, the Higher Education Student Loans Board (HESLB) disburses the instructional expenses component of the loan (the largest loan component) directly to HETIs. As a result, the students never receive these monies, and too many are not aware that they are incurring a real repayment obligation. To mitigate this common misperception that public financing of higher education is a grant rather than a loan, the HESLB requires that the student borrower sign an undertaking and also provides loan amounts to cover living costs directly to the students. Nonetheless, the number of loan defaulters by December 2010 was still high at 53 percent (figure 6.8). Only a quarter of the borrowers were making loan repayments, and more creditworthy borrowers were found in private sector institutions, some of whom had always made voluntary repayments, than borrowers in the public sector. Theoretically, it should be easier for the HESLB to get repayments from public sector workers through direct payroll deductions.

Education Finance and Spending in Tanzania: Challenges and Opportunities

Figure 6.7 Numbers of Students Eligible and Ineligible for Higher Education

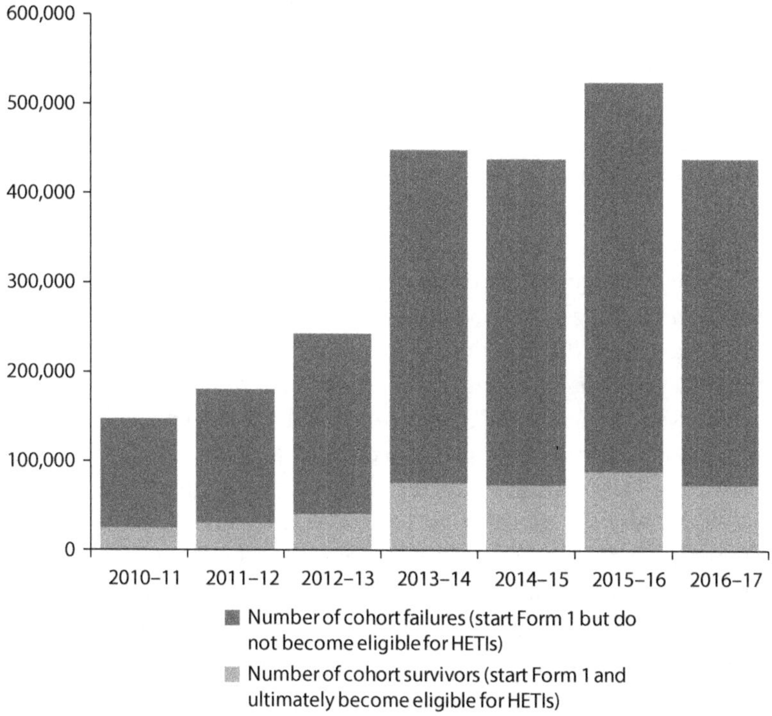

■ Number of cohort failures (start Form 1 but do not become eligible for HETIs)
▨ Number of cohort survivors (start Form 1 and ultimately become eligible for HETIs)

Source: URT 2012b.
Note: HETI = higher education training institution. Numbers for 2014–2017 are projected.

Figure 6.8 Repayment and Default Rates for Student Loans by Sector

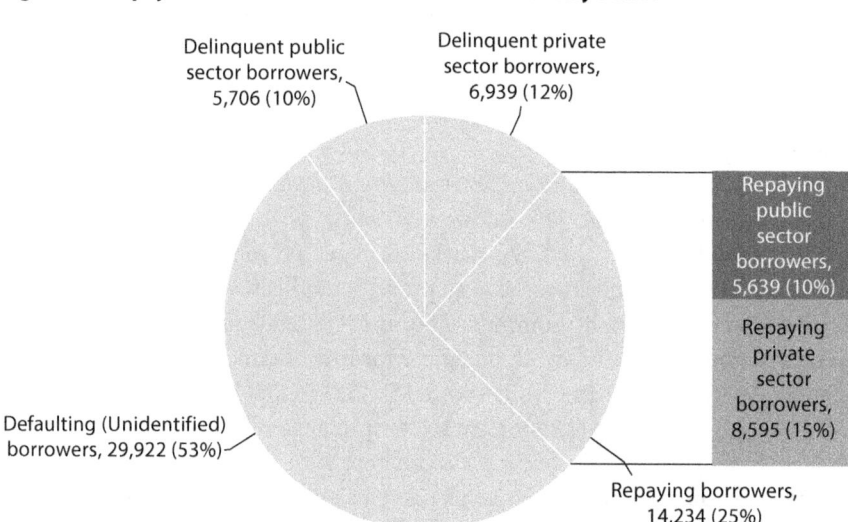

Delinquent public sector borrowers, 5,706 (10%)
Delinquent private sector borrowers, 6,939 (12%)
Repaying public sector borrowers, 5,639 (10%)
Repaying private sector borrowers, 8,595 (15%)
Defaulting (Unidentified) borrowers, 29,922 (53%)
Repaying borrowers, 14,234 (25%)

Source: URT 2010a.

Spending Patterns in the Nontraditional Education Track

Tanzania currently lags regional peers in terms of teacher availability at the preprimary, primary, and secondary levels. Tanzania's preprimary pupil-teacher ratio (PTR) is the worst for reporting countries in Sub-Saharan Africa. The PTRs at the primary and secondary levels are in the bottom third of 36 reporting countries. For 2010, there was one teacher for every 51 primary school pupils compared with a regional median of one teacher for every 44 primary school pupils.

A larger number of teachers and improvements in their deployment are required at the primary and secondary education levels with implications for the teacher education budget. The Ministry of Education and Vocational Training (MoEVT) projected the requirements for new degree-holding teachers for mathematics, sciences, and English to be about 15,600 over the six school years from 2008 through 2013. However, reflecting expected output from teacher training institutions, the projected hiring of such teachers (degree holders qualified to teach mathematics, sciences, or English) was projected to be only 3,400 over those same six years (World Bank 2008). Evidence also shows that a paucity of interest in teaching careers explains teacher shortages at the secondary education level. A recent survey indicates that most secondary school teachers in Tanzania have not chosen teaching through interest and motivation and are thus less motivated when compared with primary school teachers (Bennell and Akyeampong 2007, 28).[9] Evidence is also seen of inter-district inequities in teacher availability, with vacant positions and great difficulty associated with teacher deployment to rural, distant, and/or inaccessible locations. For instance, in 2010, at the primary level, the PTR in government-run schools was as high as 114.5:1 in Ilala district and as low as 27.6:1 in Iringa Manispaa district.

Increases in the number of teachers to meet student requirements and teacher professional development activities have resource implications. For the period 2007–08 to 2011–12, workforce compensation purposes dominated spending at teacher education institutions with more than 50 percent of spending and will only intensify as the need to expand the teacher pool intensifies.

A need exists to improve labor market readiness through mainstream as well as vocational education tracks. The number of youth with incomplete secondary schooling poised to enter the labor market is expected to surge in the next few years. This is based on cohort survival analysis that indicates that only 17 percent of the number of youth who commence Form 1 will be eligible for higher education, so that the number of youth ineligible for higher education but with some secondary education will rise from about 150,000 in 2011–12 to over 400,000 in 2015–16 (figure 6.7). It is important to complement reforms in the traditional education track (primary, secondary, and higher) with reforms in the vocational and technical education tracks, especially given significant increases in the number of Tanzanian youth that are expected to pursue additional schooling through the nontraditional track. Laderchi (2009, 2) identified the key challenges facing Tanzanian youth in their transition to the labor market as "starting too early, failing to enter the labor market, and getting stuck in jobs that do not build human capital." Those most vulnerable to these challenges are the group that are unable to complete the traditional track and can benefit from viable programs offered at TTIs.

The MoEVT's development of a strategic plan for technical and vocational education is an important first step. A surge in development spending for TTIs has occurred largely because of construction activities at the Tanzania Law School, which accounted for 46 percent of the T Sh10.5 billion spent on TTIs in 2010–11 and is expected to require 75 percent of the T Sh 15.1 billion planned for TTIs in 2011–12. The strategic plan may propose additional investments in a variety of skill categories with spending requirements.

Comparison with Successful Reform Countries

The pattern of intrasector spending is now catching up with trends in countries that experienced similar expansions at the secondary level. Countries that implemented secondary education quality and enrollment expansion reforms in the past spent between a quarter and a third of their education budget on this level of education. For example, the Republic of Korea's secondary net enrollment rate (NER) increased from 38 percent in 1970 to 85 percent in 1975, and for Singapore it increased from 44 to 49 percent over the same period. At the same time, secondary education spending in Korea fluctuated between 23 and 26 percent of total education spending, and for Singapore it was stable at 34 percent (figure 6.9). In both cases, secondary education spending was at least twice as much as tertiary education spending, whereas for Tanzania with a 2009 secondary NER of 28 percent, secondary education spending was about 40 percent of higher education spending. Further, Tanzania's public spending on the secondary education level of 13 percent in 2009 was among the lowest relative to similarly situated Sub-Saharan African countries.

The surge in secondary enrollment without adequate secondary education investments has affected student learning achievement in real and absolute terms. After a sustained period of reductions in the share of students failing the lower secondary examinations from 21.6 percent in 2000 to 8.5 percent in 2004, beginning in 2005, the share of candidates failing the lower secondary examinations has increased from 10.7 percent to 49.6 percent in 2010 (figure 6.10). The rapid increase in lower secondary student enrollment at an annual average rate of 19.6 percent from 238,194 students in 2000 to 1,711,109 students in 2011 has led to a significant rise in the number of youth that are unable to proceed to higher education institutions. The number of students that fail the lower secondary examinations has risen from 10,250 in 2000 to 156,085 in 2011. Increases in the level of spending at the secondary level need to be accompanied with reforms that ensure that student learning achievement improves, thereby improving education rates of return.

Figure 6.9 Lessons on Sector Spending from Successful Reform Countries

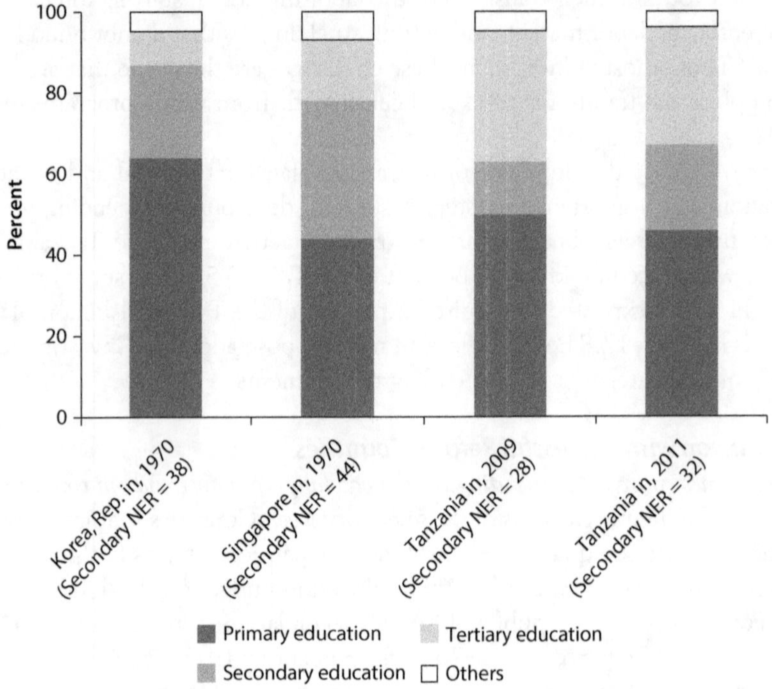

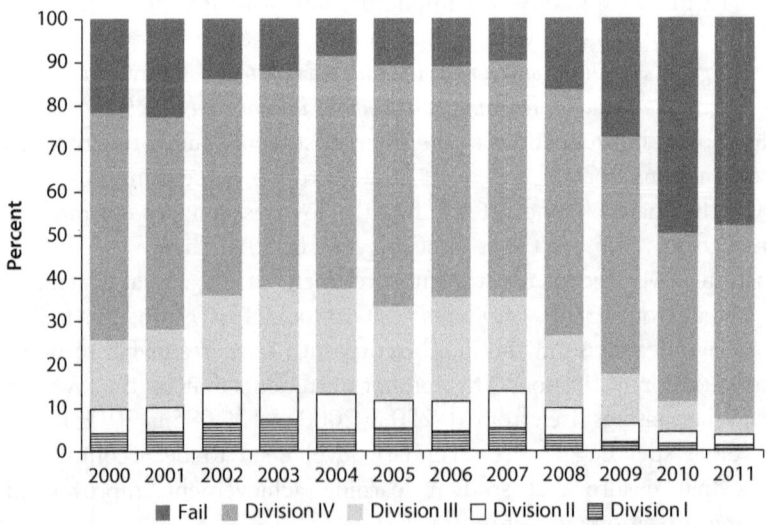

Sources: Ahlburg and Jensen 2001; URT 2012b.
Note: NER = net enrollment rate.

Figure 6.10 Declining Value Derived from Public Investment in Secondary Schooling

Source: URT 2011.

Public Education Unit Cost Estimates and Equitable Resource Allocations

Budget allocations for teaching and learning materials are fully funded for the secondary level but underfunded at the primary level. After correcting for the misclassification of T Sh 12 billion of the development budget intended for the purchase of teaching and learning materials through the government's capitation grant component of recurrent spending, the budgetary allocation for secondary-level capitation grants is consistent with the budget allocation formula of T Sh 25,000 per enrollee, unlike the experience in the 2005–09 period when lower secondary pass rates declined at the same time that resources for teaching and learning materials also declined. Recurring budget per secondary enrollee has improved dramatically in nominal and real terms from about T Sh 140,000 in 2006–07 to T Sh 264,565 in 2011–12 (table 6.7).

Capitation grants continue to be underfunded for the primary level, currently budgeted at T Sh 6,263 per enrollee in 2011–12 (compared with a target of T Sh 10,000 per enrollee per year). Budget estimates per preprimary and primary enrollee and passer are also provided given that the disbursement to primary schools is actually utilized for both preprimary and primary pupils in the absence of a budget line for preprimary schooling.[10] Planned recurrent spending per primary school enrollee is stable and will achieve its highest nominal level in 2010–11 at T Sh 121,509 (table 6.7). By comparison, planned recurrent spending per public secondary school enrollee was T Sh 100,802 in 2010–11, T Sh 96,147 in 2009–10, and T Sh 66,708.61 in 2008–09. Planned recurrent spending per public higher education enrollee has declined from an actual of T Sh 5,041,552.05 in 2010–11 to a budget of T Sh 4,236,880.92 for 2011–12, suggesting a movement toward improved cost control in higher education (table 6.8).

We find less than satisfactory outcomes from resource allocations to the primary and lower secondary levels. Crude pass rates are 53.5 percent and 50.4 percent for the primary and lower secondary education levels, respectively,[11] and these are used to estimate unit cost (public spending per Primary School Leaving

Table 6.7 Unit Costs of Expenditures Spent on Enrollees and Passers in Primary and Secondary Education Budgets

	Primary education budget			Preprimary + primary education budget			Secondary education budget		
	Per enrollee (T Sh)	Per passer (T Sh)	Share (%)	Per enrollee (T Sh)	Per passer (T Sh)	Share (%)	Per enrollee (T Sh)	Per passer (T Sh)	Share (%)
Development	6,788	12,684	5	6,052	11,309	5	56,528	108,865	18
Wages	104,669	195,584	82	93,323	174,381	82	182,968	352,369	57
Capitation grants	6,263	11,703	5	5,584	10,434	5	25,260	48,647	8
Other recurring	10,577	19,763	8	9,430	17,621	8	56,338	108,498	18
Total	128,296	239,733	100	114,388	213,745	100	321,093	618,379	100

Source: URT 2012a.

Table 6.8 Actual and Budgeted Unit Cost of Public Investment in Education

	2010–11 actual			2011–12 budget		
	Total (T Sh)	Per enrollee in public HETI (T Sh)	Share of actual (%)	Total (T Sh)	Per enrollee in public HETI (T Sh)	Share of actual (%)
Development	50,253,982,461	599,489.22	11	114,112,132,700	1,095,862.22	21
Wages	158,895,689,102	1,895,496.60	34	170,834,088,804	1,640,584.74	31
Student loans[a]	235,020,685,400	2,803,606.02	50	242,816,362,000	2,331,857.89	44
Other recurring	28,706,850,702	342,449.43	6	27,535,959,758	264,438.30	5
Total	472,877,207,666	5,641,041.27	100	555,298,543,262	5,332,743.14	100

Source: URT 2012b.
Note: HETI = higher education training institution.
a. Student enrollment in public HETIs was 83,828 in 2010–11 and 104,130 in 2011–12. Students in both public and private HEIs are eligible for student loans.

Examination [PSLE] and Certificate of Secondary Education Examination [CSEE] passer). The crude pass rate at the upper secondary level is higher at 92.1 percent. We find that on average the public unit recurrent cost of producing a PSLE passer is T Sh 1,589,344 (T Sh 227,049 per year over a seven-year period), whereas the public unit recurrent cost of producing a CSEE passer is T Sh 2,038,057 (T Sh 509.514 per year over a four-year period).

Differences of several hundred percent are found between district per capita averages for the least and best resourced districts with respect to transfers for teaching and learning materials at the primary level. For 2011–12, the allocation of capitation grants at the primary level remains inequitable, with only two districts (Sumbawanga Rural and Mpanda Urban) expected to meet the required T Sh 10,000 per enrollee in public primary schools at T Sh 11, 674 and T Sh 9,992, respectively. The lowest capitation grant allocation per primary enrollee of T Sh 1,071 is for Kilolo district. The top 20 districts have between T Sh 11,674 and T Sh 7,040 per enrollee, where the bottom 20 districts have between T Sh 5,541 and T Sh 1,071.

Apart from student learning achievement deficits (chapter 4), high levels of teacher absenteeism (chapter 5), and inefficient utilization of resources across districts (chapter 7), inequality in the availability of resources across districts is an additional challenge for the primary school system. The top 20 districts (median of T Sh 8,152 per enrollee) have more than twice the value of allocations to the bottom 20 districts (median of T Sh 3,923 per enrollee). This has been a permanent feature of public education finance over the past five years; most districts receive the same per student allocations, but a small subset receive disproportionately high or low allocations (table 6.9). The regional disparity challenge and a lack of budgetary allocations for preprimary education have a negative impact on child development.

Geographical disparity is evident in teacher and infrastructure availability. For 2011, the mean secondary school student teacher ratio varied from 46:1 in the Mara region (worst ratio) to 26:1 in the Dodoma region (best ratio) with even greater interdistrict variation. Similarly, student-classroom ratios were 55:1 and 36:1 in these regions, respectively. The situation is similar at the primary level

Table 6.9 Inequality in Recurrent Unit Cost Allocations for Primary Education
T Sh

	Minimum	Median	Maximum	Range
Bottom quintile	1,071.26	5,163.97	5,816.07	4,744.81
2nd quintile	5,847.54	6,038.23	6,138.31	290.77
3rd quintile	6,144.75	6,250.73	6,400.32	255.57
4th quintile	6,414.66	6,501.44	6,666.96	252.30
Top quintile	6,694.84	7,969.01	11,673.59	4,978.75

Source: URT 2012a.

where the student-teacher ratio varied from 59:1 in the Tabora region (worst ratio) to 34:1 in the Kilimanjaro region, whereas student-classroom ratios were 89:1 and 43:1 in these regions, respectively (URT 2012b). As a result, strong geographical correlation is found between teacher and facility shortages at the pretertiary education levels. This puts children from certain geographical locations at some disadvantage relative to their peers and reinforces existing inequalities in access to services and opportunities.

Policy Recommendations

Going forward, it is recommended that the government of Tanzania's budget try to separate and prioritize spending for preprimary education and allocate specific and adequate funding for both primary and preprimary, train more preprimary teachers, and ensure the equitable deployment of teachers to both rural and urban schools. Additionally, achieving equity in allocations and efficiency in spending at the local government authority (LGA) level should remain a priority to help boost primary and lower secondary student achievement across all districts. Mindful of the possible trade-offs involved in a context of binding resource constraints, attention should also be given to scaling up resources for secondary education to reverse deteriorating performance by investing more in quality-enhancing improvements: adequate teachers, teaching aids, and learning materials.

Higher education reforms require that interventions achieve two objectives (Shyllon 2011).

- Ensure equitable access to higher education by (a) improving the mechanisms for achieving separation between the poor and the nonpoor and (b) making higher education affordable for the poor at the point of use.
- Ensure sustainable financing of the student loan scheme before scheme maturity by (a) raising interest rates to cover at least the government's cost of borrowing, (b) increasing voluntary repayment rates including through income-contingent repayments, and (c) supplementing public financing resources with private financing resources.

Labor productivity in Tanzania is much lower than for regional peers. In 2010, output per worker (1990 purchasing power parity [PPP]) was US$1,636 for

Tanzania compared with US$2,380 for Kenya, and US$2,622 for Uganda (World Bank 2012b). Two channels for productivity improvements include (a) improving within-sector productivity by using more efficient production functions and (b) making structural change involving shifting private resources to the most productive sectors (McMillan and Rodrik 2011). Both of these require better skilled workers. Production function improvements require technology and skill advances. In addition to technical and vocational skills, employers require workers with behavioral skills such as teamwork, diligence, creativity, and entrepreneurship to succeed in rapidly evolving and technologically driven globalized economies (World Bank 2010). Reforms to improve capabilities in the technical and trade skills area will require a better understanding of education and labor market linkages through the much delayed take-off of Tanzania's Tertiary Labor Market Observatory to inform competency gaps to be accompanied by reforms that address these deficiencies and ensure a workforce with desired behavioral attitudes.

Annex 6A: Spending Patterns and National Education Strategies

Table 6A.1 Alignment of 2011–12 Approved Education Budget with MKUKUTA II Objectives

Resource-related education strategies from MKUKUTA II Cluster II	Alignment to priorities
Goal 1A: Equitable access to quality early childhood development (ECD) programs, primary, and secondary education for all girls and boys: Nominal and real increases in capital spending for secondary to catch up with primary. Recurring spending is adequate for secondary but inadequate for primary. Specific allocations for ECD is missing.	
(a) Rehabilitating and expanding school infrastructure, especially sport facilities, laboratories, water supplies, latrines and hand-washing facilities, and secondary school dormitories	Yes
(b) Providing school materials and sports equipment in the required ratios and mix	Mixed (yes for secondary education, no for primary education)
(c) Ensuring achievement of subject specific recommended textbook-student ratios	Mixed (yes for secondary education, no for primary education)
(d) Ensuring achievement of recommended classroom density, student-desk ratio, (pit) latrine ratio	Mixed (yes for primary education, no for secondary)
(e) Equipping classrooms with ICT facilities and promoting use of ICT in teaching and learning	No
(f) Supporting regular school inspection for monitoring inputs, processes, and learning outcomes	No
(g) Strengthening quality assurance, including training and recruiting qualified school inspectors for education delivery	No
(h) Effective implementation of integrated ECD policies	No
(i) Expand access of children with disabilities to all levels of education; strengthen and equip laboratories, sports, and game facilities that are accessible to children with disabilities	Yes (based on increased enrollment)

table continues next page

Table 6A.1 Alignment of 2011–12 Approved Education Budget with MKUKUTA II Objectives *(continued)*

Resource-related education strategies from MKUKUTA II Cluster II	Alignment to priorities
Goal 1B: Training an appropriate number of teachers to the required mix of subject competencies as well as equitable deployment across regions, districts, and schools: Nominal and real decrease in financing for teacher education and training from actual in FY 2009–10. Yet teacher production is less of a challenge compared with ensuring that teachers go to and stay in remote and hard-to-reach locations.	
(a) Training adequate teachers in the appropriate mix of subjects, with emphasis on science subjects and languages, including sports and physical education	Yes
(b) Promoting regular and inclusive preservice and in-service training programs	No
(c) Deploying qualified, competent, and motivated teachers in equitable and appropriate manner	Yes
(d) Devising and strengthening incentive structure to ensure recruitment and retention of highly qualified teachers, especially in underserved areas	No
Goal 2A: Ensuring quality expansion of technical and vocational education and training: Dramatic nominal and real decrease in financing for technical training institutions (regulated by NACTE). Implementation of TVDEP remains outstanding.	
(a) Expanding and improving infrastructure to expand enrollment, especially of girls	No
(b) Improving quality of teaching and learning environment	No
(c) Strengthening quality assurance	No
Goal 2B: Ensuring quality expansion of higher education: Nominal increase but no real increase in higher education financing. Unit cost control in place for higher education.	
(a) Expanding and improving infrastructure to support increased gender equitable enrollment and quality delivery	Mixed (yes for improved access, no for equity)
(b) Integrating ICT in teaching and learning	Yes
(c) Reviewing the Higher Education Loans Policy with a view to exploring other sources of financing and increasing accessibility to higher learning institutions	Yes
Goal 2C: Ensuring quality expansion of adult, nonformal, and continuing education: Nominal increase but no real increase in higher education financing. Insufficient for quality expansion.	
(a) Scaling up the "Yes I can" campaign and advocacy and awareness	Yes
(b) Expanding and improving education infrastructure, including ensuring effective use of schools and other institutions for basic and continuing education for out-of-school children youth and adults, especially in rural areas	No

Note: ICT = information and communication technology; NACTE = National Council for Technical Education; FY = fiscal year.

Notes

1. This 7 percent share is as a result of Project and Basket Funds specific to the education sector. Part of the government of Tanzania's financial contribution is through donor-afforded general budget support.
2. Mincerian regression results are presented in chapter 3.
3. The increase in the number of lower secondary students failing examinations is discussed in the fifth section.
4. Primary school enrollment increased very little over the study period because of near universal enrollment. Other levels of education had very low starting points and thus had significant room for improvement.
5. Four training institutions were upgraded to provide degree program training: Dar es Salaam Maritime Institute (DMI), Institute of Adult Education (IAE), Tanzania School of Journalism (now Institute of Journalism and Mass Communication [IJMC]), and Kikuvoni Academy for Social Sciences (now Mwalimu Nyerere Memorial

Academy [MNMA]). The four completely new institutions are Dar es Salaam University College of Education (DUCE), Mkwawa University College of Education (MUCE), University of Dodoma (UDOM), and Nelson Mandela African Institute of Science and Technology (NM-AIST).

6. Student loans will be interest bearing beginning in 2011–12.
7. This is based on administrative data from the 2011 EMIS database.
8. The cohort survival analysis was conducted using 2009–10 data on promotion rates, repetition rates, and drop-out rates for secondary education. The reconstructed cohort method was applied.
9. This study contains an interesting analysis of teacher motivation in Sub-Saharan Africa and South Asia.
10. This is different from the absence of a budget for early childhood development (ECD). In Tanzania, ECD refers to the zero-to-eight age range. Given that the official age of commencement at the primary level is seven years, the first two years of primary schooling are budgeted for by the government. The two years of preprimary education for five- and six-year-olds is, however, not budgeted for.
11. Crude pass rates are estimated as the number of examination passers as a share of the number of examination candidates, without making a distinction in the quality of the passing grade.

References

Ahlburg, D. A., and E. R. Jensen. 2001. "Education and the Asian Economic Miracle." In *Population Change and Economic Development in East Asia*, edited by A. Mason, 231–54. Stanford, CA: Stanford University Press.

Bennell, Paul, and Kwame Akyeampong. 2007. "Teacher Motivation in Sub-Saharan Africa and South Asia." Researching the Issues Series, Issue 71. Department for International Development, London.

Hoogeveen, J., and R. Ruhinduka. 2009. "Poverty Reduction in Tanzania since 2001: Good Intentions, Few Results." Paper prepared for the Research and Analysis Working Group of the MKUKUTA Monitoring System, Ministry of Finance and Economic Affairs, Dar es Salaam, Tanzania.

Laderchi, C. 2009. "Transitions and Informality: Improving Young People's Opportunities in Tanzania's Urban Labor Markets." Policy Note, Tanzania PREM Team, World Bank, Washington, DC.

McMillan, M., and D. Rodrik. 2011. "Globalization, Structural Change and Productivity Growth." Working Paper 17143, National Bureau of Economic Research, Cambridge, MA.

Shyllon, O. 2011. "Tanzania's Higher Education Student Loan Scheme: Financial Sustainability for Equitable Access." Briefing Note, Tanzania Education Team, World Bank, Washington, DC.

URT (United Republic of Tanzania). 2007. *Household Budget Survey*. National Bureau of Statistics, Dar es Salaam, Tanzania.

———. 2010a. "Higher Education Students Loan Board Database." Higher Education Student Loans Board, Dar es Salaam, Tanzania.

———. 2010b. *Tanzania's Demographic and Health Survey*. National Bureau of Statistics, Dar es Salaam, Tanzania.

———. 2011. "Rapid Budget Analysis 2011: Synoptic Note." Tanzania PER Macro Group, Dar es Salaam, Tanzania.

———. 2012a. "Budget Database." Ministry of Finance, Dar es Salaam, Tanzania.

———. 2012b. "Education Management Information System (EMIS) Database." Ministry of Education and Vocational Training, Dar es Salaam, Tanzania.

World Bank. 2008. *Tanzania Science and Technology Higher Education Project—Program Appraisal Document*. Report 40775-TZ, World Bank, Washington, DC.

———. 2010. *Stepping Up Skills: For More Jobs and Higher Productivity*. Washington, DC: World Bank.

———. 2012a. "Education Statistics Database." World Bank, Washington, DC.

———. 2012b. *World Development Indicators*. Washington, DC: World Bank.

CHAPTER 7

Value for Money in Education

Stevan Lee

Summary

An increasingly large share of the budget is allocated to the education sector in Tanzania. This has allowed increasing necessary inputs and expanding access to education at all levels. Unfortunately the quality of education seems to have fallen recently, evidenced by declining Primary School Leaving Exam (PSLE) and Certificate of Secondary Education Exam (CSEE) pass rates. Quality-adjusted unit cost (in terms of recurrent spending per passer) shows that the recent declines in primary and secondary examination pass rates have already increased the cost per passer in both subsectors and thus lead to a substantial decline in value for money.

Regionally disaggregated data show further persistent high inequality across districts in terms of public spending on education per capita, educational outcomes, and social conditions. Generally the poorest districts tend to receive fewer resources than their wealthier counterparts. At the same time, a strong positive relationship is seen between resource allocation and educational outcomes, suggesting that the uneven resource allocation across districts is at least partly responsible for the observed unequal results, thus further exacerbating existing inequalities in social conditions and living standards. Moreover, these regional inequalities in public spending are also inefficient, given the existence of diminishing returns. This suggests that a more equitable distribution of public education spending would lead to improvements along the efficiency and the equity dimensions.

However, unequal spending and social conditions cannot explain all the variation in educational outcomes. The empirical evidence suggests substantial inefficiencies in some districts, which are most likely related to local managerial effectiveness and/or teachers' incentives. An examination of quality-adjusted unit cost (per passer) shows extraordinary variation across districts. This notion of regional differences in efficiency is confirmed using a more sophisticated efficiency measure, which conditions on the underlying social conditions. Although we can identify a group of highly efficient districts, with low unit cost per passer, most districts, unfortunately, are far below the efficiency frontier curve. Further analyzing and addressing the causes of these inefficiencies is of great policy relevance, because this would either lead to considerable cost savings, in order of magnitude of 1 percent of gross domestic product (GDP) in 2010, or, if spending levels are kept constant, to greatly improved educational performance.

Introduction

Tanzania has achieved considerable increases in the number of enrollments at all levels of the education sector. In many ways, expansion and access were the right focal points over the last decade, captured under the slogan "education for all." But education is supposed to be an investment in human capital, and this can work only if schooling produces useful learning outcomes. These learning outcomes have so far received little attention in budget analyses in Tanzania. This chapter provides an assessment of value for money in the education sector to move from "education for all" toward "learning for all."

Education Spending and Results: National Trends

Tanzania Has Shown a Strong Commitment on Spending Levels with a Current Bias toward Higher Education

Tanzania has a long history of continued substantial increases in education funding. The sector has consistently claimed the highest spending in the country's budget. Figure 7.1 shows strong growth in overall education spending averaging 15–20 percent per year in 2007–08 to 2010–11. Within this, the bill for higher education is growing fastest, so higher education is increasing its share. In most years, spending in the big primary and secondary schooling subsectors grows in real terms, although there have been some exceptional years.

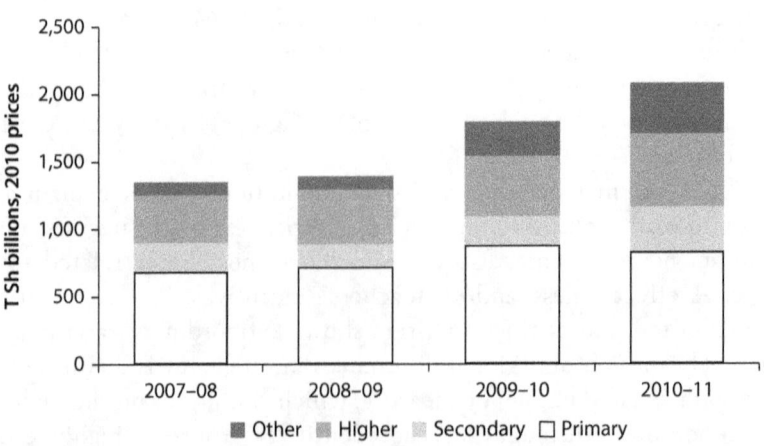

Figure 7.1 Public Spending by Subsector

Worsening Primary Enrollment and Quality Present a Threat to Value for Money

Learning outcomes and even enrollment rates have started to deteriorate in primary education. During the early 2000s, substantial gains in primary school enrollment rates were linked to universal primary education policies. Examination performance also improved during this period (figure 7.2), such that the number of children completing school and passing exams increased substantially—a major gain in learning outcomes. Since 2008, however, these performance benchmarks have been in decline. Primary school enrollment reached a plateau despite rapid population growth, which caused a drop in official gross enrollment rates. In addition, PSLE pass rates, which had been improving until 2007, had fallen from 70 percent to 50 percent of candidates by 2009 and have fallen even further since then. These factors combine to produce a decline in the proportion of children completing Standard 7 (the final year of primary schooling) with a PSLE pass.

Part of the explanation for deteriorating quality is linked to rapid expansion that started more than seven years earlier. The first universal primary education cohorts entered the primary system in 2002 and therefore started to exit in 2008 and 2009. These large numbers of children stretched resources, and most were educated in much larger class sizes than children a few years older, or a few grades ahead, in the same schools. So some deterioration in average quality was to be expected in this "universal primary education vanguard," and this could partly explain the deterioration in the proportion of 13-year-olds passing PSLE in 2008 and 2009.

The issue of declining quality still represents a serious threat to value for money in education if it cannot be addressed. We can use a quality-adjusted unit

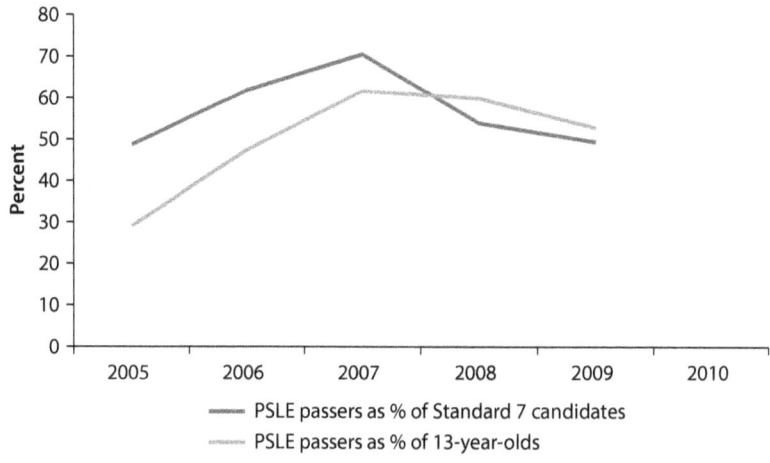

Figure 7.2 Primary School Leavers Pass Rates

Note: PSLE = Primary School Leaving Examination.

cost to measure value for money in a very simple way; this is just the recurrent spending in education divided by the number of exam passers in a given year and approximates to "cost per passer."[1] The decline in PSLE pass rates has been sufficient to raise the cost per passer in 2009 (in real terms) to a level that is almost 40 percent higher than it was in 2007, which represents a substantial decline in value for money (figure 7.3).

Outcomes Deteriorated in 2007–09, but the Level of Outcomes Achieved in Tanzania Was Too Low Even in 2007

Evidence indicates that the quality of Tanzania's primary education is low compared with that of neighboring countries and that the level of achievement is fundamentally inadequate as well as deteriorating. A report by Uwezo (2011) shows Tanzanian students performing much worse than students in Kenya and Uganda on comparable English, numeracy, and Swahili tests designed to represent a Standard 2 (eight-to-nine-year-old) level of learning.[2] It shows that many Tanzanian pupils take seven years to acquire the skills they should have acquired in two years. Figure 7.4 shows mathematics results. In Tanzania, only 18 percent of children in Standard 3 could pass the Standard 2 level test. Even by Standard 7, when children are at least 13 years old, only 68 percent pass the Standard 2 level test. Learning outcomes at this level mean that near-universal access to primary school will not generate the benefits associated with a much stronger basic skills set in the population. In the worst case scenario, very poor quality in primary education has the potential to undermine the demand for education and threaten universal primary education gains.[3]

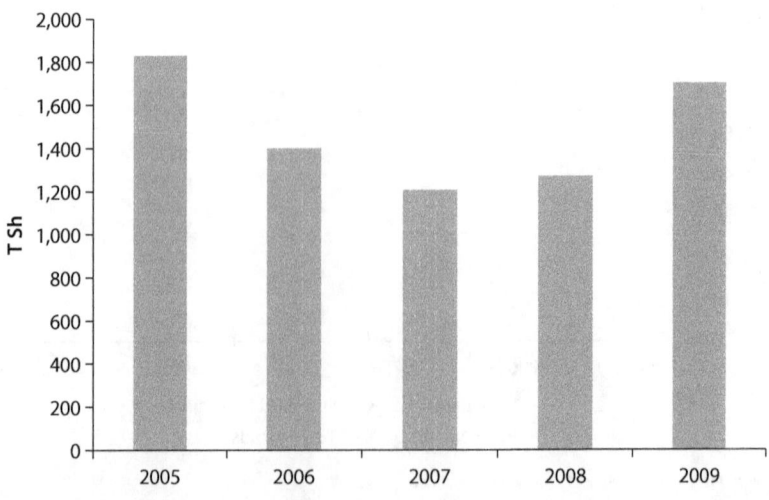

Figure 7.3 Public Expenditure per PSLE Passer ("Cost per Passer")

Note: PSLE = Primary School Leaving Examination.

Figure 7.4 Results of Uwezo's Standard 2 (8-to-9-Year-Old Level) Mathematics Test among Pupils from Standard 3 to Standard 7 (9-to-14-Year-Olds)

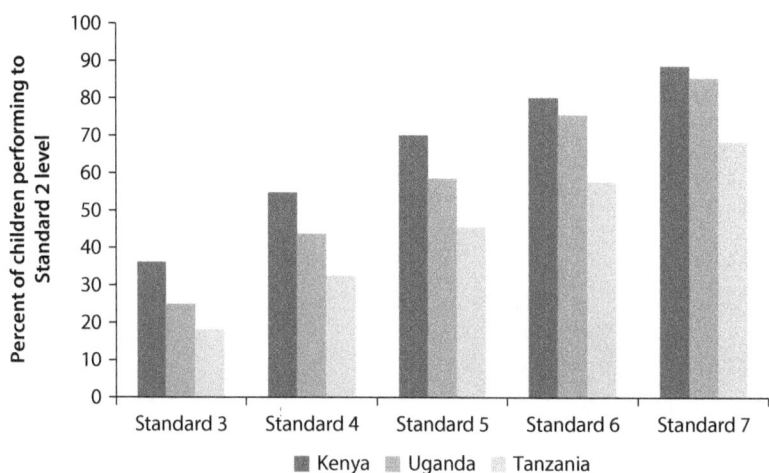

Secondary Education Sees Impressive Expansion but Also Suffers Severe Quality Problems

Historically, participation in postprimary education in Tanzania has been low by any standards, certainly by the standards of the East African Cooperation. In 2000, just 47,000 students—approximately 5 percent of 17-year-olds in the country—were candidates for Form 4 exams.[4] It was vital to address this very low level of postprimary education, which would form a real constraint to labor-intensive, poverty-reducing growth in the country. This has been addressed very impressively. In 2005, 355,000 students were enrolled in government secondary schools (figure 7.5); another 65,000 were enrolled in private schools. By 2010, the numbers had grown to 1.4 million in government schools and 237,000 in private schools, which represents an annual growth rate of 31 percent; with that growth rate, the secondary gross enrollment rate rose from 9.4 percent to 32.4 percent in five years. Even higher enrollment rates are already built into the system because of student numbers in Forms 1 and 2 (first two years of secondary school).

During this period of enrollment expansion, public spending grew fast at 19 percent per annum in real terms, but at a rate that failed to keep up with the expansion of the school population. As a consequence, by 2008–09, real expenditure per student had fallen to half the 2005–06 level. There was some recovery in 2010–11, but spending rates continue to fall short of increased rates of enrollment.

Severe quality problems in Tanzania's secondary education sector pose serious current and future challenges with regard to value for money. Quotation of pass rates is hampered by the existence of "Division IV," which is the lowest division in the Form 4 CSEE above a fail and is not sufficient to allow entry to Form 5. Therefore, a useful pass is one in Divisions I to III. If Division IV is treated as a pass

Figure 7.5 Children in Government Secondary School

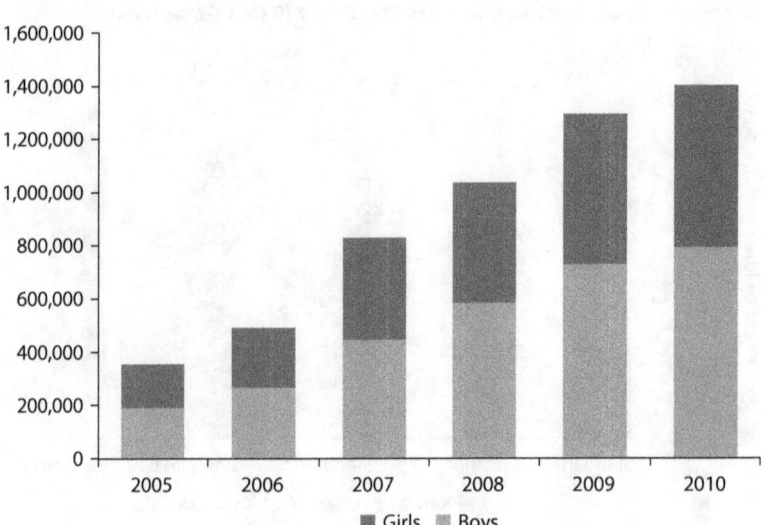

Figure 7.6 Percentage of CSEE Candidates at Grade

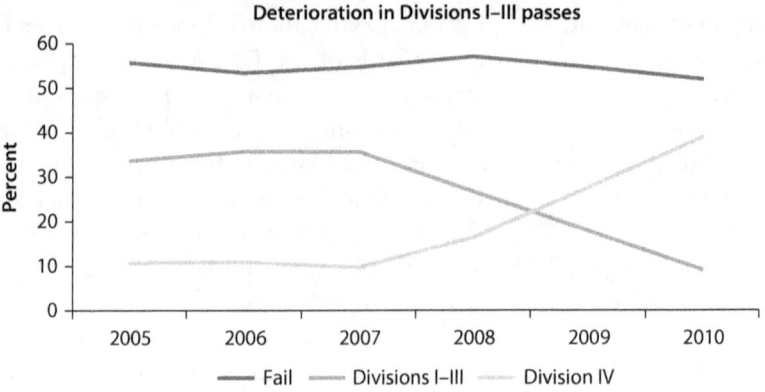

CSEE = Certificate of Secondary Education Examination.

in the main Form 4 exam, public spending per CSEE passer is now increasing: The cost per CSEE passer rose from T Sh 826,000 in 2008 to T Sh 1.04 million in 2009. Since 2007, the number of Division IV passes has been increasing to the point where a majority of students fail CSEE and the majority of the rest get a Division IV, quasi-fail. Divisions I–III fell from 27 percent in 2008 to 18 percent of students in 2009, and in 2010, this has fallen to just 9 percent of candidates (figure 7.6). Therefore, a better measure of value for money looks at "costs per passer," including only Divisions I–III passers. This cost per passer is high and increasing fast—from T Sh 3.8 million in 2008 to T Sh 8.2 million in 2010—a clear indicator of current value for money problems. For comparison, recall that cost per passer in primary is only T Sh 1.6 million.

Other signs indicate that severe quality problems are pervasive in secondary schools. In 2009, approximately 4 percent of secondary schools had an average grade point average (GPA) score of 3 or less (in Tanzania, GPA equates to average "division," so 4 is average Division IV, and 1 represents the best, Division I pass achieved in everything). This means that the average candidate in 96 percent of schools scored either Division IV or Fail on the CSEE exam. Without attention to quality, Tanzania risks producing large numbers of very poorly educated and unemployable Form 4 "graduates." This would not represent value for money.

Signs also indicate that secondary school teachers in the hugely expanded system may not be equipped to teach the course. A study of Service Delivery Indicators tests teachers against the curriculum they are teaching. In mathematics, fewer than 50 percent of teachers passed the tests necessary to teach for CSEE, and in English language, which is the language of instruction in Tanzanian secondary schools, only 25 percent of teachers passed the test. This suggests that overstretched resources and the lack of available staff could be causing serious quality problems.

Key Issues Are Different in Higher Education: Unit Costs Are under Control, but without Student Loan Reflows, Affordability Is in Doubt

Historically, Tanzania has had very, very low participation in higher education, but as with secondary education, the country has made great strides in recent years, with enrollment growth the same as in secondary education, 31 percent per annum between 2005 and 2010. Table 7.1 shows that Tanzania now approaches neighboring countries in terms of higher learning enrollment rates. No data are available, however, to assess quality in tertiary education. Public spending in higher education has been increasing faster than that for secondary education, but spending per enrollee has still fallen so unit costs are under control.

There is a cost-recovery instrument for higher education, but currently it generates very little revenue—higher education is becoming very expensive for government. Since 2005, a large and increasing share of the higher education budget has been financed through the student loans scheme. This is intended to reduce the burden of higher education on the public purse, and in fact the public spending per student other than the loan has decreased substantially since 2005 (figure 7.7). Cost recovery is important because by 2010, higher education was taking 28 percent of the education budget, compared with just 16 percent for

Table 7.1 Trend in Tertiary Gross Enrollment Rates in East African Countries
Percent

Country	1985	2001	2002	2004	2009
Burundi	0.55	1.14	1.81	2.33	2.68
Kenya	1.28	2.81	2.81	2.90	4.05
Rwanda	0.34	1.71	1.94	2.66	4.82
Uganda	0.79	2.75	3.04	3.48	3.69
Tanzania	0.26	0.69	0.81	1.25	3.86

Figure 7.7 Public Expenditure per University Student per Year

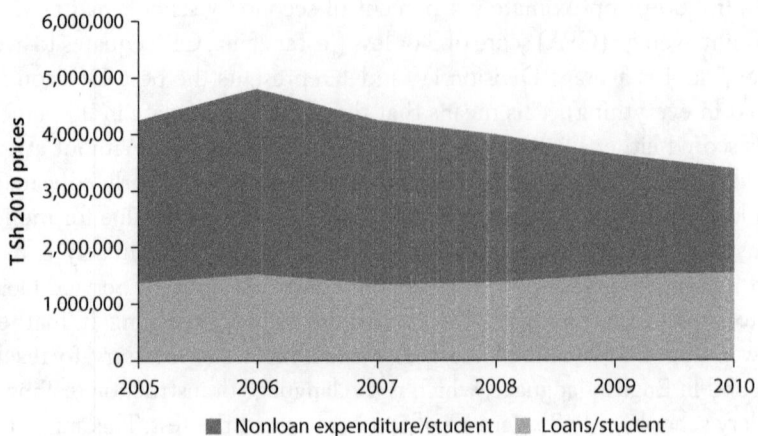

secondary and 40 percent for primary. A major challenge for the whole education sector, therefore, is how to generate reflows (repayments) under the student loan scheme.

Student loan reflows are more about affordability than value for money. They are also an issue for equity, since the majority of higher education students are from, and stay within, the top 20 percent of Tanzania's income spectrum, and the individual education subsidy they enjoy under current arrangements is unjustifiably high (without loan repayments). Public expenditure per 20- to 23-year-olds in higher education is higher than public expenditure per 7- to 13-year-olds in primary education, despite the fact that there is only 4 percent enrollment of 20- to 23-year-olds and near universal enrollment of 7- to 13-year-olds. Having tertiary education is a very good predictor of having a high income.

Beyond the Averages: Unequal Funding, Unequal Outputs, and Local Inefficiencies

At the District Level, Funding, Social Conditions, and Educational Outcomes Are Persistently Unequal

This chapter draws on analysis of district-level data gathered from the Education Management Information System (EMIS), National Examinations Council of Tanzania, various household surveys, and financial data from the Ministry of Finance and President's Office, Regional Administration and Local Government. It is already well known that there is persistent high inequality across districts in Tanzania in terms of public spending per capita (figure 7.8), educational outcomes, and social conditions. This produces significant variation in the "universal" service offered: In some districts, fewer than 30 children are found for each primary school teacher, whereas in others, the number is closer to 80 (figure 7.9). This variation carries through to outcomes: In some districts, 15 percent of 13-year-olds can expect to pass PSLE, whereas in others, more than 90 percent

Figure 7.8 Primary Education Budget per Capita across Districts—Persistent Inequality

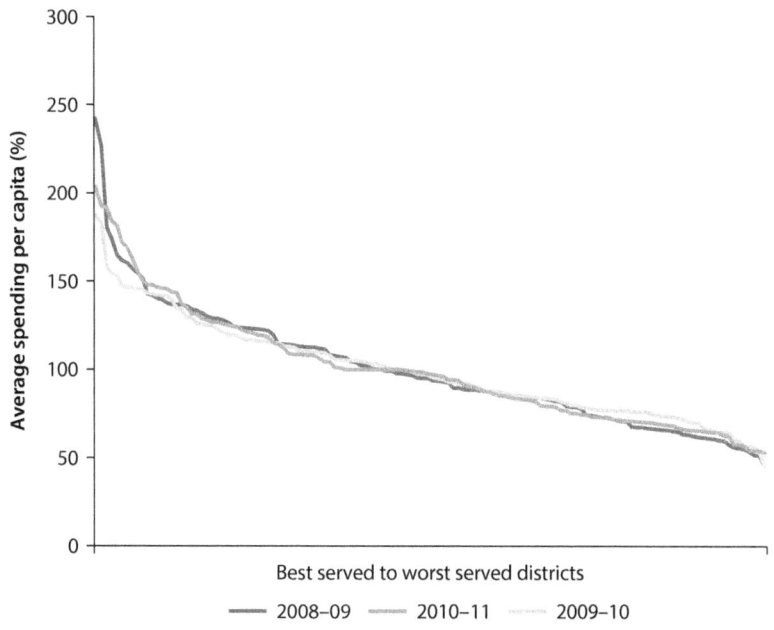

Figure 7.9 Children per Primary School Teacher—District Average Ranges from 30 to 80

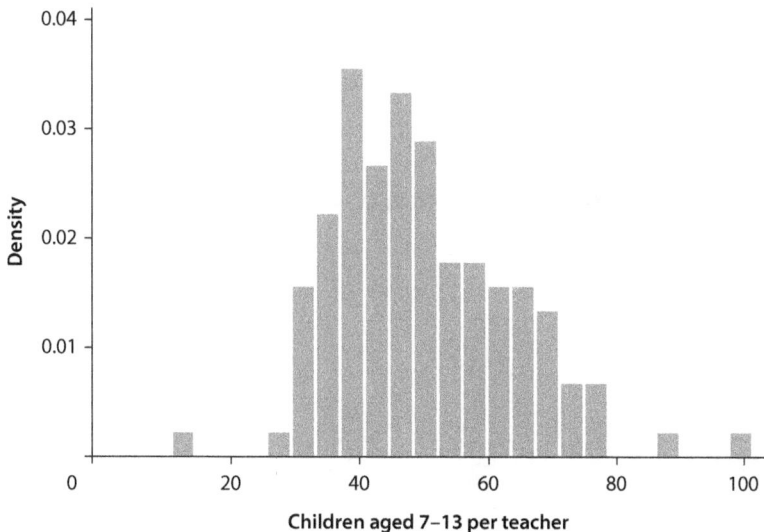

can expect to pass (figure 7.10). In general, the worst served districts tend to have worse social conditions—probably because it is more difficult to attract teachers to these remote, poor areas.[5] Figure 7.11 shows higher poverty in districts with the least education spending.

Social Conditions Affect Outcomes

We would expect poor social conditions to make learning outcomes more difficult to achieve, and we know that poor social conditions tend to mean less resources too, so it is no surprise that poor social conditions are strongly correlated with worse educational performance (figures 7.12–7.14).

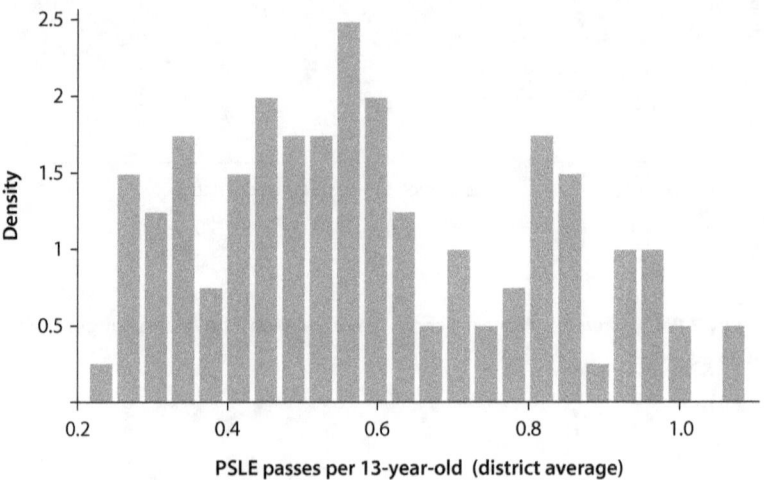

Figure 7.10 PSLE Passers per 13-Year-Old—District Average Ranges from 0.2 to 1.1, 2008

Note: PSLE = Primary School Leaving Examination.

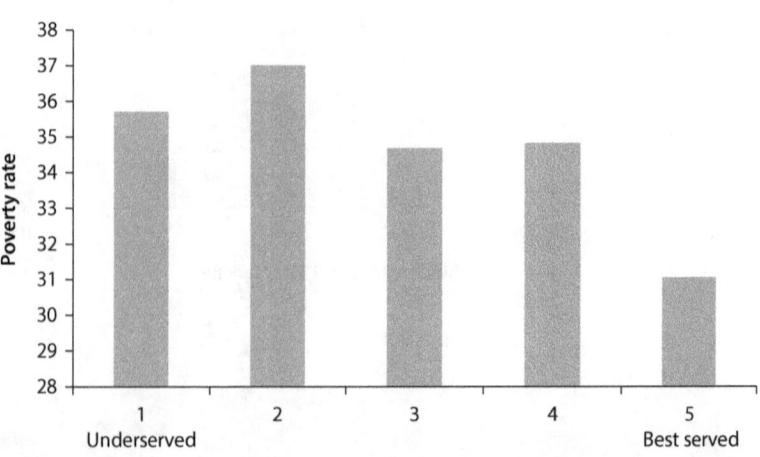

Figure 7.11 Poverty Rates in Districts by Level of Spending
Percent

Figure 7.12 Poverty and Passers per 13-Year-Old, 2008 (−32% Correlation)

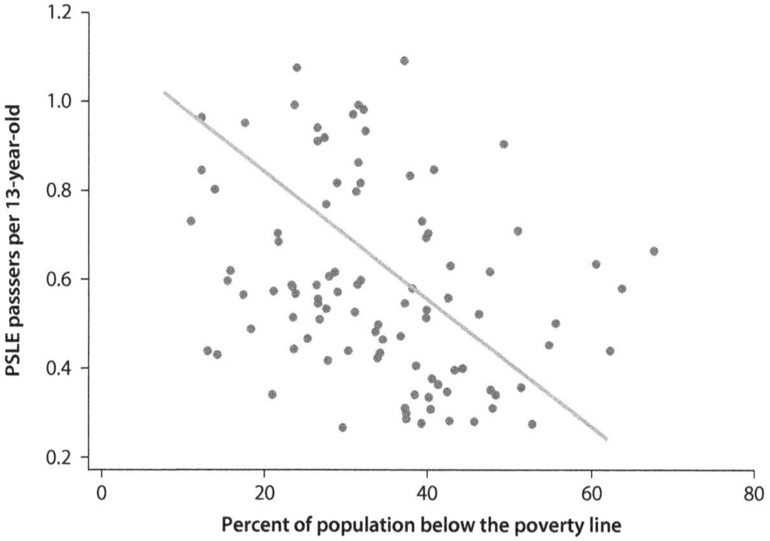

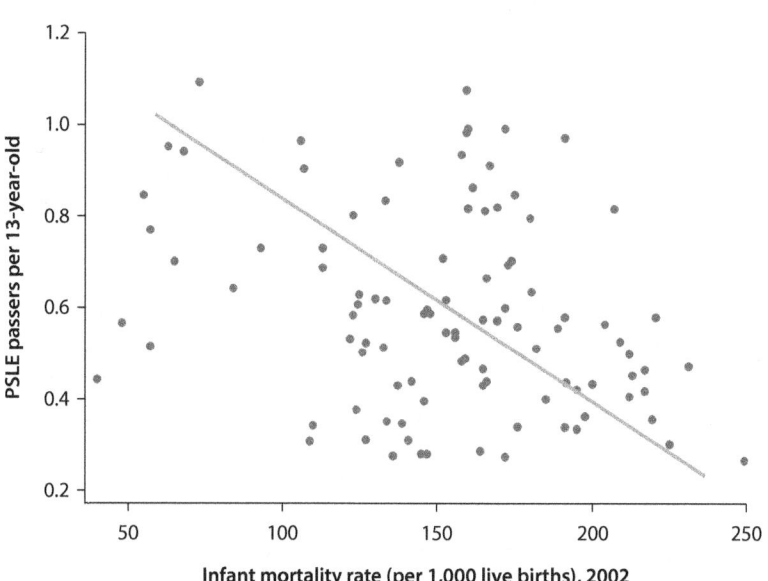

Note: PSLE = Primary School Leaving Examination.

Figure 7.13 Child Health and Passers per 13-Year-Old, 2008 (−28% Correlation)

Note: PSLE = Primary School Leaving Examination.

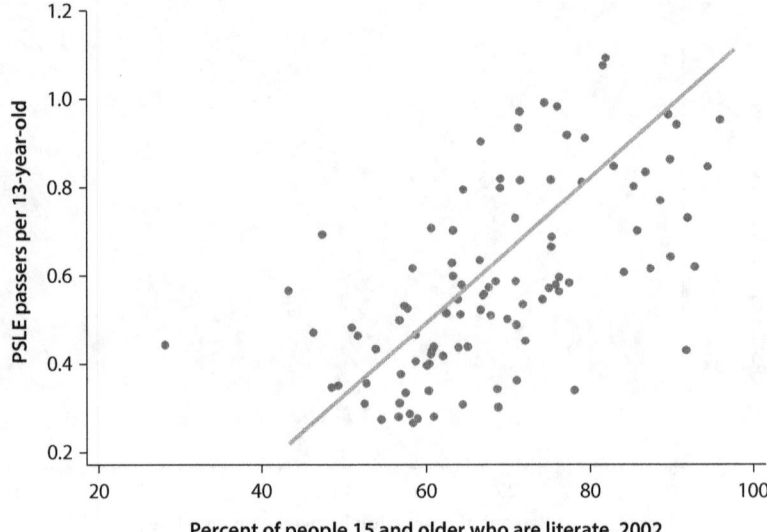

Figure 7.14 Adult Literacy and Passers per 13-Year-Old, 2008 (60% Correlation)

Note: PSLE = Primary School Leaving Examination.

A Strong Relationship Can Be Observed between Different Levels of Spending and Different Results, So Unequal Spending Patterns Really Matter

Strong theoretical reasons lead us to think that, all else being equal, increased resources should produce improved results in education. This is why we have public spending in education. However, it is often difficult to find empirical evidence for this relationship. In many international settings, usually where average levels of resources are higher and the differences between resource levels in different schools and districts is less pronounced, it is difficult to see this relationship or confirm this theory. Other factors seem to dominate: things such as the children's ability, the unobserved quality of teachers, and managerial effectiveness/teacher incentives, which are also very hard to observe. All these other factors exist in Tanzania too, so it is not obvious that we will see a strong relationship between resources and outcomes in Tanzania.

By modeling educational outcomes as a function of resources, controlling for social factors, we do in fact see a strong correlation between resources and outcomes in Tanzania. This actually explains 72 percent of the wide variation in outcomes (PSLE passes) in primary education in Tanzania. The relationship is also observable in secondary education, but weaker (40 percent fit). Figure 7.15 gives an idea of the strong relationship between an input (teachers) and exam passes looking across districts in Tanzania. This is an important result because it suggests the highly unequal resource allocation in Tanzania is at least significantly responsible for highly unequal results.

Figure 7.15 More Teachers Means More Exam Passers (Controlling for Social Conditions)

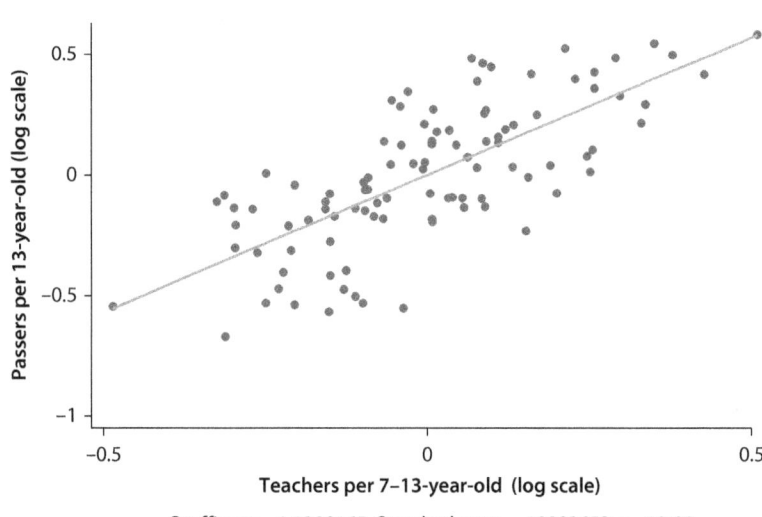

Coefficient = 1.1398165, Standard error = .10883653, t = 10.47

Strong Evidence Indicates That Uneven Spending Patterns Are Inefficient

The level of spending in a given setting relates to efficiency if returns or variable scale economies are diminishing; in Tanzania, clear evidence indicates that this is the case. Without using too many economic terms, we might theorize that an extra teacher or other input would have a lot more impact in very underserved areas (where there are hardly any teachers) than in other areas where there are already many teachers. In fact, the standard estimation supports this.[6] Estimates of exam passers against expenditures show decreasing returns at all levels, which means that all else being equal, the cost per passer is lower in underserved districts than in better served districts and that the expected impact of an additional teacher or more resources would be greater in underserved districts than in much better served districts. Little additional return on any investment was made in excess of T Sh 18,000 per capita. Thus, efficiency and equity would be served by the same incremental changes to resource allocation, because a more equitable distribution of resources would also be more efficient.

Social Conditions and Resources Do Not Explain It All: There Is Substantial Inefficiency in Some Districts

Social conditions and resources have an important impact on school system performance, but local managerial effectiveness and/or local teacher incentives seem to cause very significant variations in performance too. For example, evidence is at hand of substantial absenteeism in Tanzania: Chapter 5 shows that teachers are not in the classroom more than half of the teaching time, and that on average, children can expect only two hours of contact per day with a teacher in a classroom in primary school. If the rate of absenteeism is highly variable (the results show, for instance, much worse absenteeism in urban areas), it would be likely to have an impact on learning outcomes. This effect might be completely separate from the effects stemming from the level of resources and social conditions. The previous discussion describes the estimation of a simple production function that seemed to explain a substantial share of the variation in performance, but this leaves out the determinants of local managerial effectiveness and/or teacher incentives. They may well be as important as the other factors in explaining performance.

An examination of quality-adjusted unit cost (cost per passer) shows extraordinary variation across Tanzania, from approximately T Sh 0.5 million to over T Sh 2.0 million (figure 7.16). This alone suggests that local managerial effectiveness and/or local teacher incentives have a major impact on value for money in Tanzania, because it is impossible for such a variation in cost per passer to arise because of diminishing returns to scale alone.

We can create a better measure of efficiency that allows for the impact on unit cost of other factors like social conditions and the level of spending/diminishing returns. Previous paragraphs described the relationship between resources and outputs from an estimate that controlled for social conditions. This relationship makes it possible to estimate the level of exam performance each district should be producing with average efficiency for Tanzania. The ratio of actual to predicted performance is then a measure of efficiency; a ratio greater than one means high efficiency, and a ratio below one means low efficiency. Unlike cost per passer, this measure controls for other cost factors (in this case, social conditions and diminishing returns). Overall the efficiency measure is correlated

Figure 7.16 Distribution of Average Unit Cost: Recurrent Expenditure per PSLE Passer, 2008

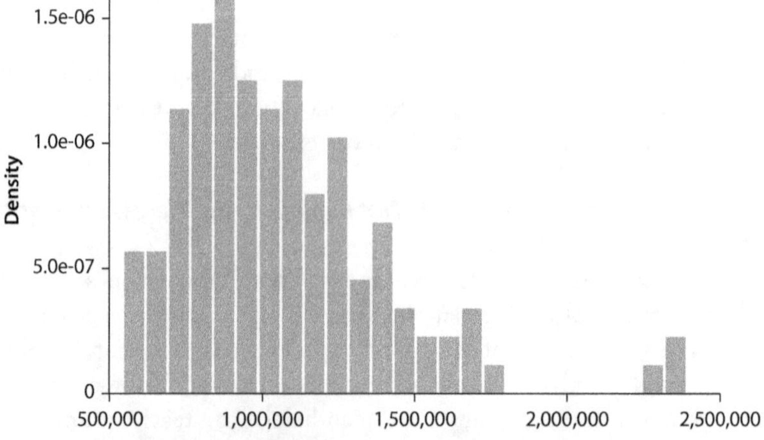

Note: PSLE = Primary School Leaving Examination.

We Can Identify Specific Districts with Very High Efficiency and Low Unit Cost

The following group of seven districts did very well on unit cost (cost per passer) and on the efficiency measure (table 7.2). They are not necessarily the most efficient districts in Tanzania, but they are certainly among them on both unit cost and technical efficiency ratio measures. On average, the unit cost of producing a PSLE passer in this group is T Sh 659,000 in 2008. This is 38 percent below the national average of T Sh 1,062,499 per passer in the same year.

The group has social indicators and spending levels that are close to the national average. In fact, social indicators are slightly better than average: Only 87 percent of the national average for poverty, average (though variable) mortality rates for children under the age of five years, and above average adult literacy rates. Education spending is about 5 percent above the average level. In view of these indicators, this set of districts should perform modestly better than the national average in terms of learning outcomes and costs per passer.[7]

In fact, this group has far better learning outcomes than could be expected given social conditions and spending levels, and this is why their efficiency measure is so high. The background factors mean that in comparison with the national pattern, these districts should be able to generate an above average rate of 69–72 passes per 100 13-year-olds. These districts manage to achieve slightly

Table 7.2 Some of the Most Efficient Primary School Districts in Tanzania
2008 data and prices

	Public expenditure per passer (unit cost)	Efficiency[a]	Public expenditure per capita (for primary)	Child population per primary teacher	PSLE passers per 100 13-year-olds	Poverty rate (%)	Under five mortality per thousand	Adult literacy rate (%)
Sumbawanga urban	690,360	1.36	15,657	45.3	100.2	27.4	138.0	77.2
Ludewa	722,647	1.37	19,195	37.8	117.3	24.1	159.5	81.6
Kyela	736,148	1.43	18,020	42.0	108.1	23.8	172.0	74.4
Njombe rural	718,514	1.46	10,499	43.0	88.6	25.0	165.5	79.0
Kilombero	574,287	1.47	11,581	46.6	89.1	29.0	160.0	75.2
Mufindi	624,326	1.54	15,128	40.7	107.0	32.3	159.5	76.0
Mbulu	553,223	1.76	12,332	40.1	98.5	49.3	107.0	66.6
Average this group	659,929	1.48	14,630	42.2	101.3	30.1	151.6	75.7
Average all districts	1,062,499	0.99	13,869	45.6	64.5	34.3	151.0	68.5

Note: PSLE = Primary School Leaving Examination.
a. High is good.

more than 100 PSLE passes per 100 estimated 13-year-olds in the district. This puts them on Tanzania's productivity "frontier" and provides a useful benchmark group by which to assess the performance of other districts in Tanzania.

We Can Also Describe a Group with Very Low Efficiency and High Unit Costs

The next group comprises 16 districts that perform badly both on simple unit cost measures (cost per passer) and the efficiency measure; they are far from Tanzania's efficient production frontier (table 7.3).

Again, social conditions are close to average in this group, as is the level of public spending on education. If anything, these districts are slightly disadvantaged, compared with the national average, and much variation is seen within the group. They are also funded slightly worse, on average. Relative to the national pattern, this group of districts is predicted to achieve only slightly worse than average results of about 56 or 57 passers per 100 13-year-olds.

This group has performed much worse, however, than the national pattern would predict given local conditions. Exam performance is very poor—just

Table 7.3 Some of the Least Efficient Primary School Districts in Tanzania
2008 data and prices

	Public expenditure per passer (unit cost)	Efficiency[a]	Public expenditure per capita (for primary)	Child population per primary teacher	PSLE passers per 100 13-year-olds	Poverty rate (%)	Under five mortality per thousand	Adult literacy rate (%)
Kondoa	1,489,672	0.60	12,581	50.5	37.3	20.9	110.0	68.6
Masasi	2,278,683	0.61	12,344	52.0	33.0	37.4	225.0	68.7
Ukerewe	1,488,731	0.61	12,522	50.1	37.2	48.4	176.0	78.1
Ruangwa	1,729,542	0.62	11,352	58.5	29.0	29.7	249.5	58.4
Shinyanga rural	1,719,680	0.63	11,941	62.4	30.7	42.7	145.0	56.6
Kasulu	1,475,025	0.63	11,236	62.4	33.7	40.4	109.0	64.4
Kibondo	1,519,330	0.63	10,376	87.2	30.2	39.4	136.0	59.0
Kishapu	1,541,079	0.64	10,679	67.1	30.6	45.7	147.0	60.9
Sikonge	2,390,588	0.64	20,467	66.0	37.8	42.5	139.0	48.6
Lindi urban	1,686,152	0.67	20,354	46.5	53.3	18.3	159.0	70.9
Mpanda rural	1,608,936	0.69	10,098	67.6	31.3	37.6	164.0	58.0
Same	1,371,369	0.69	21,743	33.4	70.0	34.1	84.0	89.8
Meatu	1,609,327	0.69	10,886	64.6	29.9	52.9	172.0	54.5
Nachingwea	1,389,183	0.70	12,439	52.4	39.6	41.4	197.5	71.0
Kahama	1,413,736	0.71	10,883	68.8	34.0	37.3	127.0	56.7
Kongwa	1,342,471	0.79	11,105	62.2	36.5	40.2	195.0	57.5
Average this group	1,628,344	0.66	13,188	59.5	37.1	38.1	158.4	63.9
Average all districts	1,062,499	0.99	13,869	45.6	64.5	34.3	151.0	68.5

Note: PSLE = Primary School Leaving Examination.
a. High is good.

37.1 passers per 100 13-year-olds on average—which means a 13-year-old from these districts has half the normal chance of passing the PSLE. The efficiency scores are all low: averaging 66 percent compared with 148 percent in the previous group. As a result, unit costs/costs per passer are also very high; these districts spend T Sh 1,628,344 for each PSLE passer produced in 2008, 60 percent above the national average.

Unfortunately, Most Districts Are Quite Far from the "Efficiency Frontier" in Tanzania

Figure 7.17 shows that most of Tanzania's districts are far from the green "efficiency frontier" and that some are extremely inefficient. The figure plots expenditure per capita against PSLE passers per 13-year-old in each district. The most efficient districts are highlighted in green, most inefficient in red. Districts in vertical alignment have the same public spending per capita. At around T Sh 12,000 per capita (purple vertical dashed line) clusters are seen near the green line and the red line, where spending is very similar but where exam performance is about three times better on the green line than the red line. Far to the right of the panel, there is also a subgroup of three inefficient districts (Sikonge, Lindi Urban, and Same) that are well resourced and have mostly

Figure 7.17 "Frontier" Group Circled in Green, Highly Inefficient Districts Circled in Orange, 2008

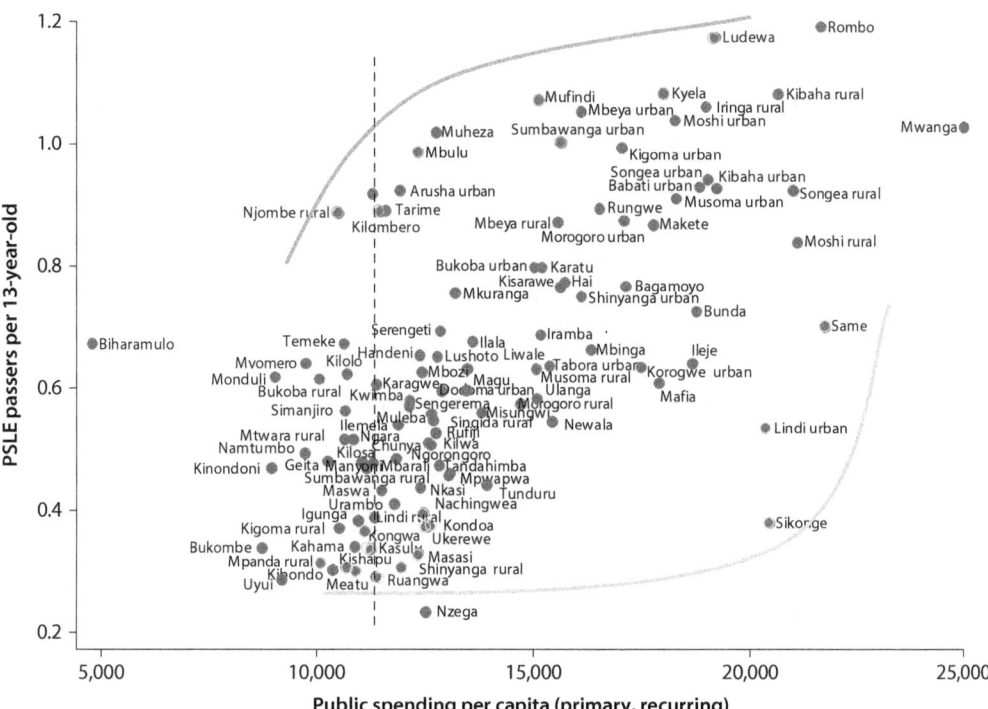

Note: PSLE = Primary School Leaving Examination.

good social conditions. These districts' primary education spending rises above T Sh 20,000 per capita, and they have below average poverty rates and above average adult literacy rates. They are predicted to generate over 80 PSLE passers per 100 13-year-old but actually they manage only 53, which demonstrates that even districts that enjoy relative advantages can be inefficient.

The evidence documents how some seriously underperforming districts in Tanzania have unexplained high local costs and/or are wasting resources. This sometimes has nothing to do with insufficient resources or poor social conditions but is due to much more local factors. In some ways, this is good news, because managerial or teacher inefficiency should be a more tractable problem than poor social conditions.

The Scale of Inefficiency

Potential Efficiency Savings, If Causes Can Be Identified, Could Be Up to T Sh 310 Billion per Annum in Primary Education Alone, 1 Percent of GDP

What is the potential for savings if laggard districts could be made more efficient? How much would the 16 districts identified as having high cost and low efficiency save were they to achieve average efficiency? Or what if all Tanzania's districts achieved the same sort of efficiency as exhibited by the green group of districts close to the efficiency frontier?

If the districts in table 7.4 were to move to average efficiency, they would save T Sh 38.3 billion. For example, Kasulu should be able to achieve 33.7 passers per 100 13-year-olds for an outlay of just T Sh 4,501 per capita, whereas the district now spends T Sh 11,236 per capita, wasting T Sh 6,735 per person or T Sh 4.14 billion per annum in total. Current waste in these districts totals T Sh 38.3 billion.

Finally, what would be the cost savings if all districts achieved a similar unit cost to the "frontier" districts? This would be an average T Sh 660,000 per passer compared with the average (in 2008) of T Sh 1,062,000, or a 38 percent saving across the entire recurrent primary education budget. For 2008, this would have meant saving more than T Sh 250 billion. By 2010, this saving would have risen to an estimated T Sh 310 billion, equal to nearly 1 percent of GDP being wasted on inefficiency in primary education each year.

It Would Be Equitable and Efficient to Direct Resources to the Least Served Districts

Tanzania's very unequal distribution of resources for primary education has been persistent over time. Somehow, the system continues to deliver the bulk of discretionary resources to districts that are already well served and may not be very efficient. The finding was that additional resources for the best served districts had hardly any impact, whereas much greater impact would be predicted, in general, in less well served districts. However, this is a stylized finding, holding other things equal. The finding might be mitigated by the fact that less well served areas are often those with worse social characteristics and higher poverty that could be underlying causes of higher costs. Many of them might also have

Table 7.4 District Expenditures on Education
2008 data and prices (T Sh)

	Public expenditure per passer (unit cost)	Current public expenditure per capita	Current PSLE passers per 100 13-year-olds	Predicted expenditure/ capita to achieve given PSLE (from normal prediction)	Population-weighted savings/current waste (T Sh billion)
Kondoa	1,489,672	12,581	37.3	4,518	4.10
Masasi	2,278,683	12,344	33.0	4,549	2.96
Ukerewe	1,488,731	12,522	37.2	4,688	2.43
Ruangwa	1,729,542	11,352	29.0	4,360	1.03
Shinyanga rural	1,719,680	11,941	30.7	4,723	2.37
Kasulu	1,475,025	11,236	33.7	4,501	5.01
Kibondo	1,519,330	10,376	30.2	4,211	3.03
Kishapu	1,541,079	10,679	30.6	4,374	1.79
Sikonge	2,390,588	20,467	37.8	8,427	1.90
Lindi urban	1,686,152	20,354	53.3	9,195	0.54
Mpanda rural	1,608,936	10,098	31.3	4,771	2.30
Same	1,371,369	21,743	70.0	10,352	2.86
Meatu	1,609,327	10,886	29.9	5,165	1.69
Nachingwea	1,389,183	12,439	39.6	6,123	1.21
Kahama	1,413,736	10,883	34.0	5,466	3.82
Kongwa	1,342,471	11,105	36.5	6,929	1.23
Mean	1,628,344	13,188	37.1	5,851	
Total savings					T Sh 38.3 billion

Note: PSLE = Primary School Leaving Examination.

severe management problems causing inefficiency. Factoring all this in, is it still a good idea to direct resources to the worst served districts?

This question can be examined by estimating the impact of an additional T Sh 50 billion in primary education spending in different groups of districts: quintiles arranged according to 2008 primary education spending per capita. In figure 7.18, underserved districts are shown on the left and better served districts on the right.

Figure 7.18 shows the T Sh 50 billion spent in underserved/middling or better served districts under two different sets of assumptions. The first assumption is constant unit cost. This is just a comparison of the average unit costs in underserved and better served areas. In fact, they do not differ very much, so the T Sh 50 billion produces about 50,000 new PSLE passers regardless of which quintile receives it. Poorer social conditions in the underserved areas are not enough to push up the unit cost very much, on average. However, this assumption is not realistic, as unit costs are not constant. Rather, costs increase with scale. The constant unit cost assumption produces very significant overestimates. This itself is instructive: This is why we should not expect a doubling of per capita primary education expenditure to produce a doubling of results.

Figure 7.18 Estimated PSLE Passers for an Extra T Sh 50 billion Spent in Each of Five Groups of Districts, Underserved to Best Served

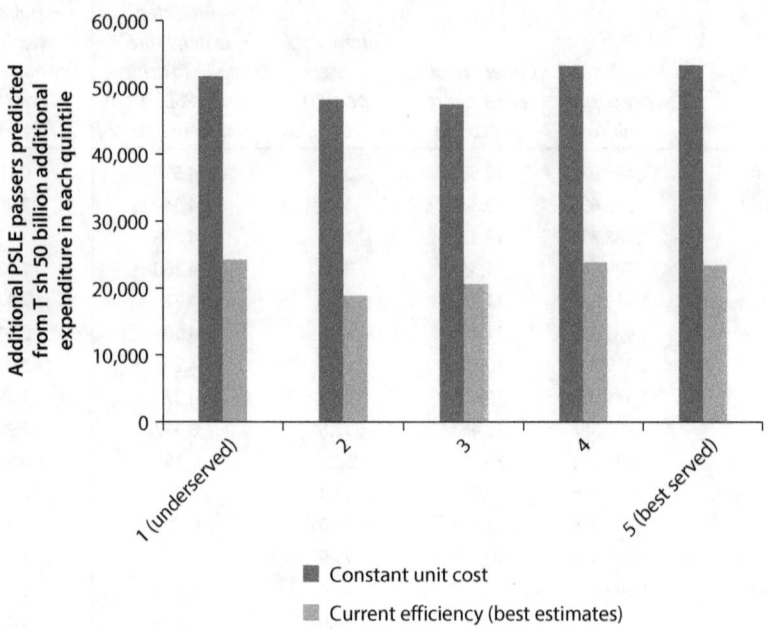

Note: PSLE = Primary School Leaving Examination.

The second set of assumptions produces the bars highlighted in red because it should produce the best estimates. Here, the assumption is that the managerial/teaching inefficiencies observed with current resources are preserved in the use of the new resources in each district, and the Cobb-Douglas production function described above is used to estimate the impact of an extra T Sh 50 billion in each set of districts, holding social conditions and efficiency constant. This assumption has a great impact on individual districts because some are so much more efficient than others. Across quintiles, however, the effect is greatly muted. Results are similar to the constant unit cost estimates except that far less extra performance is estimated. However, also note that the least well served areas get more out of an extra T Sh 50 billion than the rest.

Overall, these are strong arguments in favor of distributing incremental resources, or the proceeds from efficiency savings, to the worst served districts, although this presents difficulties in administration and implementation.

District-Level Information Could Be Used to Target Incremental Resources in an Even Better Way

In the interests of equity and efficiency, the authorities could try to target districts that are both underserved and efficient. If resources could be absorbed in those districts (which would require that staff could be persuaded to work in these areas) then very good learning impact could be expected. Table 7.5 shows

Table 7.5 Underserved Districts with Good Efficiency
2008 data and prices (T Sh)

	Expenditure per capita	Cost per passer	Efficiency score	Passers per 13-year-old (%)
Biharamulo	4,794	810,584	2.18	74
Monduli	9,046	1,077,606	1.48	68
Namtumbo	9,735	871,840	1.03	54
Mvomero	9,747	673,216	1.22	70
Bukoba rural	10,065	1,181,949	1.07	68
Geita	10,255	945,251	1.07	53
Njombe rural	10,499	718,514	1.46	97
Temeke	10,631	699,482	0.99	74
Ngara	10,647	913,169	1.00	57
Simanjiro	10,660	837,316	1.01	62
Kilolo	10,697	758,269	1.08	69
Mtwara rural	10,842	929,555	1.29	57

12 districts with very low levels of spending but reasonable or good efficiency and with average or low cost per passer. It would be good for equity and efficiency to target these districts for extra resources using the current education system, but with measures to make sure staff could be retained (an exception might be Njombe Rural, which is so efficient that it manages to achieve great results even with meager resources). The list in table 7.5 excludes underserved districts that are very inefficient.

In very inefficient districts, underserved or otherwise, outcomes are bad but extra resources cannot be expected to help very much unless something is done to address the chronic inefficiency. This might involve management innovations or new service delivery models.

The Way Forward

This chapter has proposed a direction for improving value for money in Tanzania's education system. This should not detract from the fundamental finding that the country's bold changes in education policy in the last decade overall have been highly beneficial and have either represented value for money already or should represent good value for money in the future. Tanzania has achieved significant progress toward the primary education Millennium Development Goal at low cost. Room is seen for efficiency gains in primary education, but there is still a need for more resources in that subsector. The rapid expansion of postprimary education is overdue and developmentally strategic. In higher education, cost recovery needs to be improved. In secondary education, quality problems are undermining the benefits so far, but that does not mean the expansion was a mistake; continuing to enroll only

5 percent of the age group in secondary education would be disastrous for Tanzania's future growth and poverty reduction. In secondary education, the expansion policy needs to be followed up, not reversed:

- It is essential to find a way to shift resources for primary education to the worst served areas. Inequalities are pronounced, and strong evidence from the analysis presented in this chapter shows that shifting incremental resources to the worst served areas is likely to improve efficiency rather than reduce it. District-specific knowledge could be used to target underserved yet efficient districts, with different treatment for highly inefficient districts.

- A strong need exists to examine what's going on in districts identified as highly inefficient, unrelated to the level of resources or social conditions, but probably related to local management effectiveness or teacher incentives ("governance" issues). These districts might be able to generate efficiency gains or greatly improve their performance. More resources with no other change probably will not improve things much in these districts.

- Overall, we can identify a major problem with quality in primary education. Given that Tanzania now spends significant sums on primary education, poor quality is a value-for-money issue across the system. Moreover, at a national level, poor quality could undermine the demand for education among poor groups in the future.

- Secondary education is both a triumph and a problem. The triumph is that the speed of expansion has been extraordinary, and Tanzania has made great progress in rectifying its historic deficit in postprimary education. The corresponding problem is that resources are spread more and more thinly over the increasing number of pupils, which is creating a critical quality problem in secondary education outside a small group of excellent schools. This destroys value for money, as in 2010, Tanzania spent more than T Sh 8 million for every Division I–III CSEE passer. Part of the cause is probably the low availability of suitably skilled teachers.

Notes

1. This unit cost is selected partly because it is simple, also because it relies on spending and exam results data. A theoretically superior indicator can be created using enrollment data and attrition rates to estimate costs of pupil-years per passer. However, this measure is rejected because of accuracy problems in enrollment data.
2. This is based on first-round Uwezo surveys in Kenya (2009) and Tanzania and Uganda (both 2010). See chapter 4 for further information of the Uwezo methodology and a more in-depth discussion of the results of the second round.
3. Uwezo notes that the tests results are not good in any of the three countries, but they are worst in Tanzania.

4. Most secondary school students leave at Form 4, but some stay on into "6th form" before university.
5. Strong evidence is already available that the high variation in expenditure per capita on education (and other services) in each district mainly occurs in wage expenditure and is driven by very unequal deployment of staff. Annual efforts to redeploy staff to underserved areas are defeated by in-year transfers to other areas. There are no effective limits on the recruitment of staff in highly staffed districts, and very little scope is available for creating incentives for staff to remain in districts with recruitment and retention difficulties (see URT 2008 and World Bank 2010).
6. This is based on a Cobb-Douglas (or log-linear) production function, which gives decreasing returns. Variation in functional form, for example, a polynomial function, confirms the decreasing returns of the production function.
7. Note that there is variation within the group; Njombe Rural, for example, has a low level of spending.

References

URT (United Republic of Tanzania). 2008. "Background Analytical Note for the Annual Review of General Budget Support 2008. Equity and Efficiency in Service Delivery: Human Resources." United Republic of Tanzania, Dar es Salaam, Tanzania.

Uwezo. 2011. "Are Our Children Learning? Numeracy and Literacy across East Africa." Uwezo East Africa managed by Twaweza, Dar es Salaam, Tanzania

World Bank. 2010. *Equity in Public Services in Tanzania and Uganda*. Policy Note, Report 56511_AFR, Washington, DC.

Environmental Benefits Statement

The World Bank Group is committed to reducing its environmental footprint. In support of this commitment, the Publishing and Knowledge Division leverages electronic publishing options and print-on-demand technology, which is located in regional hubs worldwide. Together, these initiatives enable print runs to be lowered and shipping distances decreased, resulting in reduced paper consumption, chemical use, greenhouse gas emissions, and waste.

The Publishing and Knowledge Division follows the recommended standards for paper use set by the Green Press Initiative. Whenever possible, books are printed on 50 percent to 100 percent postconsumer recycled paper, and at least 50 percent of the fiber in our book paper is either unbleached or bleached using Totally Chlorine Free (TCF), Processed Chlorine Free (PCF), or Enhanced Elemental Chlorine Free (EECF) processes.

More information about the Bank's environmental philosophy can be found at http://crinfo.worldbank.org/wbcrinfo/node/4.

www.ingramcontent.com/pod-product-compliance
Lightning Source LLC
Chambersburg PA
CBHW082124230426
43671CB00015B/2795